Orsolya Kolozs

Second Edition

Gender, Marriage & Families

From the Individual to the Social

Kendall Hunt
publishing company

Cover Image © Shutterstock

Kendall Hunt
publishing company

www.kendallhunt.com
Send all inquiries to:
4050 Westmark Drive
Dubuque, IA 52004-1840

Copyright © 2016, 2019 by Kendall Hunt Publishing Company

ISBN 978-1-5249-8814-2

Printed in the United States of America

CONTENTS

Part 3. Families around the World 279

Part 1

Romantic Relationships and Marriages

CHAPTER

1

"We're not together, but we're together:"
ONLINE RELATIONSHIPS

Avery Ross could hardly contain her excitement as she was getting ready for her date. She rummaged through her closet for something extraordinary to wear. She decided on a yellow sundress, which accentuated her curves and slim waist. She wanted to look more gorgeous today than he had ever seen her. She fervently brushed her auburn hair, each vehement stroke matching the velocity of her heartbeat. She rarely wore makeup, but now she put on some eyeliner and lip gloss. She sprinkled her favorite perfume on her neck and lit a candle, and the scent of lilacs immediately filled the room. She knew he wouldn't notice either the perfume or the fragrance of the candle, and it felt like a waste, but she still yearned for the aroma to embrace and calm her.

Her younger brother, Logan, suddenly burst through the door, completely forgetting the rule to knock first.

"Hey, let's go to the beach. We could hang out and watch the fireworks later. Are you coming?" He sounded exhilarated, and she hated to disappoint him.

"You know I have a date, Logan. I told you. I'm sorry."

"You gotta be kidding. How can you not come? It's the Fourth of July." His face shone with utter incredulity.

"I know," Avery sighed. "Just go without me this time, okay?"

3

Logan frowned, but eventually said, "Your call. You're really missing out though." With that, he turned and ran out of the room.

Logan might have disappeared, but his reminder of the Fourth of July stayed. Avery loved the beach and the fireworks after sunset. She reluctantly admitted to herself that it saddened her a bit to miss the Fourth of July festivities. But it would have upset her even more to cancel her date with Tibor.

"Tibor Lantos," she said aloud. After months of practice, his name now sounded familiar; it was like a warm blanket that engulfed and reassured her. At the same time, the syllables were still somewhat foreign, exotic, and electrifying as they rolled off her tongue.

The abrupt buzzing of her phone harshly interrupted her daydreaming.

"Hey, Chase," Avery said, glad to talk to one of her closest friends. She still had almost an hour until her date with Tibor, and she welcomed a distraction.

"Hey, Ave," Chase said, his cheerful voice exploding in her ear. "So, how is your Fourth so far?"

"So far so good. We had a backyard barbecue with my family. The usual."

"So, how about more of the usual? Are you ready to head down to the beach later and watch some fireworks? I heard they're going to be awesome this year." Chase's voice was full of smile and anticipation of a memorable evening with friends. But Avery was looking forward to making different kinds of memories tonight.

"Chase, I can't," she sighed. "I have a date."

"A *date*, huh?" Chase asked, with just a hint of sarcasm. It was barely audible, but Avery knew him, and she instantly felt her defences rising.

"Yes, a *date*," Avery answered, enunciating every word. "Today is our two-month anniversary with Tibor."

"Well, congratulations, I guess," Chase shot back. He paused for a second, then added, "I just think it's kind of funny to talk about dates and your anniversary when you haven't even met the guy."

His comment stung. Avery had to catch her breath before responding. "Don't be like that, okay? Tibor and I, we're not together, but we're together. We *are* a *couple*. Please be happy for me."

"I want to be happy for you, Ave," Chase sighed. Suddenly all the sarcasm was gone, and his voice was filled with concern instead. "I just don't get it, and I'm worried about you. I mean, you don't know the guy. That's a fact. He could be anyone. Yeah, he could turn out to be the greatest guy in the world, but he could also be an axe-murderer. And he's halfway across the world. How could you even meet him? You can't even pronounce his name."

"I can pronounce his name just fine, thank you," Avery said, heat rising to her face. "And we're *getting to know* each other. We talk every day. I do know him. And I do know he's right for me. You're right about one thing, though: you don't get it. But I wish you at least tried."

"I am *trying*, Ave," Chase breathed, sounding weary. "I just don't want you to get hurt. But I'll shut up for now and let you get ready for your date."

"I appreciate that," Avery finally smiled. "And I appreciate your concern, but believe me, I'm fine. I'm happy. Enjoy the fireworks, okay? Talk to you later."

"Talk to you later," Chase echoed.

As they hung up, Avery still felt a little shaken by their exchange. Why did Chase have to ruffle her sea of happiness, and why on her anniversary? And why did he have to call? Why couldn't he just text like a normal person, like he usually does? Then they could have avoided this futile back-and-forth.

To get her mind back on Tibor and evoke the excitement about their date again, Avery conjured up her first memories of him. They had met on Second Life, a huge online virtual world, 9 months ago. For the next 3 months their avatars ran into each other occasionally. Then they started seeking out those meetings and talking more. First, they strictly communicated through their avatars, as avatars, and mostly about the things they were doing or aspiring toward in Second Life. Then one day, about 3 months ago, Tibor's avatar suddenly blurted out that his real-life name was Tibor Lantos, and he was a 23-year-old law student from Hungary. His admission changed the game. Avery also told him her full name, that she was 20 years old, she lived with her parents and younger brother in Daytona Beach, Florida, and that she was a freelance personal care aid for the elderly. They exchanged Skype account names, and while they still spent time together and chatted on Second Life as avatars, they gradually migrated more to Skype. Avery remembered how self-conscious, nervous, and giddy she was the first time they saw each other on webcam. Tibor's deep-set, warm brown eyes and cute accent instantly charmed her.

Their Skype sessions really helped them open up and share a lot about themselves. About 3 weeks after they had begun to talk on Skype, on May 4, Tibor seemed uncharacteristically quiet and melancholic. After some prodding from Avery, he blurted out that he saw some lilacs on his way home. They were in season in Hungary, and their exceptional beauty and soft fragrance reminded him of Avery, which made him realize how much he would like to walk hand-in-hand with her among the lilacs and give her a bouquet. Once he started talking, words were flooding out of him. He

CHAPTER 1: "We're not together, but we're together." Online Relationships

5

told Avery how much their conversations meant to him, and how beautiful she was, inside and out. Finally he whispered that he loved her. Then it was Avery's turn to grow quiet. She might have appeared serene, but on the inside she was battling mammoth waves of emotion that his words stirred in her. She felt more elated, but also more scared than ever. She had a simultaneous urge to laugh aloud and to cry. Eventually she didn't succumb to either, just simply and evenly told Tibor that she loved him, too.

They decided to make it official and changed their Facebook status from "single" to "in a relationship" that day. Since then they spent almost all their free time together on Skype, at least 2 to 3 hours per day during the week, around 12 hours per day on weekends (including sleep), and once a record 24-hour stretch. The 6-hour time difference could be tricky, but they learned to work around it. This meant that sometimes they had to stay up late or get up very early, or go to bed at odd times when they both slept with Skype on. The difficulties of time management didn't faze them; in fact, they often felt as if they were masters of time and space by synchronizing their lives and carving out a time and mutual virtual space for themselves. On Second Life they were literally in the same space and on the same time. Physical distance and time zones ceased to matter and disappeared. Their time together online *was* their space together. Couples tend to be defined by "being together," and they were together *all the time*, so how could Chase or anyone else question that they were a couple?

Avery glanced at the clock on her laptop and noted that she still had about 15 minutes until their date. She reached for the stuffed bear that Tibor had mailed her. She clutched it and breathed in Tibor's cologne that he had sprayed on it before sending it for their 1-month anniversary. The scent was getting faint now, but closing her eyes it still helped her imagine Tibor next to her.

After gently putting the bear back on her bed, Avery pulled up the "Loving From a Distance" website on her computer. She loved the advice, inspirations, and activities she found there for long-distance couples. Her favorite were the forums and blogs, where she could chat with others in long-distance relationships. Unlike Chase, they always seemed to completely understand what she was going through. While most posts were extremely helpful and reassuring, a few bothered her. When people complained about their sweetheart being 300 to 500 miles away and "only" seeing them every few weeks, once a month, or every couple of months, she couldn't feel very sympathetic. Didn't they realize how good they had it? Tibor lived about 5,000 miles away, and he once said that he could kill for a distance of "only" 300 to 500 miles. Of course, he was talking about kilometers, not miles, and she had had no idea what distance he had in mind until she looked it up on a measurement converter online. That was not the only thing she had to look up; for example, when he first mentioned he was from Hungary, Avery only had a vague recollection of where that was, but luckily she was sitting in front of her computer, and Google maps quickly came to the rescue. In the last few months Avery often stared at the two dots on the map: Daytona Beach and Budapest. Sometimes they didn't seem that far, but other times they seemed to be worlds apart.

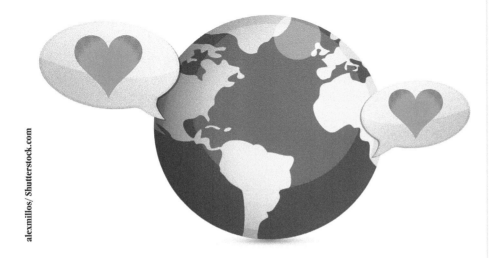

alexmillos/ Shutterstock.com

Avery decided to take a quick look at another website, "In Love Abroad," which had useful tips for international long-distance couples. Before she could have immersed herself in a sea of valuable information, she heard the easily recognizable tune of an incoming Skype call, which became the familiar soundtrack of her life. Her heart jumped, and she answered the call with a wide smile, "Hey, love."

Tibor's face filled the screen. "Hi, szerelmem," he said. Avery knew that "szerelmem" meant "my love" in Hungarian, and she let the cadence of those foreign, but now oddly familiar, unique words reach into her heart.

"How was your day?" Avery asked.

"You know, just the usual. Pretty busy day at my internship. Then I went for a run on Margaret Island." As Avery learned, Margaret Island was a beautiful island on the Danube in central Budapest. Tibor lived close to it and loved to run the track around the entire island, which was about 5

CHAPTER 1: "We're not together, but we're together." Online Relationships

7

kilometers, or 3.1 miles, as Avery figured out later. "What about you? Did you have a busy day at work, too?" Tibor asked.

"No, I had the day off. Fourth of July, Independence Day, remember?" Avery laughed. She knew that Tibor grew up in a different culture and Independence Day in the United States didn't mean anything to him, but she still found it funny that he would completely forget about it.

"Right," Tibor said, sounding a little embarrassed. "I knew that. But working all day, I guess I just forgot. So did you have a good time with your family?"

"Yes, definitely," Avery smiled. "Logan was a little disappointed that I'm not going to the beach for fireworks, but he'll be fine."

"Were you? I mean, were you disappointed, too?" Tibor suddenly sounded serious, his voice full of concern. "I don't want you to miss something important."

"That's OK," Avery assured him, not admitting that she *was* slightly melancholic about the fireworks, and not mentioning Chase's comments, which unexpectedly just popped into her mind. "I have seen like 20 Fourth of July fireworks, I can miss one. But I have never had a 2-month anniversary with you, I can't miss that."

"Alright, if you're sure," Tibor was now grinning. "Hey, check out the attachment I've just sent you in chat."

Avery clicked on the file, and a picture of blooming lilacs filled her screen. She felt moved; Tibor did manage to give her a bouquet of lilacs after all.

"Thank you! I have the scent to go with them," she said, moving her laptop closer and pointing to her candle.

Shulevskyy Volodymyr/ Shutterstock.com

Christian Jung/ Shutterstock.com

"Cool," Tibor said as he sent a kissing face emoticon on Skype. "Love your dress, by the way. You look very pretty."

"Thanks," Avery breathed as she sent a kissing face emoticon back.

"Are you hungry? Do you want to eat dinner yet?" Tibor asked.

Avery felt stuffed after the family barbecue earlier, and it was only 3 o'clock in the afternoon, so technically it wouldn't be dinner, but she didn't want to miss out on the chance of a romantic meal with Tibor on their anniversary, so she nodded. "Sure. Let me get my food."

They returned with their food a few minutes later. Avery got some left-over salad from the barbecue, and Tibor had something that she couldn't identify, so she had to ask, "What are you eating?"

"Oh, it's cottage cheese noodles," Tibor explained. "It has sweet cottage cheese, noodles, and bits of bacon. It's good."

"Hmm, that sounds… I could say it sounds and looks appetizing, but actually not really," Avery laughed as Tibor pushed the plate right in front of the webcam so that she could see it better.

Tibor put on some soft background music to accompany their dinner. They talked about their food, trying to describe its smell and taste, and about Tibor's internship at his father's office. Tibor was studying to be a lawyer, following in his father's footsteps. Avery knew nothing about law, especially Hungarian law, but she enjoyed listening to him. After dinner Tibor grew quiet, stared at her, and said, "Avery, I want to tell you something. Or maybe ask you something."

"OK," Avery said, feeling a little apprehension rising in her chest. Everything was going so well, and she was hoping Tibor wasn't about to say something that would shatter her illusions. He looked so serious, and she didn't know what to expect.

"Avery, I love you, and I think it's time for us to take the next step in our relationship. Or at least start thinking about it," he said.

"I love you, too," Avery whispered, waiting for him to elaborate. She was wondering what he meant by the next step. Maybe sex. Probably sex. He was a guy, after all. But they had discussed this about a month ago, and Tibor seemed understanding when she said she wasn't sure if she was comfortable with virtual sex, at least not before they slept together in real life. Despite the obvious chemistry between them that transcended the screen, it might be awkward before they actually met. Their avatars often kissed on Second Life, but that was the furthest they had gone in physical intimacy. So, was he going to bring up sex again, or was it something else?

"I think we should start planning our first meeting," Tibor said.

Avery was instantly relieved and exhilarated. While she enjoyed their online relationship, she was hoping to meet Tibor offline one day.

"I'm pretty busy at my internship during the summer and then with school from September, but if you came sometime in August, or even September or October, I think we could make that work. If you can get time off, of course," Tibor mused.

"I think I could get some time off, especially because I'm my own boss, and my clients would probably understand. And I'd love to see your country," Avery said. "But Tibor, I don't have a passport. I have never gone anywhere. I haven't even traveled further North than Tennessee. I have never been on a plane before."

"Well, you can get a passport, can't you? I don't think it would take you that long. And flying is cool, you're going to like it," Tibor assured her.

"I don't even think my parents would be crazy about the idea," Avery admitted. "I know I'm 20, but I'm still their little girl, and I know they would be really worried."

"You just need to talk to them, they might surprise you," Tibor suggested.

"I guess I can talk to them and see. I don't have money for a plane ticket either. How much do you think it is? I bet it's like $500," Avery said.

"Of course, we would split the cost. I think the ticket would be closer to $1,000 or even more," Tibor said.

"What?" Avery couldn't hide her shock. "That's crazy. And what if you came to visit me first?"

"I don't know. I mean, with my internship and school and everything, I don't think I could before next summer or something, and I don't want to go that long before seeing you," Tibor explained.

"I would like to see you much sooner, too," Avery confirmed. "So how about we both look into it more, like how much tickets are, dates, and I'll talk to my parents."

"OK, sounds good," Tibor said. "I just wanted us to start planning it, so let's do that. The point is that we really want to meet, so we'll make it happen sometime, somehow."

"Yes, we will," Avery smiled. She imagined Tibor hugging and kissing her, and the image was so vivid, she could almost really feel it. As their conversation was winding down, Tibor was "pretend" holding her while he fell asleep. She turned off her lights and lay there for a while. It was only 6:30 p.m., but she forced herself to fall asleep. She listened to Tibor's calm breathing across Skype and dreamed about being in his arms for real.

*

Six and a half months later Avery's dream came true. She was lying in Tibor's arms and could hardly believe how lucky they were that they could finally meet. She was listening to Tibor's even breathing while he was sleeping soundly. She could not sleep and was aimlessly staring at the ceiling. It had been a very long road from their first meeting on Second Life to Budapest, Hungary. They had been so naïve and hadn't been counting on the numerous obstacles that they encountered on this journey. The plane ticket turned out to be the first roadblock. Tickets ran over $1,000, which was considerably more than what either of them could afford. They had to take a reality check and postpone Avery's trip until they both put some money aside. It took them almost six months to scrape that huge sum together. The cost might have been negligible for some, but it was almost insurmountable for Avery and Tibor. Tibor was too proud to borrow money from his parents, and Avery didn't even ask her own parents, as she knew they were dead set against her trip anyway. In fact, she had never seen them so terror-stricken before. Her mother was begging her not to go, almost constantly in tears for weeks and forecasting various potentially catastrophic scenarios. She predicted that Avery would end up kidnapped, a sex slave, dead, or all of the above. After all, what else could happen if you met a stranger in an Eastern European country, fraught with communism? It took so much energy from Avery to soothe her that she didn't even bother to correct her and explain that Hungary was technically in Central Europe, and communism had been over before Tibor was even born. Her father's stern expression, but petrified eyes struck Avery just as hard as her mother's vocalized panic. Eventually they were mollified by several talks with Tibor and his parents, but convincing them that she wasn't crazy, reckless, and irresponsible for going was one of the most difficult things she had ever had to accomplish.

While they were putting money aside for the trip, and Avery's passport application was pending, the wait became almost unbearable. Time had never seemed to pass as slowly as it did then. They felt that they would give anything for a magic power to speed things up. Once it became clear that meeting in September was impossible, they were shooting for Christmas. However, as plane tickets were even more expensive then, and Avery's parents would have been wary of letting her go for Christmas, Tibor and Avery settled on a January visit. Once they had the dates, and she had the ticket, Tibor came up with the idea to set up a countdown clock on both of their laptops until the day they met. Avery loved the idea, as it made her feel more in control of time. Every day, when she woke up and glanced at the clock to acknowledge that another day had passed, she was filled with an incredible sense of accomplishment. On the other hand, staring at the clock could really agitate her sometimes. While change from one day to the next felt exhilarating, watching seconds and minutes pass gave her a frustrating sense that the wait would last forever.

The plane ride to Hungary, with two layovers, turned out to be the longest 18 hours of Avery's life. She was throbbing with anticipation to finally see and be able to touch Tibor. They had both been convinced that when they finally saw each other, they would be locked in a never-ending embrace and kiss. Surprisingly, when they met at the airport, they just stared at each other sheepishly, neither of them making a move toward the other. Although they had been a couple for more than 8 months at that time, it took them nearly 2 days to finally kiss and almost a week to make love. This timidness took both of them by surprise, given the unbelievable chemistry they had experienced online. After a transitionary period of awkwardness, their online attraction eventually translated to an offline, physical relationship. And once that happened, there was no turning back.

Avery's visit was scheduled for 2 weeks, which had seemed like infinity before they met, but appeared to be so short now that they were together. Just as time had been dragging before her visit, it seemed to be zipping by at the speed of a race car now. One day felt no more than a blink. They did their best to make the most of their time together. They were fully in the present and immersed in making memories. They hardly slept to lengthen days. Tibor showed her all his favorite places and introduced her to his family and friends. Although it was late January, they celebrated Christmas late and Tibor's February birthday and Valentine's Day early. They squeezed months' worth of special events into 2 weeks.

Tibor's parents were good sports and played along. They put up a Christmas tree again, complete with beautifully wrapped candy and sparklers, which turned out to be the Hungarian custom. Avery was surprised to learn that Christmas constituted of 3 days in Hungary (December 24, 25, and 26), people ate a poppy seed cake as a traditional Christmas dessert, and it was the little Jesus who brought presents, not Santa. Avery also discovered that Hungarians celebrate name days, based on their first names. As there was no name day for Avery in the Hungarian calendar, Tibor suggested that they dedicate the name day for Eva (pronounced "Ava") as Avery's name day. As that name day fell on December 24, they threw a "belated," makeshift name day party for Avery as well. Tibor's grandmother was the only one not thrilled by this idea, as she insisted that Avery was not an actual Hungarian name. She was even less happy with Avery's last name, Ross, which sounds like the word for "bad," or "wrong" in Hungarian. She was afraid that it was a bad omen, indicating that Avery might be wrong for Tibor. Of course, Avery didn't understand a word his grandma was saying, but once Tibor translated it, Avery and Tibor just laughed it off. Tibor's laugh was loud and genuine, while Avery's a little forced and uncomfortable.

Now the two most intense weeks of Avery's life were winding down. She was leaving tomorrow. She and Tibor decided not to sleep at all to have more time together. They were both exhausted, and Tibor finally succumbed to sleep, but Avery was determined to stay up and not miss a moment with him. A pang of fear and deep sorrow was squeezing her heart. She found it inconceivable to say goodbye to Tibor. While she had enjoyed their online romance immensely, she couldn't fathom how she could go back to that now. She was suddenly shaken by an enormous wave of sobs. She tried to suppress it and not wake Tibor. He stirred and, half asleep, reached out to caress her face. He felt the tears and suddenly jerked awake, turning to her.

"Are you crying, szerelmem?" he whispered. "It's OK, don't worry, it's going to be OK."

"No, it won't," Avery sobbed. "How can it be? I'm leaving. Tibor, I don't want to leave. I don't think I can be apart any more."

"Maybe we don't have to be," Tibor smiled gently.

"What do you mean? My plane is leaving tomorrow, I can't stay," Avery said breathlessly.

"Well, maybe you can't stay now, but it doesn't mean we have to be apart much longer," Tibor suggested reassuringly.

"But… but, we could hardly make this one visit work, when are we going to have money for another trip again?" Avery cried. "It might be another six months or more. And then what? A couple of weeks together and six more months apart?" She felt panic rising in her chest. "Tibor, I don't know how we can do this."

"Don't worry, szerelmem," Tibor tried to soothe her. "I have a plan. It's a great one, believe me, and then we can soon be together."

"A plan? What's your plan?" Avery perked up slightly, but she couldn't succumb to hope entirely.

"Look, you know that I'm almost done with college. Once I graduate in the summer, I can start working at my dad's law firm and make some serious money. I know it's a lot to ask, but I want you to come back in the summer, this time for good. It's just 6 more months apart, we can make that work, and then we can always be together," he spoke fervently, his eyes shining with passion and determination.

Avery was overwhelmed with emotion. Her heart leaped with joy, realizing that Tibor wanted to spend his life with her. She had never felt more ecstatic and more certain of wanting the same herself. Still, a small voice was nagging at her, clawing away at her bliss. For a moment she was puzzled by that recalcitrant voice. What was that about? She knew she loved Tibor and wanted to be with him forever. So, why not feel pure elation? It took her a moment to recognize what was bothering her.

"Tibor, I want to be with you, too," she said slowly. "I've never wanted anything more. But does it have to be here? Is that the only option? Can we at least consider you coming over to Florida?"

"Sure, I'd like to visit," Tibor affirmed. "I want to see where you come from."

"You mean you moving to the United States is not even on the table?" Avery exclaimed. "Can we not entertain that idea at least?"

"Yes, of course, we can talk about it," Tibor said, sounding cautious. "But like I said, I'm about to graduate from college and get a great job here."

"I'm sure you could get a great job in the United States. It's the land of opportunity. So many immigrants go there every year. You could be one of them," Avery beamed.

Tibor didn't smile back, "I wish I could do that. But not with my degree. I have a degree in Hungarian law. What could I do with that in the United States? Nothing. I'd have to start school all over again. I have the job all set here, and my dad is counting on me, too. He's always thought I'd take over the firm one day."

"I get that," Avery sighed, her smile disappearing. "But at least you speak English. You could still have good opportunities over there. But what could I do here? I don't even speak the language."

"You could learn," Tibor tried to console her. "Yes, it's a pretty hard language, but you could learn it, and almost everyone speaks English anyway."

"Like your grandma?" Avery pointed out.

"OK, maybe not my grandma, and not some other people, but mostly you could get by with English and then slowly master Hungarian."

"But you know I love my job, working with the elderly. Yes, it's not much, it's a part-time job, but it's important to me," Avery breathed. "And it's the elderly here who are the least likely to speak English. And how could I help them with errands and stuff when even I don't know where everything is, and how everything works?"

"Those are valid points," Tibor said thoughtfully. "But I'm not worried. In a year or two you'd know all that stuff, plus the language. Of course, we'd have to figure out the bureaucracy and all that, but we can do that together. And I'll help you with everything. I'll stand by you all the time. We'd most likely have to get married right away so that you can live and work here, but actually that's kind of nice, too, as eventually we'd want to get married anyway," Tibor grinned.

Avery was stunned, "Are you proposing to me right now? And that's the way you're going about it? It's not very romantic. I don't want to get married for bureaucracy, I want to get married for love."

Tibor's smile grew even wider, and he hugged Avery, "I want to get married for love, too, and that's why I want to marry you. Yes, maybe it'd have to be a little bit faster than we'd prefer, but I want to make this happen. And don't worry, I'll propose to you in a *very* romantic way. This wasn't the proposal yet; this is just a discussion to try to be on the same page."

"Hmm…," Avery hesitated. "You really see me here? You think I'd be fine here?"

"I think you'd be great here," Tibor squeezed her hand. "You love it here, don't you?"

"I love that you are here," Avery mused. "I love how your parents have accepted me, and how close you guys are. It's different from my family. In a good way. Your friends are pretty cool. And Budapest is beautiful. The Danube, the hills, the architecture. The opera, the museums, the history. I love the bakeries with all the cakes, gelato, and great coffee. Although probably I could end up weighing a ton living here," she laughed. "Especially with the Hungarian hospitality. Everyone is always feeding me, and when you're a guest, you don't have to lift a finger. I could get used to that. And it's kind of neat how people dress up more here. I like dressing up, and I wouldn't have to have an excuse for that here. This whole thing is like a storybook. A far-away kingdom with my own prince in it."

"You see, I'm so glad you love it," Tibor smirked.

Avery smiled back, but her smile grew slightly faint as she reflected on the sides of Hungary that she wasn't keen on. First of all, it was so cold, at least now, in January. Coming from Florida, Avery was always shivering, even in the thick coat she borrowed from Tibor's mom. And it got dark so early in the winter, which already made her a little depressed. Tibor's family and friends were nice, but strangers were somewhat grumpy. When she smiled at them passing by, they didn't smile back and many gave her a disapproving look. And everything was so small, the roads, cars, houses, bathrooms. Tibor's family was not poor, but they still lived in a two-bedroom condo with one bathroom, which was common for middle-class families here. Avery had always imagined living in a four-bedroom, three-bathroom house near the beach. Well, living here would be as far as it gets from that.

She also imagined having children with Tibor. The thought warmed her heart, but, at the same time, scared her. She envisioned giving birth here and not even understanding the instructions of a doctor. What's worse, would she understand her own children? They'd be speaking to their father and almost everyone in Hungarian, and what if she never learned enough to catch what they're saying? She wouldn't admit it to Tibor, but the thought of learning Hungarian terrified her, especially because she honestly didn't even like the sound of it too much. And would it be little Jesus who brought her children Christmas gifts, not Santa? Or would it be both? How would they merge Hungarian and American culture? Maybe she could give up her country, but she couldn't fathom giving up her language and culture. Could she still remain an American in Hungary without losing herself? Could she stay in touch with her parents and brother? Now instead of a long-distance relationship with Tibor, would she have a long-distance relationship with everyone else?

The questions came flooding, but there were no answers at this point. Only time could tell. She glanced at Tibor's face, which shone with hope and love. She felt immensely close to him, but at the same time, in a way, she vaguely sensed some unfamiliar distance between them, which had not been there, even when they had been so far away geographically. She hoped that this sudden gap could be overcome the same way they had conquered physical distance. She pushed away her doubts and fears and pulled Tibor closer, resolving that, for now, only the present moment mattered, and the future could be decided later.

Neirfy/ Shutterstock.com

Tonis Valing/ Shutterstock.com

Discussion Questions

1. What do you think will happen to Tibor and Avery?

   I think they will go through immense

2. Goffman (1986) used the term *stigma* to describe a strong negative label that people attach to individuals who do not conform to social norms. Would you say that there is any stigma attached to online relationships? Why/why not? Are there any examples of this in Tibor and Avery's story? Do you expect changes in perceptions of online relationships in the future? Why/why not?

3. What role (if any) do you think gender plays in this story?

4. What role (if any) do you think socioeconomic status plays in this story? What could be different if Tibor and Avery had more money (or less), or if they had different occupations?

5. Discuss the role of cultural differences in the story. Also, would it make a difference if Avery and Tibor lived in the same country, or if they lived even further apart from each other?

6. Many online couples report falling in love before meeting face-to-face (Baker, 2005; Ben-Ze'ev, 2004). Illustrate this by the case of Avery and Tibor. Do you believe in love *before* first sight? Why/why not?

7. Zerubavel (1991) explained that "[t]o define something is to mark its boundaries, to surround it with a mental fence that separates it from everything else" (p. 2). Berger and Kellner (1964) stated that couples construct their own definitions of couplehood, and others around them could reinforce or challenge those definitions. Apply these theories to the story of Tibor and Avery.

8. Long-distance partners (including online couples) often experience both temporal compression and protracted duration. Temporal compression is the sense that time flies, whereas protracted duration is the perception that time is passing slowly (Adam, 1995, 2004; Flaherty, 1991, 1999; Flaherty & Meer, 1994). Also, geographically distant couples frequently assign extraordinary meaning to an ordinary day—that is, they are converting profane time into sacred time (Durkheim, 1995). Mention examples for all three from the story. Are they engaging in temporal agency, too? In what ways? Temporal agency is an "intrapersonal and interpersonal effort directed toward provoking or preventing various temporal experiences" (Flaherty, 2011, p. 11).

9. Chayko (2008) defined a sociomental space as an "environment in which people derive a sense of togetherness by being mentally oriented toward and engaged with one another" (p. 10). Simultaneity is "the creation of a shared present irrespective of the number of people and spatial distances involved" (Adam & Groves, 2007, p. 202). Zerubavel (1981) referred to the same phenomenon as temporal symmetry. Mention examples of creating a sociomental space and simultaneity/temporal symmetry from the story.

Find the Answers

Go to http://www.pewresearch.org/fact-tank/2016/02/29/5-facts-about-online-dating/ to find answers to the following questions.

1. About what percentage of Americans believe that online dating is a good way to meet people? Has that percentage increased in the last 10 years? Are you surprised by these numbers? Why/why not?

2. Which age group is the most and least likely to use an online dating site or app? What could be the reasons for these groups being the most and least likely to use online dating?

3. Do most people who use online dating sites go on a date with someone they met on these sites? Why/why not?

4. About what percentage of Americans have met their spouse or long-term partner online? Is the percentage about what you expected? Why/why not? How do you think the number might change in the future?

Mini Research Assignments

1. Review long-distance relationship activities at http://lovingfromadistance.com/things-forldrcouplestodo.html. Which ones did Avery and Tibor also do? Which ones do you consider the best and worst ideas? Why? Can you add any ideas to this list? Do you think activities like these can enhance the stability and longevity of long-distance relationships? Why/why not? Do you think that such activities work any better for online couples, versus couples that had started out close-distance and then became long-distance? Why? Discuss the role of age, globalization, and technology in today's long-distance relationships.

2. Browse through articles at http://www.ldrmagazine.com. Read at least three articles carefully. Find parallels between the articles and the story of Avery and Tibor. What kind of messages do these articles convey about long-distance romances? Do you find them helpful? Why/why not? What kind of messages are stressed or implied about gender, sexual orientation, social class, age, time, and space?

3. Watch a movie that depicts an online or other type of long-distance romance. In what light are such relationships portrayed in the movie? Is there any obvious or latent stigma? Why/why not? What kind of messages are conveyed or implied about gender, sexual orientation, social class, age, time, and space? Would it make a difference if the movie were set at a different location or in a different era? How so?

4. Interview a couple in an online or other type of long-distance relationship, or interview someone who has ever been in such a relationship. Ask them at least seven questions. Ask them questions that you are curious to know, but also ask questions that might get to the core of any controversies regarding online/long-distance relationships. Draw parallels with the story of Tibor and Avery and analyze the role of gender, social class, age, and any other similar factor you choose in their relationship.

References

Adam, B. (1995). *Timewatch: The social analysis of time.* Cambridge, MA: Polity Press.

_____. (2004). *Time.* Malden, MA: Polity Press.

Adam, B., & Groves, C. (2007). *Future matters: Action, knowledge, ethics.* Leiden, The Netherlands: Brill.

Baker, A. J. (2005). *Double click: Romance and commitment among online couples.* Cresskill, NJ: Hampton Press.

Ben-Ze'ev, A. (2004). *Love online: Emotions on the internet.* New York, NY: Cambridge University Press.

Berger, P., & Kellner, H. (1964). Marriage and the construction of reality: An exercise in the micro-sociology of knowledge." *Diogenes, 12,* 1–24.

Chayko, M. (2008). *Portable communities: The social dynamics of online and mobile connectedness.* Albany, NY: State University of New York Press.

Durkheim, E. (1995). *The elementary forms of religious life* (K. E. Fields, Trans.). New York, NY: The Free Press. (Original work published 1912)

Flaherty, M. (1991). The perception of time and situated engrossment. *Social Psychology Quarterly, 54,* 76–85.

_____. (1999). *A watched pot: How we experience time.* New York: New York University Press.

_____. (2011). *Textures of time: Agency and temporal experience.* Philadelphia, PA: Temple University Press.

Flaherty, M., & Meer, M. D. (1994). How time flies: Age, memory, and temporal compression. *The Sociological Quarterly, 35,* 705–721.

Goffman, E. (1986). *Stigma: Notes on the management of spoiled identity.* New York, NY: Touchstone. (Original work published 1963)

Smith, A., & Anderson, M. (2016). 5 facts about online dating. Washington, DC: Pew Research Center. Retrieved from http://www.pewresearch.org/fact-tank/2016/02/29/5-facts-about-online-dating/

Zerubavel, E. (1981). *Hidden rhythms: Schedules and calendars in social life.* Chicago, IL: University of Chicago Press.

_____. (1991). *The fine line: Making distinctions in everyday life.* New York, NY: Free Press.

CHAPTER 2

"How can you be married and not live together?"
COMMUTER MARRIAGES

Stacey Newman/Shutterstock.com

Caitlyn Hollis suspected that this Fourth of July afternoon at her in-laws might turn out to be more explosive than the fireworks later on that evening. As she walked up the stairs to her in-laws' house, she glanced at her husband, Nate, apprehensively. He squeezed her hand and whispered, "Don't worry, it's all going to be fine." Before his words had time to sink in and soothe Caitlyn, his mother, Elaine, opened the door with a wide smile and pulled Nate into an affectionate embrace. She faltered only slightly before hugging Caitlyn. Her hesitation was so faint and imperceptible that no one, but Caitlyn, sensed it.

"Hi," Elaine burst out cheerfully. "I'm so happy you're finally here. Please come in; it's too hot out here. I'm sure y'all are just parched after the trip, let me get you some iced tea."

Caitlyn followed Elaine to the living room, with Nate in tow, and wondered how quickly her mother-in-law's southern hospitality and politeness would evaporate after Caitlyn shared her big news. Caitlyn had no illusion that her mother-in-law would ever truly like her; Elaine was simply too protective of her only son for that. But so far she had at least managed to stay civil most of the time, and Caitlyn fretted that after this afternoon even that might change. She had always been eager to please, and she didn't want to disappoint her mother-in-law. More importantly, she didn't want to let Nate down.

As Caitlyn saw her father-in-law, Richard, some of her tension dissipated.

"Hey, pretty lady, hi son," Richard exclaimed, grinning. His words and embrace seemed more heartfelt than those of Elaine, and Caitlyn was suddenly thankful to have him there. His presence always reassured her somehow, and his calm, quiet demeanor reminded her of Nate. Caitlyn was convinced that Richard liked her and secretly thought of her as the daughter he never had, but he adored his wife too much and hated to disagree with her, so he rarely showed his genuine fondness of Caitlyn when Elaine was around.

As Elaine disappeared into the kitchen, and Nate and his father launched into an analysis of yesterday's game, Caitlyn sank onto the cushy sofa and became immersed in her own thoughts. She caught a glimpse of her wedding picture, displayed on a small end table by the sofa. The photo transported her back to her wedding day. It had been a warm, perfect day last March, with everything exactly the way she and Nate had wanted. They had an outdoor ceremony on Tybee Island, near Savannah. She wore an understated lace gown, and as she walked barefoot on the makeshift sandy aisle toward Nate, she felt more confident than ever before. The small, intimate wedding symbolized their feelings for each other, and so did the waves of the ocean stretching before them. Those waves were calm, solid, and constant that day, but they could be wild and consuming at other times. This dichotomy of the ocean encapsulated the essence of their relationship. Most people would have described their love as placid affection, a stalwart union of companionship, similitude, and respect. Yes, it was all that, but only Caitlyn and Nate knew that when they were alone, it also had a strong undercurrent of unbridled passion.

Caitlyn's parents didn't approve of the kind of wedding she and Nate had decided on, but Nate gave her a boost of confidence and determination to be able to stand up to her parents for the first time in her life and not seek their approval. They attended the wedding but looked out of place. Caitlyn had used to feel that no matter how hard she tried to meet her parents' expectations, she often fell short of them, and her older sister, Cassidy, always managed to surpass her. Cassidy seemed to be a better version of Caitlyn. They looked slightly alike, but while Caitlyn had a nondescript face, the same features, but fuller lips, higher cheekbones, and eyes of a more vivid color made Cassidy's face uniquely pretty. Caitlyn was short and skinny with A-cup breasts and narrow hips. Cassidy was slightly

taller, and she had a fuller and curvier, but still slender figure. She had looked spectacular in a traditional ballgown at her own wedding, deemed *proper* by their parents. It was held at one of the oldest and most ornate Catholic churches in their native Charleston, followed by a reception at a five-star hotel in the historic downtown area.

Cassidy had always outperformed Caitlyn in school, and following in their parents' footsteps, she had become a pharmacist. Caitlyn had enrolled in college as a pre-pharmacy student as well and completed 3 years of education, but she decided to take a break from school because she wanted to figure out if pharmacy was something she really wanted to do, or if she was simply trying to please her parents. That break led to her moving from Charleston to Savannah more than 3 years ago and working as a receptionist at a chiropractor's office while trying to figure out her life. As it turned out, her job at the chiropractor's office had a momentous impact on her life. That's where she met Nate, who walked in as a patient, and it had also contributed to an imminent change of direction in her life, which she was now about to divulge to her in-laws.

Elaine returned with some sweet tea, which pulled Caitlyn back to the present.

"So, what's going on with y'all?" Elaine asked. "I feel like I haven't seen you in ages."

"Yeah, sure, mom. We were here for Memorial Day, remember?" Nate laughed. As he caught Caitlyn's nervous glance, his smile froze. He moved next to her on the sofa and held her hand. "Actually, there is something going on. Caitlyn has, I mean we have some news to share," he said, clearing his throat.

"You're having a baby," Elaine shouted, jumping up and giving both of them a truly genuine hug this time. "I knew it. It's about time. You've been married for more than a year; I was beginning to wonder when this would happen. I'm going to be a grandma! Hey, grandpa," she beamed at her husband.

"Mom, calm down, this is not about a baby," Nate sighed, exchanging an exasperated glance with Caitlyn. They hadn't anticipated this reaction and his mother hijacking the conversation this way before it could even begin. It would be even harder to get her to focus now. "Caitlyn, do you want to explain it to them?" he asked. "Probably you can explain it better."

Caitlyn would have preferred if Nate had just told them instead of passing it on to her; they were *his* parents after all. But it was *her* decision, and in a way she understood why she should be the one telling them. "You know, lately I've been thinking a lot about my life," she began slowly. "I like my job, but something still seems to be missing. I think I finally know what I want to do. Watching my boss at the office I realized I want to become a chiropractor like him. I have to go back to school for that, though. So, I applied and got accepted. I'm starting next month."

"Wow, that's wonderful, honey," Elaine interjected. "But what about your pharmacy education? You're not finishing that?"

"No, I'm not," Caitlyn confirmed. "I think that was probably decided a long time ago when I took a break. I think I knew I wasn't going back, just wasn't ready to admit it."

"So, what do your parents think?" Elaine asked. "Were they disappointed?"

"Yes," Caitlyn sighed, her mind traveling back to the heated phone call she had with them a week ago. "Yes, they were. But this is what I want to do. They'll just have to accept that. And I'll still be in healthcare, although a completely different field, I admit. Completely different. Maybe that's what I like about it, actually."

"The exciting part is that she can apply a lot of the courses she did in pre-pharmacy toward a chiropractic degree," Nate added, and Caitlyn looked at him gratefully.

"This sounds like a great plan, Caitlyn. And it's a big deal that you got accepted," Richard said with a reassuring smile.

"Yes, congratulations, honey," Elaine chimed in. Maybe she thought that a college degree would make Caitlyn ever so slightly more suitable for her Ph.D. graduate son. "So which school are you going to?"

Caitlyn took a deep breath. "I'm going to a school in Atlanta."

Elaine seemed confused for a moment, then utter shock took over her expression. "You're kidding, right?" Her eyes darted around the room, expecting affirmation from either Nate or her husband that Caitlyn was indeed joking. "But you live in Savannah. Couldn't you find a school in Savannah?"

"No, not a chiropractic school," Caitlyn sighed. "The one in Atlanta is the closest, and it's a great school, so it makes sense."

"It makes sense?" Elaine asked in disbelief. "No, it doesn't make sense at all. Why don't you do a degree online then? Now *that* would make sense."

"I can't do it online," Caitlyn said, her voice weary. "I looked into all options, believe me. But I can't do a chiropractic degree online; I need hands-on education and practice."

"So, is it only a couple of classes you need to take, and then you're done, or how long is the program?" Richard asked sensibly.

"Well," Caitlyn looked at Nate hesitantly. "The classes would probably take about 4 years to complete. Maybe 3 years if I'm really pushing it."

"Four years?" Elaine screamed. The Fourth of July explosions Caitlyn had anticipated seemed to have arrived. "You mean you are going to live in Atlanta, away from your husband for 4 years?"

"Come on, mom," Nate jumped in, trying to pacify his mother. "Don't be so dramatic. This is really important for Caitlyn's career. And it's not that far, about a 4-hour drive. We'll see each other every 2 to 3 weeks."

"But you won't *live* together," Elaine protested loudly. "How can you be married and not live together?" Suddenly her face turned aghast. "Oh my Lord, you're getting a divorce, right? Is that what you're trying to tell us? You're getting a divorce?"

Now it was Caitlyn and Nate's turn to look stupefied. "No, we're *not* getting a divorce, mom," Nate finally said, slowly recovering from his shock that his mother would even think that.

"But married couples don't live apart unless there are problems, and they're ready to separate," Elaine argued vehemently.

"What about military families?" Caitlyn asked, struggling to remain calm. "Married couples in military families have lived apart since, well, since forever."

"That's completely different," Elaine contended sternly.

"Why is that different?" Caitlyn asked quietly. "Because most of them are men, and they're okay leaving and their wives waiting for them at home?"

"Why, yes," Elaine didn't falter. "That, and they don't have a *choice*. They're fighting for their country. Don't tell me that a woman leaving her husband for *years*, for a whim is the same thing."

"Now, mom, careful here," Nate interrupted. "Caitlyn's not leaving me. We've talked about this and agreed that it's good thing in the long run. She needs this. And it's not a whim; it's her education, her future, and I'm proud of her."

"Are you telling me you're okay with this?" Elaine asked, astonished.

Nate only hesitated for a second before answering, "Yes, I'm okay with this. It's not ideal, I don't love it, but I'm okay with it."

Caitlyn looked at him, her heart full of gratefulness and love. She knew this wasn't easy for Nate. He had had a long-distance relationship in high school that failed miserably. He and Maribel, an exchange student from Venezuela, had fallen in love fast and hard. After a year she had to return to Venezuela, but they vowed to keep the relationship going. This was almost 17 years ago, in the early days of the Internet. Maribel didn't have Internet access or an email address, and the cost of international phone calls would have greatly surpassed the allowance of high school students. Nate and Maribel exchanged letters for a few months, but communication was slow, and they had slim hopes of being able to meet face-to-face more than once a year, if that. Eventually they had a very reluctant and agonizing breakup. While Caitlyn knew these memories left a scar, the situation was completely different now. With cell phones, Skype, and the Internet, constant communication would be no problem. Plus, they were older, more mature, and completely committed to each other. Caitlyn fervently disagreed with her mother-in-law, who seemed to imply that a long-distance relationship was an even more preposterous idea for a married couple than an unmarried one. For Caitlyn, being married actually provided a sense of reassurance, a level of commitment that elevated the chances of being able to stick it out and make it work. She wasn't sure if Nate felt the same way, but she suspected and hoped that he did.

Her mother-in-law's relentless voice tugged Caitlyn back to the present.

"But what about children?" Elaine lamented. "I was so looking forward to grandchildren. And I thought you wanted to have children soon. It's time, you know. You're not getting any younger."

Caitlyn glimpsed at Nate. They had talked about waiting to have children for 3 to 5 years anyway, but they hadn't actually discussed how a temporary long-distance marriage might play into this.

"Mom, we have plenty of time," Nate said. "Caitlyn is only 27, and I'm 32. We're not in a hurry. Sounds like you are, though."

"OK, I admit it," Elaine threw up her hands. "I do want to be a grandma so bad. But if you're really going through with this silly long-distance thing, and I'm not happy to say this, then you *should* wait. How could Caitlyn take care of a child all by herself and go to school? That wouldn't be right. Children need both parents."

Caitlyn was about to protest and point out the successes of single parents, single mothers *and* fathers, but deep down she agreed with her mother-in-law for once. She and Nate had both grown up with two parents, and she wanted the same for her children one day. She applauded the efforts of single parents, but she knew she wasn't cut out to be one of them.

Abruptly abandoning the topic of children, Elaine suddenly came up with another worrisome thought. "Oh my Lord, Nate, I hope you're not considering leaving your job. You've worked too hard for that."

"No, mom," Nate sighed. "That didn't even come up. Of course I'm not leaving my job."

Nate worked as an Assistant Professor of English. This was his fourth year, and if everything went well, he would be coming up for tenure in about 2 years. If he left now, his work would most likely not be transferable toward tenure at another college.

"In fact," Nate added, "with Caitlyn gone during the week I might be able to get even more work done. We can both work hard during the week and come together and have fun over the weekend. Well, over every second or third weekend."

"So, how is this going to work?" Richard asked with genuine interest. "Who's going to visit?"

"We both will," Nate answered. "We'll alternate. Caitlyn will want to come home, but it wouldn't be fair to her to have to do all the driving."

"My, this is going to be mighty expensive, you know," Elaine predicted. "All that gas money and maintaining two homes."

"Thanks for pointing that out, mom," Nate said with a hint of sarcasm. "We know. But it's all worth it; we're investing in her future, in our future."

"You mean, *you're* investing in her future," Elaine remarked, her tone not only matching, but grossly exceeding Nate's sarcasm. "With all those classes I'm guessing she won't have time to work, so you'll be the only one making money. So guess who's going to have to cover all the costs?"

"Now, mom, that's going too far," Nate said firmly. "Our finances are our business, and we're going to handle them in any way *we* see fit."

"I'm sorry, honey," Elaine said, doing her best to soothe him. "I just don't know if you thought this over, and I'm trying to help you anticipate the challenges."

"We *are* anticipating challenges," Nate said quietly. "We know it's not going to be easy. But we decided to give it a try, and we have no doubt that we can make it work."

The heated debate continued on for a few more hours, and by the time the fireworks came along, they were all worn out, so they just watched them in silence, having had more than enough explosions for one day. They made an unspoken pact to agree to disagree, at least for now. Caitlyn felt drained, having to justify herself all afternoon. Her parents didn't support her decision because they disapproved of her career choice and questioned her ability to go through with her studies. After all, she had left school before. And her in-laws, or Elaine at least, disputed her commitment to Nate and their marriage to even survive going long-distance. It was all too much to absorb. Actually she tried her best *not* to absorb it all. She had always been indecisive and unsure of herself, but she was entirely confident in her love for Nate and her desire to become a chiropractor. As

both of those were suddenly questioned, she felt some inner turmoil slowly starting to boil. She firmly held on to her convictions and Nate's declaration to have no doubt to be able to make this work. She purposefully went through her mind to weed it from small seeds of doubt that had been planted there. She was relieved to find that most were removable, but she wasn't completely convinced that she managed to get rid of them all.

*

Six months later Caitlyn was sitting in front of her computer, staring at the screen, in the tiny bedroom of the apartment she shared with two roommates. Lisa was talking on the phone, or rather, yelling into the phone, which was her usual conversational tone, especially when she had another fight with her boyfriend. Their other roommate, Jack, was listening to music way too loud, disregarding Caitlyn's repeated requests to keep it down. Caitlyn had a paper that was due the next day, and at the rate she was going, she wasn't sure if she could finish it by the deadline. Most likely she would have to stay up almost all night again. At least Lisa and Jack were quiet then, except when Jack threw a party.

It was far from ideal to live with two roommates, but when Caitlyn and Nate sat down to make a budget for maintaining two households, they quickly realized that they didn't have the funds for Caitlyn to live on her own, at least not in a safe neighborhood, close to the college. They made it work on a shoestring budget, but it cost Caitlyn dearly in terms of sacrificing privacy. In fact, it was a sacrifice they both had to make. After having lived together on their own for nearly 3 years, it felt strange to have others around and be forced to renounce privacy. For this reason, Nate usually wasn't keen on visiting; he prompted Caitlyn to come home instead. She would have loved to do that, but sometimes she was too busy in school to make the trip. Occasionally she couldn't leave Atlanta before 6 or 7 p.m., then she hit rush-hour traffic and was utterly exhausted by the time she got to Savannah shortly before midnight. Nate had more free time during the weekends, and as he drove faster, he could squeeze the drive into less than 4 hours. Caitlyn joked from time to time that this way the distance was not as far for him, so that's why he should be the one visiting more often. Ordinarily what ended up happening was that they met once every 3 or 4 weeks, which diverted from their original plan.

In addition, the roommate situation raised another issue. Nate gradually grew jealous of Jack. He had been slightly surprised to learn that one of Caitlyn's roommates was a guy, but at that point he had acquiesced to the idea. However, when he first came to visit and was introduced to Jack, jealousy took root. He couldn't help but notice Jack's striking face, bulging muscles, and charismatic personality. Even that hadn't bothered him significantly, at least not until he discovered that Jack liked to tease Caitlyn, and his light-hearted jokes ever so slightly crossed over to the territory of flirting.

At first, Caitlyn was amused by Nate's increasingly apparent jealousy. She reminded Nate that Jack was 6 years younger than her, he was aware of her marital status, and he was simply a ladies' man, who threw tiny flirt bombs indiscriminately at every woman who crossed his path. Caitlyn was convinced that Jack regarded her as an older sister or pal, not as a potential romantic interest. Nate was not completely reassured, however, which bothered Caitlyn, as jealousy had not been part of their relationship before. Caitlyn even suspected that Jack was one of the reasons why Nate was reluctant to visit and preferred her to go home. She found it ironic that she used to be the insecure one (never about Nate, though), and now this situation seemed to generate some insecurities in Nate. Caitlyn had an inkling that it might be related to residual pain about Maribel and the failure of that past long-distance relationship. She didn't want to bring her up, but she wished she could remind Nate that the two scenarios were widely different. First, they were married, which was a huge difference, at least to Caitlyn. As far as she was concerned, they had a rock-solid commitment, no matter what. Second, while they couldn't see each other as often as they had planned, they still got together at least once a month, and they talked, texted, Facetimed, and Skyped all the time. Caitlyn felt that they were indivisibly linked by their emotions, marriage vows, and the invisible lines of modern communication technology.

Caitlyn continued to stare at the screen and realized apprehensively that words for her paper were not about to materialize. The cacophony of the apartment sneaked into her ears and filled her mind completely. She sighed, missing the peace and quiet of her home with Nate. She was suddenly grasped by a wave of missing Nate as well. This was a familiar feeling by now, and she knew that sometimes she just had to ride out those strong and unpredictable currents of emotion instead of resisting them. This way they passed sooner. She had been used to the constancy of her feelings for Nate and their relationship and was first taken aback by the emotional rollercoaster of a long-distance marriage. A few days before their visits she began to sense some giddiness and impatience overtaking her, feeling like a schoolgirl preparing for a first date, as opposed to a grown woman about to see her husband. Physical intimacy had always been an important part of their relationship, but now they were more consumed by passion than ever, which could be especially awkward when Nate came to visit, and they had to take roommates into account. Goodbyes could be astonishingly agonizing, and as they shared just one last kiss, and then another, and another, they occasionally ended up joking that no one had told them that one could have so much zest, yearning, and lovesickness in marriage.

Caitlyn also missed her home, but it puzzled her that sometimes it didn't feel like her home any more. Nate kind of overtook the space and made it his. His office, which used to be located in the second bedroom of their home, gradually flooded into the living room and dining room. His books and notes occupied nearly every square inch of their home now. When Caitlyn visited, she had to break through the clutter to get to the bedroom or bathroom. Nate had always been prone to messiness, but he made a genuine effort and improvement when they shared a space. However, while Caitlyn was away, he backslid and took possession of the entire space. When Caitlyn returned home, she hardly felt like it was *their* home anymore; it was *his*. Her tiny rented room was definitely not *their* space either; it was *hers*. She reluctantly admitted to herself that in a way she enjoyed having her own, clean and uncluttered space, and didn't miss Nate's mess. At the same time, she would have chosen being able to cuddle in an unkempt home over loneliness and longing in a clean space of her own.

She felt the urge to call Nate, but glancing at her watch she realized that he was probably working now. He was working a lot these days, doing research and submitting manuscripts for publication. She was immersed in studying most of the time herself. They had their separate lives. Lately more of their lives was separate than shared. Caitlyn sometimes felt as if she had two lives and two selves: one just for herself and one she shared with Nate. She noticed that they used the word "I" much more frequently than "we" these days. She knew this was a result of their current arrangement, but once in a while it still led to a sense of fragmentation. At the same time, she felt more fulfilled and whole than she had in her previous life with Nate, as she still had him, but she could pursue her own goals as well. She was aware that she was the one to move away from "we" toward a focus on "I," at least for now, and while occasionally she felt a pang of guilt (or loads of guilt when talking to her mother-in-law), she was convinced that this was the right course of action for her and, in the long run, even for both of them. If Nate ever tried to hold her back, she could grow resentful, and she was extraordinarily grateful that he never attempted to do that. In fact, he was incredibly supportive.

Caitlyn smiled affectionately at imagining Nate hard at work. She decided not to call. It would just throw off their routine anyway. As they used to have their rituals while together, they formulated some new ones in their long-distance marriage now. They always talked at 7 a.m., right after they woke up, both drinking coffee and giving each other a rundown for their plans for that day. It was a brief call, but it started their day with a boost. Then they talked around 10 p.m., for about an hour, before going to bed. They always said goodbye with "goodnight, sleep tight, like I'm with you all night." It sounded silly, but these rituals became extremely meaningful for them. They provided a sense of security and continuity.

Caitlyn glanced at her watch and grudgingly realized that tonight she was not going to bed right after talking to Nate, or at all. She had to accept that she was not getting any work done while Lisa and Jack were awake and so loud, and while she was so distracted by musing about her long-distance marriage. She decided to take a break, call a friend, and finish her paper later. Then she abruptly recognized that she didn't have a friend who truly understood her. Although they had never been friends, she knew what her sister, Cassidy, would tell her. She would make her feel like a failure for not having graduated yet and for not standing by her husband. Her best friend in Savannah, Kristen, usually kept repeating disbelievingly how courageous and strong she was for sticking to her goals and making it on her own. Kristen added that she could never do the same. For some reason, her words didn't resonate as a compliment in Caitlyn. Caitlyn suspected that Kristen meant that she wouldn't leave her husband behind and opt for a long-distance marriage. Also, she hardly ever saw Kristen anymore, so their closeness started to erode. She and Nate tended to have couple dates with Kristen and her husband, Joel, who was Nate's friend. Even when Caitlyn traveled home now, they rarely got together with others, as they became somewhat protective of their limited time alone. Caitlyn had the sense that Kristen was less interested in her as an individual than as a member of a fellow couple.

She couldn't make new friends with married couples in Atlanta either. A couple of times married couples invited her with Nate, but when she showed up alone, they looked uncomfortable, and Caitlyn didn't feel welcome. Everyone kept asking where her husband was, and she got tired of having to make excuses or explain their situation. Most people reacted by confusion or pity when they learned about their long-distance marriage. Some cynics assumed that they had an imminent separation, while incurable romantics speculated how soon one of them wouldn't be able to tolerate this any longer and rush to be with the other. Single acquaintances were even more wary of inviting Caitlyn anywhere, knowing that she was married and not wanting to tempt her with the funs of single life.

As a result, Caitlyn often felt caught in the middle and marginalized. Finally she reached out to others in long-distance marriages, hoping that they would understand her. She found a meetup group for individuals in long-distance marriages and went to their events a couple of times. She quickly recognized the diversity of this group, but she still found some common ground with them. She decided to call one of the members, Heidi. She took a long time to answer, and when she did, her voice sounded tearful.

"Hey, Heidi, how are you?" Caitlyn asked, forcing some cheerfulness on herself, anticipating that Heidi might need support instead of being able to offer it.

"Well… not too great right now," Heidi admitted. "The twins are acting up. They're not listening to me at all, and their teachers keep complaining about them. They're driving everyone crazy, including me."

"I'm sorry to hear that," Caitlyn sympathized.

"Yeah, well, that's how they are," Heidi sighed. "This always happens when Craig is away. They're fine for a few weeks, and then hell breaks loose. I don't know what to do with them. They're boys, they just need their father."

"That must be hard," Caitlyn commiserated, but she couldn't fully comprehend what Heidi was saying. She found a long-distance marriage difficult enough without children; she couldn't even fathom how children might play into this picture. While she got the baby fever once in a while, she was firm on postponing the baby project until she and Nate lived in the same household again.

"Yes, it is," Heidi conceded. "But that's nothing. Craig told me about a mission he's going on in a couple of days. I mean, he told me as much as he could, which is practically nothing, and I didn't catch half of it because of the poor Internet connection, but it still sounded dangerous. I'm worried about him. What if something happens to him? I know that's always a possibility. I knew that was a possibility when I married a guy in the army. You can get used to the fear, but it doesn't get any easier. I'm still terrified. I can't lose him, Caitlyn, I just can't, especially now, with the twins and another baby on the way," Heidi was sobbing.

Caitlyn was stunned and speechless. What could she say to that? How could she reassure Heidi? She mumbled some words of consolation, and as Heidi calmed down a little bit, Caitlyn got off the phone. She felt ashamed and as if she let Heidi down. However, their situations were immensely different. First off, most people accepted or even praised absence in military families with pride, which diverted from Caitlyn's experience. People were more likely to question her choice of absence. Second, she never had to worry about literally losing Nate. Yes, they were apart for now, but they could end it any time they chose to, and Nate's life was not in danger.

To get her mind off of Heidi's agony, Caitlyn decided to call another member of the long-distance marriage meetup group, Mandy. In contrast with Heidi, Mandy answered after the first ring, her voice perky and full of smile, "Hey, Cait, what's up?"

"Hey," Caitlyn began. "I'm fine, just working on a paper and not making any progress… Kind of missing Nate right now."

"Oh, come on," Mandy exclaimed. "Not that stuff again. No feeling sorry for yourself. You live in a great city. You do what you want to do, getting closer to your own goals every day. Enjoy it. Enjoy every minute of it."

"I'm trying to," Caitlyn laughed, not being able to resist Mandy's vehemence and releasing some of the tension that the call with Heidi stirred in her. "Just right now I kind of wish Nate was here."

"No, you don't," Mandy interjected. "Do I wish Steven was here? No, I don't. I look forward to seeing him in 2 weeks, like I do every 2 weeks, and we have a mighty good time when together, I mean, mighty good," she laughed.

"But I sure don't want him here all the time. I'll enjoy every minute of the next 2 weeks. I have the best job in the world. I live in one of the greatest cities on Earth. Well, OK, at least more exciting and warmer than rural Minnesota. I'll leave that for Steven, thank you very much. And I'm not crying a river every night because he's not here. I don't *need* him. I *want* him—*sometimes*. I'm telling you, seeing him for a weekend every 2 weeks is perfect. I get the best of him. I don't get his snores, well, at least not each and every day, 24/7. I don't have to look at his unshaven face each and every day, and when we see each other, he actually shaves and dresses up for that now. You need to freshen up your marriage? Try long-distance, that's what I'm telling everyone now. We never knew what we were missing for 15 years. We're in love again, and he respects me more than ever. I'm never going back to living in the same house again. And he agrees; he likes having the house to himself and the excitement of our biweekly visits and romantic getaways. I was always looking for a way to have some space to myself and feel like myself *and* his wife, but I could never do that living in the same house. This job offer came at the best time. I'm telling you, the last 2 years have really enriched me *and* our marriage. Who says you have to live together when married? Who comes up with those rules? I'm glad Steven and I are making our own rules now."

"I'm happy for you, too," Caitlyn echoed. "You *do* sound happy. I'm so glad it works so well for you and Steven."

"Thanks," Mandy chirped. "And it can work just as well for you and Nate."

As they said goodbye, Caitlyn wondered if it indeed could work so well for her and Nate. They would be long-distance for years while she was studying. Might they get so used to it that they end up *preferring* a long-distance arrangement? Will they ever go back to *normal*? Do they have to go back to normal? What *is* normal? She was getting confused. She couldn't quite associate with Heidi, as their situations were so vastly different. She couldn't entirely identify with Mandy's viewpoint either, especially as she was still pining for Nate. She found it peculiar how her marriage, Heidi's, and Mandy's were all referred to as long-distance marriages, but were they really in the same category, being more similar to each other than to "regular," non-long-distance marriages? The questions left her perplexed, but finally it was time to call Nate. It was time to *live* her marriage instead of thinking about it. She couldn't envision a clear-cut future yet, but she was confident that she and Nate would make it work somehow, in their own way.

Discussion Questions

1. What do you think will happen to Caitlyn and Nate?

2. Discuss the role of gender in the story of Caitlyn and Nate and the other couples that they encounter.

3. Do you think a long-distance marriage leads to fragmentation and separate lives, or can it lead to unity and harmony instead? Discuss examples from the story for each.

4. Do you think children make a difference in a long-distance marriage? Why/why not? How could Caitlyn and Nate's situation be different (if at all) if they had at least one child?

5. Durkheim (1984) explained that rituals could strengthen solidarity in a group. How do you apply this to long-distance marriages? Mention examples of solidarity-enhancing rituals from the story of Nate and Caitlyn.

6. Blumer (1969) identified three premises of symbolic interactionism. The first is that humans act toward things based on the meanings those things have for them. The second is that meanings are created through social interaction. The third is that meanings are understood and potentially transformed through an interpretative process. Apply this theory to definitions of marriage, including a long-distance marriage.

7. Brekhus (1996) argued that when we mark a category, we not only differentiate it from other categories, but we also make it seem as less natural or potentially more problematic than an unmarked category. Do you think that marking long-distance marriages by placing the term "long-distance" in front of them distinguishes them from non-long-distance (unmarked) marriages and potentially defines them as unnatural and problematic? Why/why not?

8. Goffman (1986) referred to stigma as a strong negative label that people apply to individuals who do not conform to social norms. Do you think that long-distance marriages carry a stigma? Why/why not? Is the stigma the same, stronger, or weaker than the stigma of long-distance (unmarried) relationships? Why?

9. Compare and contrast the different types of marriages in the story. Do you use more lumping or splitting in your comparisons? Lumping is emphasizing similarities between certain groups and neglecting their potential differences, whereas splitting is focusing on, or even exaggerating, differences between certain groups (Zerubavel, 1991, 1996).

10. Couples discuss and delineate the boundaries of couplehood together. However, their definition of couplehood could either be strengthened or challenged by others who might or might not accept the social legitimacy of the relationship based on social norms (Berger & Kellner, 1964). List a few examples to illustrate this from the story.

11. Use an ethnomethodological approach to discuss norms of co-residence and monogamy in marriage based on the story. Ethnomethodology is the study of how norms of the social world are created and understood (Garfinkel, 1984). Ethnomethodologists deliberately breach social norms to shed light on the rigidity of those norms. How can we see norms about co-residence and monogamy at play in marriages when those norms are questioned or violated?

Find the Answers

Go to http://www.bbc.com/capital/story/20150807-your-house-or-mine to find answers to the following questions.

1. What is living apart together? Is it the same as a commuter marriage?

2. How many married people in the United States live apart from their partner? Do you expect this number to grow, stay the same, or decline in the next decade? Why?

3. List some statistics for living apart together couples from other countries. Do you think this mostly happens in high-income nations? Why/why not?

4. The article lists some essentials to make a living apart together arrangement work. Which three do you find the most important? Why?

Mini Research Assignments

1. Find at least two websites or blogs devoted to military families. Compare and contrast them. How do they depict military families? What issues/concerns do they focus on? Then, find at least two websites or blogs dedicated to living apart together families/commuter marriages/long-distance marriages. Compare and contrast them with each other. How do they portray LAT families/commuter marriages/long-distance marriages? What issues/concerns do they stress? What significant differences (if any) do you perceive between the sites for military families versus LAT families/commuter marriages/long-distance marriages?

2. Survey at least seven individuals, asking them to rate their agreement with the following statements on a scale of 1–10 (1 meaning complete disagreement and 10 indicating full agreement): 1. "If you are married, you need to live together with your spouse." 2. "It is honorable for military spouses to make the sacrifice of living apart when one of them is deployed." 3. "It is completely understandable for dual career married couples to live apart if they can't both get a job in the same city." 4. "A long-distance marriage that involves children is less acceptable than a long-distance marriage without children." Summarize your results and discuss why you might have received these answers. Draw parallels with the story of Nate and Caitlyn.

3. Interview a couple in a long-distance marriage *or* in an unmarried long-distance relationship. Ask them the following questions: For how long have they been in a long-distance marriage/relationship? What has prompted this arrangement? Do they see it as temporary or permanent? How do others view their relationship? Might those perceptions change if they were not married/married? Would anything be different in their long-distance arrangement if they were not married/married? Why? What do they see as the main challenges and upsides of a long-distance marriage/relationship? Summarize the results and discuss whether anything surprised you in their answers and why. Draw parallels with the story of Nate and Caitlyn.

References

Ashford, K. (2015). Your house or mine? The life of couples who live apart. London: BBC. Retrieved from http://www.bbc.com/capital/story/20150807-your-house-or-mine

Berger, P., & Kellner, H. (1964). Marriage and the construction of reality: An exercise in the micro-sociology of knowledge. *Diogenes, 12,* 1–24.

Blumer, H. (1969). *Symbolic interactionism: Perspective and method.* Englewood Cliffs, NJ: Prentice-Hall.

Brekhus, W. (1996). Social marking and the mental coloring of identity: Sexual identity construction and maintenance in the United States. *Sociological Forum, 11,* 497–522.

Durkheim, E. (1984). *The division of labor in society* (W. D. Halls, Trans.). New York, NY: The Free Press. (Originally published 1893)

Garfinkel, H. (1984). *Studies in ethnomethodology.* Malden, MA: Polity.

Goffman, E. (1986). *Stigma: Notes on the management of spoiled identity.* New York, NY: Touchstone. (Originally published 1963)

Zerubavel, E. (1991). *The fine line: Making distinctions in everyday life.* New York, NY: Free Press.

_____. (1996). Lumping and splitting: Notes on social classification. *Sociological Forum, 11,* 421–433.

CHAPTER 3

"He's fine to be your friend."
INTERRACIAL RELATIONSHIPS

alexandre zveiger/ Shutterstock.com

Tara Maynard dreamily closed her eyes, thoroughly enjoying the breeze that stroked her long, blonde hair. It was warm outside, but not too hot, and it just felt perfect in the car with the windows down. She stretched out her long legs and took a deep breath, which relaxed her even more. She caught a whiff of Marcus's cologne and let it permeate her nose. His alluring scent had captivated her from the very beginning. She was engrossed in the moment and happily recognized that she had never been so much in love before. As the car was speeding toward Florida and the port to get on their cruise, she was fully cognizant that even more bliss was awaiting them in the next few days.

They were on spring break, hauling from their college in North Carolina, about to embark on a trip of a lifetime. Tara could hardly contain her excitement. She had never been on a cruise before, and she had never taken a vacation with Marcus. She felt that two long-term dreams were being attained at the same time, and there was no place she would have rather been, and no one she would have rather been with. She reached for Marcus's hand and squeezed it. He clutched her hand and kissed it. Her heart did a backflip, or rather, a series of somersaults and jumps. She was caught up in the moment and her euphoria. Her mind flew back to the first time she had seen Marcus.

It was 7 months ago, during a boring chemistry class in college. Chemistry wasn't Tara's major, and it didn't interest her too much either. She was mindlessly glancing around the room, her eyes desperately trying to find something enticing to settle on. The professor posed a question, which sounded like a foreign language to Tara. A tall guy raised his hand and answered the question flawlessly. At first, Tara didn't realize the response was impeccable, but she quickly deducted that from the professor's laudatory reaction. The tall guy seemed to speak the language of chemistry as well. Tara felt a sudden desire to understand chemistry more; maybe it would help her understand this guy, too. She was taken aback by her unexpected eagerness, as she had never found herself so interested in someone at first sight. She abruptly felt as if she knew all about chemistry, just not the kind of chemistry the class was focusing on.

As the class was progressing, Tara became more and more confused by the material. She was in grave need of tutoring, and when she sheepishly approached the tall guy for help, it was unclear what she was hoping for more: an enlightenment and better grade in chemistry or exploring the chemistry that attracted her to him. Either way, the guy, Marcus, was zealous to come to the rescue. He soon turned out to be interested in delving into both types of chemistry. Tara earned a strong B in the class, as well as a boyfriend. They were inseparable ever since.

Marcus was a chemistry major, preparing to go to medical school, following in his father's footsteps. Tara was enthralled by his high ambitions, especially because she was not so set on her future career. She started out with an undecided major, then opted for English, but felt dissatisfied, as if she was not on the right track. Her parents urged her to become a teacher, but she gradually realized that it was not her path. She discovered political science and fell in love with it despite her parents' concerns that she would end up in a career that wasn't the best fit for a woman, or, even worse in their minds, she would become a liberal. Her decision to attend a large university in Charlotte had already stretched their comfort level. They had pushed for a community college near her hometown in the North Carolina mountains, where she would launch into a respectable, preferably feminine, major and career and maybe even meet a nice, honorable young man and get married soon after college. Even better, she could just make up with Josh, the son of their next-door neighbor, and start dating him again. Tara and Josh dated in high school, and her parents were befuddled and despondent when they broke up, as they couldn't imagine a guy more perfect for Tara. Josh was kind and stable, but Tara was often bored and unfulfilled during their relationship. She was looking for something that Josh was unable to offer, and she found it in Marcus.

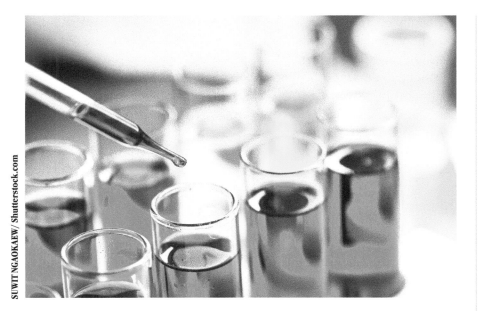

SUWIT NGAOKAEW/ Shutterstock.com

After Tara and Marcus had been dating for 3 months, he introduced her to his parents. They lived in an expansive home in a coveted suburb of Charlotte. Marcus still lived at home, in an apartment above the three-car garage. It was a private and comfortable 800-square-foot space. Tara was really impressed, but was quietly wondering why they had always met in her cozy dorm room when they could have had more space and privacy here. Well, in fact, she wasn't too surprised; she had a pretty clear idea why Marcus hadn't brought her here before.

Marcus's parents stirred even more awe in her than the house. His father appeared to be a distinguished, elegant, powerful, and respectable man, towering above everyone in the room at 6.6 feet. His mother was not petite either, but shorter than Tara, with carefully groomed hair, meticulous makeup, a master's degree, and an established career. Tara was well aware that it was not easy to impress such parents, and she felt slightly intimidated. At first glance, the eyes of Marcus's mother trailed up and down on Tara's body. They rested for a moment on Tara's long, blonde hair, voluptuous figure, and porcelain skin. There was a fleeting cloud on her face, but, beyond that, if Tara wasn't what she expected, her expression didn't give that away. Tara put her hair behind her ear and pulled down her skirt to show less skin, suddenly self-conscious about her appearance, which was unfamiliar territory, as she couldn't remember how many times people had complimented her on her looks.

Apart from the first awkward nanosecond, Marcus's parents were very polite and welcoming. Although they hardly asked any questions about her family or upbringing, they were inquisitive about her likes and dislikes, hopes and dreams. Marcus's face shone with pride as he was watching their exchange. He frequently interjected with praises of Tara. She ended up having a pleasant time and wondered why she had ever thought that she might not.

Shortly after their visit to his parents, Marcus began to ask when she would introduce him to her parents. Tara turned out to be very resourceful in procrastinating the trip. As both of them were busy, she could put off the visit for a while almost imperceptibly. After about a month Marcus started pushing the issue a little bit more forcefully, and he was clearly growing frustrated. Finally he asked Tara if there was a reason for postponing the introduction, and if the reason was what he thought it was. His question quickly sobered Tara, and she knew that it was time for the visit. She hadn't told her parents about Marcus, and she considered doing that before they just dropped in, but somehow she didn't get to it.

As they drove to Tara's parents' house, even the view of the mountains couldn't lighten her soul the way it usually did. Walking up to the house, she took a deep breath. Marcus reached for her hand, but she slid it out of his touch to ring the doorbell. The wide smile on her parents' faces froze as they saw them. They took a moment to recover and glanced at Tara questioningly.

"Hi honey," her mother greeted her. "I see you brought a friend."

Marcus held out his hand, and Tara's mother slowly shook it. Before Marcus introduced himself, Tara quickly interjected, "This is Marcus."

"Marcus, huh?" her father asked, shaking his hand. "Do you go to school together?"

"Yes," Tara asserted. "Marcus was in my chemistry class. He's saved me from failing that class. I owe my B to him."

Marcus gave Tara a bewildered look and opened his mouth to add something, but finally he stayed silent.

Tara's parents invited them to the house and sat them down in the living room. They asked some questions about school and student hangouts in Charlotte, but they were a little stiff and sometimes sunk into an uncomfortable silence. They did their best to snap out of it right away and keep the conversation going. They seemed almost too eager to fill the silence. After about 15 minutes, Tara's younger brother, Clay, walked in, and Tara's parents appeared incredibly relieved to see him.

"Clay, come here, meet Tara's friend from school, Marcus," their father bellowed, his volume louder than usual, with a forced enthusiasm in his tone.

Clay did a double take of Marcus, then a grin overtook his face.

"Hey, Marcus," Clay smirked. "It's a pleasure to meet Tara's friend from school."

"Clay, honey," their mother began. "Why don't you take Marcus outside and show him the yard? You could shoot some hoops. You like basketball, Marcus, don't you?"

"Yes, ma'am, of course, I do," Marcus sighed, with a nearly undetectable hint of sarcasm in his voice.

Marcus and Clay walked outside, and Tara braced herself to face her parents' inquisition.

"So, you know Marcus from school," her mother began slowly. "How interesting that you haven't mentioned him before."

"I don't talk about all my friends, mom," Tara responded.

"No, honey, apparently you don't," her mother said, pursing her lips.

"You might not mention all your friends, but you don't bring all of them home either," her father inserted.

Tara opened and closed her mouth, and her parents exchanged a worried glance.

"Tara, honey, Marcus is your friend, right?" her mother queried.

Tara squinted and didn't say a word.

"What's going on? Why don't you answer your mother?" her father growled.

"What do you want me to say?" Tara asked, exasperated. "Do you want me to say that he's my friend, then we have a pleasant dinner, and everyone's happy?"

Her mother paled. In fact, Tara had never seen her face so ghostly white before.

"You mean he's not your friend?" her mother inquired, her voice shaking. "You mean, he's your...?"

"Yes, mom," Tara blurted out. "He's my boyfriend."

"What do you mean? When did this start?" her father shouted, while her mother was staring, with tears in her eyes.

"Six months ago," Tara whispered.

"Six months, and you never told us? You're telling us now, and like this?" her father roared.

"Yes," Tara sighed. "I was afraid that this is how you'd react, so I kept putting it off."

"I can't believe you," her father continued, sinking down to the sofa and burying his face in his hands. "How can you put us into this situation? He's right outside with your brother. What do we do with him now?"

"Well, you could start by inviting him in and being nice to him," Tara said, on the verge of tears. "You could ask him questions and try to get to know him. You don't know him, but I do. He's smart and strong and generous and noble. If you just tried to get to know him, you'd see all of that."

"Maybe I would. Maybe he's all that. But what I see now is that he's black," her father retorted, his last word piercing the air.

Tara started to cry and felt as if she would never be able to stop. Finally she gathered herself and addressed her father, "You're a racist, dad; you're such a racist."

"How can you say that?" her father yelled, while her mother was staring at both of them, terrified. "A racist? Me? I have a black guy living across the street, and do you see me having a problem with that? No. I've gone to school with black people; I've worked with several black guys. Have I ever had a problem with any of that? No."

"Tara, honey," her mother jumped in. "Of course, your father is not a racist. Neither of us is. That's not what she meant, Ned. Nobody is a racist here. We love black people. We love all of God's creation. Sweetie, I'm sure Marcus is a nice young man. He looks smart and polite. I'm so glad he can help you in school. But you're going a little far. Maybe you're just confused. You confuse friendship with something else."

"Mom, I'm not confused," Tara declared. "I love Marcus. *We're in love.*"

"My, my, Tara, you're so young, you probably don't know what love is," her mother smiled, shaking her head.

"I do now, with Marcus," Tara countered. "But you're right that I hadn't known love before him."

Her mother paled again, "Like I said, honey, he seems like a nice person. He's fine to be your friend. He's fine to be your friend, but I hope you'll reconsider being involved with him."

"No, I won't," Tara sighed. "I can't. This is much more than friendship."

Her mother suddenly looked horrified, "Do you think you might *marry* him?"

"She's not going to marry him, Martha, don't say such silly things," Tara's father exclaimed.

"Actually it's not silly," Tara protested. "I'm not saying I will, but I'm not saying I won't either. It's too early to tell, and I'm still young."

"My Lord," her mother cried. "I've always thought you'd end up with Josh. I've still had hopes for that. Or a guy *like* Josh."

"You mean a guy who's white?" Tara asked with a slightly sarcastic tone.

"It's so rude for you to say that," her mother complained. "I meant a guy that we've known all our lives, whose family we've known all our lives."

"I'm the rude one?" Tara blurted out. "Wow. I knew you wouldn't be happy, but I didn't think you'd be like this. Especially you, mom. You've always taught me to follow my heart; you just failed to mention that it's only up to a certain point. I think this is enough for today. I'm leaving. With my *friend*. Just keep thinking that if that makes you feel better and forget I said anything."

Tara stormed out, grabbing Marcus on the way to the car. When he asked what was going on, Tara replied, "You don't want to know. And it doesn't matter. What does matter is that I love you," she asserted, kissing him hard on the mouth. Since then Tara resisted Marcus's attempts to elicit more information from her and only had a few strained conversations with her parents, and they all avoided referring to Marcus.

Tara suddenly snapped back to the present as they were pulling into the cruise port parking lot. Her excitement returned as she caught a glimpse of the mammoth ships. After boarding and dropping off their luggage in their cabin, they set out to discover the ship. It had 15 stories, with no thirteenth floor to avoid bad luck. It had two pools, several hot tubs, a gym, sauna, two beauty salons, mini golf, a casino, two theaters, two night clubs, numerous stores, and five restaurants. All of a sudden, Tara wondered if 4 days were enough to fully enjoy every opportunity this swimming city had to offer. While she was looking forward to seeing the Bahamas, she now was almost sorry to ever have to leave the ship.

After the first quick tour of the ship they returned to their cabin, stared at the ocean view for a while, made love, and then were restfully lying in each other's arms. Tara was already bursting with the abundance of new, thrilling experience the ship was graciously bestowing on them. She felt that there was something unique about the ship that she hadn't been able to put her finger on, but she couldn't figure out what. Then it dawned on her that she had been so occupied with all the novelty that she hadn't really paid attention to the people around them. She now realized that she hadn't seen any kids, only couples. There weren't any kid pools or slides either.

"Hey, Marcus," Tara began. "Is this a couples' cruise? I haven't seen any kids."

"Yes, baby, it sure is," Marcus affirmed with a grin. "I like kids, don't get me wrong, but I thought we needed some peace and quiet and some romance. On a couples' cruise everything is about romance."

"I like that," Tara smiled. "I'm all about romance, too," she said, leaning to Marcus to kiss him. Something else was stirring in her, demanding recognition, but it took her a few more moments to put it into words, "You know what else? I've just realized that there're so many other interracial

couples on this ship. More than what you usually see."

"Have you seen any couples that aren't interracial?" Marcus queried, sneering.

"I don't know," Tara mused, trying to visualize the people they had passed. "Maybe. Or maybe not. Wait, what? What are you saying?"

"I'm saying this is a cruise for interracial couples," Marcus blurted out, bursting into a laugh.

"What?" Tara asked, astonished. "I didn't know there was such a thing."

"I didn't know either," Marcus declared. "I just came across this ad and thought it was so cool. Finally some people who get it. Finally some people who're like us. Finally some people who don't stare."

"Yes, that's true, I guess," Tara mused, overwhelmed by a wave of relief. She hadn't been cognizant of this, but she just realized now that occasionally she had held her breath for a second before entering somewhere with Marcus, especially holding hands or hugging. This didn't happen so much in Charlotte, but it occurred more in small towns or rural areas of the South, such as her hometown. She sometimes felt people staring, giving them a questioning or doubtful look. She usually just straightened her back and glared back at them defiantly. On occasion, she smiled back instead, trying to show them that she and Marcus were happy and hoping that they might understand. Didn't these people know that they were well into the twenty-first century?

Apart from her parents, she had only encountered blatant prejudice once, but it was enough to shake her. She and Marcus had been shopping, but she forgot something and went back to the store. A petite old lady walked up to her and bluntly said, "Dear, you're such a beautiful girl. You could get any man. Just any man you'd want. Do you have to settle for this fellow?"

"Not that it's any of your business, ma'am, but he's the man I want," Tara retorted. Her voice sounded firm, but she felt rattled on the inside. The scariest part was that the old woman seemed so innocent, full of good intentions, and she wouldn't have acknowledged that she was doing anything wrong.

Tara was bothered even by the seemingly approving reactions. A guy patted Marcus on the back once, smirking at him and looking Tara up and down. A girl winked at Tara at a club once, after glimpsing at Marcus, and she even gave her a thumbs-up. An interracial couple gave them a high-five once, just passing them by. A few times a stranger walked up to them and said that they were such a cute couple, or that they looked great together, and they shouldn't let anyone tell them otherwise. Tara was annoyed by these gestures and comments because these people still looked at them and treated them differently.

Besides relief and joy, Tara felt an unexpected wave of discomfort about the idea of a cruise for interracial couples only. Couldn't they just go on a couples' cruise and be left alone? Couldn't they just be a couple? Did they have to be an interracial couple? Did they need, did the *world* need, a separate, almost segregated, ship for interracial couples only? And why was there an assumption, even from Marcus, that all these people were like them, and that they would understand? Would sharing one thing, that is,

Rido/ Shutterstock.com

being in an interracial relationship, override everything else? These people probably came from different families, backgrounds, age groups, parts of the United States, or even the world, so would they all really share a common ground and develop a profound understanding for each other? Tara doubted it, but she didn't want to ruin Marcus's fun, and she couldn't deny that a part of her saw the advantages of such a specialty cruise, too.

Later on that day, while Marcus was swimming, Tara was trying to catch some sun. She forgot her suntan lotion, but as if the woman on the lounge-bed next to her read her thoughts, she held out her suntan spray, "Here," she addressed Tara. "You'll probably need this."

"Thanks," Tara smiled appreciatively and sprayed some lotion on herself.

"I'm Kiesha, by the way," the woman declared, reaching out her hand.

"Tara, nice to meet you," Tara introduced herself, while she couldn't help admiring the woman's athletic, but still immensely feminine figure. Kiesha was one of the most beautiful women Tara had ever seen.

"Which one is yours?" Kiesha asked, her face full of smile.

Tara pointed out Marcus.

"Nice," Kiesha responded, pointing to a handsome, masculine guy in the pool. "That's my guy."

Tara nodded and added, "Good-looking guy."

"I know what you're probably thinking," Kiesha asserted teasingly. "You're probably trying to figure out how we're interracial. He's pretty dark, I know, but he's not black. He's three-quarters Native American, one-quarter white. He's from Colombia, so he's also Hispanic, although that's not a race, of course, despite what many people think. So, being from Colombia, naturally, he's a likely drug dealer in my parents' eyes. If not that, he's with me to get a green card through marriage. Maybe I shouldn't have told him my parents said that; he got so offended. No wonder. And he's so proud, now he won't propose to me until he has a green card of his own. That sucks. We've been together for almost 4 years, and this little finger could really use a ring now," Kiesha grinned, holding up her ring finger. "Although my parents would definitely flip then. I've already betrayed our kind; I've been so disloyal, yada, yada. I'm sure you know that kind of talk. Your man has probably heard it a million times. And Andres's parents would like a nice Catholic girl, of course. I'm fully prepared to be that. I'll be Catholic, I'll be whatever, as long as I get to marry him already. Anyway, at least our friends don't give us a hard time. In fact, most of my friends think Andres is pretty hot, so if anything, they're a little bit jealous. And you just gotta love his cute accent. I know I'm lucky to have him. And he's lucky to have me, too, of course."

Tara's head was spinning as Kiesha's flow of words saturated her mind. She was actually *not* trying to figure out what interracial combination Kiesha and Andres were. She didn't think it mattered or that it was any of her business. It crossed her mind that the label that could fit Kiesha and Andres the most was intercultural, but then she discarded the term, as she was not a fan of any kind of label. What did occupy her mind for a few moments was Kiesha's assumption that Marcus had probably been accused with betraying his "kind," too. If he had encountered that type of prejudice, he hadn't told Tara. Anxiety squeezed her stomach for a second. She was hoping that Marcus didn't have to struggle because of their relationship even more than what she was cognizant of. Not that she told him everything about *her* negative encounters, but she wished to protect *him* at least.

A few hours later, at dinner, Tara and Marcus were seated at a table for four. They could have waited for a table for two, or they could choose to be seated at a larger table. As the ship had originally been designed for a wider variety of travelers, couples *and* families, they had some bigger tables. Tara was looking forward to a romantic dinner for two, but they were both ravenous and hesitant to wait for a cozy table. Also, Marcus seemed to be enthusiastic about meeting other interracial couples, so he didn't mind sharing a table with another couple. So, a few minutes after they had been seated, another couple joined them. They looked nice enough, so now Tara felt any resistance she might have had about sharing the table evaporating.

"Hi," the guy from the couple began. "I'm Jacob, and this is my wife, Midori. May we join you?"

"Sure, come sit," Marcus waved. "I'm Marcus, and this is my girlfriend, Tara."

They all smiled at each other and expressed how nice it was to meet one another. Although Tara didn't enjoy it too much when she and Marcus were told how good they looked together because it made her wonder if people meant that their *contrasts* looked good together, she could hardly resist telling Jacob and Midori the same. Jacob was very tall, while Midori very petite, but both of their faces shone with the same benevolence and intelligence. After they had all ordered, Marcus's curiosity got the best of him, and he started asking some questions, "So, where are y'all from?"

"I'm from Connecticut, but we live in New York," Jacob replied.

"And I'm from Japan originally," Midori explained, smiling. "My parents moved to California with me and my brother when I was 5. I grew up there but moved to New York to do my master's degree. I fell in love with it, both my career and New York, so I've lived there ever since."

"Cool," Marcus beamed. "Where in California?"

"Near San Francisco," Midori responded.

"I've been to San Francisco. And New York," Marcus added. "Loved them both. You guys are lucky."

Tara had known that Marcus had been to New York, but she hadn't realized he had visited California as well. He was undeniably more widely traveled than her, courtesy of his parents. Tara had hardly been outside of North Carolina and never outside of the South.

"So, you are married, huh?" Marcus asked.

"Yes, we sure are," Jacob affirmed, squeezing Midori's hand. "We've been married for 4 years."

"Yes, and we have a 2-year-old, Mia," Midori elaborated, pulling out her phone to show them Mia's picture. "That's her."

"She's so cute," Tara and Marcus asserted in unison.

"We miss her already, but we need time on our own once in a while," Midori sighed. "But we're lucky. We couldn't be happier."

"And who would've thought we'd get here?" Jacob mused. "She was a tough one. It took me a while to get her to go out with me."

"Well, I'll admit it," Midori laughed. "I *was* a tough one. Oh, but not because of what you might think. It had *nothing* to do with race. I didn't care that he was white. I didn't care about what my parents might think at that point. I was 31. And frankly I had never been a docile little girl anyway. Yes, I knew that my parents were secretly hoping for a guy with Japanese descent, but my brother had married a white girl by then, and my parents realized that I had never dated a Japanese guy and hadn't intended to. So, they weren't surprised about Jacob. Maybe they were a little amazed about me actually settling down and getting married. I had always been all about my career."

"I can attest to that," Jacob chuckled.

"Yes, dear, you can," Midori conceded. "Poor Jacob. We met at the art gallery where I worked as an assistant creative director. He was one of the artists. He asked me out after his first exhibit, but I turned him down. I viewed myself as a professional, and I wasn't about to get involved with one of the artists. Even after he changed galleries, I turned him down at least three times."

"It was more like five," Jacob interjected.

"OK, maybe five," Midori admitted. "I was about to be promoted to creative director, and I wasn't going to jeopardize my career. I thought I didn't have time for dating anyway. But eventually I just couldn't resist him. He showed me that he was so hard-working and persistent not only through his work, but through pursuing me."

"That's a great story," Marcus said fervently. "So, being an interracial couple has never been an issue for you in any way? I don't mean to pry, I'm just curious, and I think being on this ship could be a great way to learn from each other. If we're not open and honest here, with each other, where or how can we do that?"

While Tara partly agreed with Marcus, she was also stunned that he was so forward. Jacob and Midori didn't seem to mind, however, as they were both still smiling.

"Yeah, man, I hear you," Jacob began. "Those are perfectly legitimate questions. I look forward to the day when they're not, when it becomes a non-issue entirely, but I have to admit that we're not quite there yet."

"I think we're lucky," Midori contemplated. "We live in New York, so nobody cares. Nobody would've cared in San Francisco either. And we're mostly surrounded by the art community, who are very open. Frankly, I think most people don't even realize that we're interracial or wouldn't call us that. A white guy and Asian girl is the most common interracial combination, so people are used to it. Also, being Asian American I'm the model minority, remember? I'm the 'honorary white.' So, in many ways we're not even seen as interracial."

"Yes, that's very true," Jacob confirmed. "So, in most contexts it's not really an issue. Some people in my family, or even a few of my acquaintances, I wouldn't say they had an issue with it, but some seemed to have some stereotypes. After hearing that Midori was from Asia, some assumed that she was this quiet, passive, obedient woman, and knowing me, they were surprised that I'd go for that."

"The surprise was on them," Midori grinned. "They didn't expect me. I'm about as far from that stereotype as you can get."

Tara and Marcus laughed along with Midori and Jacob, as even they realized by now how true that was.

"You know, my brother encountered some stereotypes, too," Midori continued. "Actually, his wife's parents had some positive stereotypes. They assumed he was hardworking and highly educated with a good income. So, they were happy that their daughter scored such a guy. Coincidentally, these stereotypes were true for my brother, but, of course, they can be very inaccurate for others. Oh, it just occurred to me that some of my sister-in-law's friends had some other assumptions about my brother. Some were worried that he might not only be hardworking, but a workaholic, who'd never be home and never spend any time with his wife. Also, at her bachelorette party a few of her friends, after consuming some liquid courage, were wondering if my brother was sufficiently well-endowed… Apparently they had some incorrect ideas about the anatomy of Asian American men…"

Tara and Marcus laughed, but they were both slightly horrified. It abruptly crossed Tara's mind that a couple of her friends had the opposite presumption about Marcus, and one of them was bold enough to ask, but she quickly shook off the memory, and would have been too embarrassed to share it with Midori and Jacob, or even with Marcus.

After dinner Marcus and Tara waved a convivial goodbye to Midori and Jacob. Marcus seemed pumped about meeting another *interracial couple* and sharing their experience. Tara wasn't necessarily as thrilled as Marcus, or rather, she wasn't elated for the same reason as Marcus. She was simply delighted to have met a nice *couple*.

The next day they arrived at the Bahamas. While Tara enjoyed the cruise, she was suddenly ready to get off the ship and dive into more novel experiences. She was even more keen on having some alone time with Marcus. She wanted to immerse herself into being a couple and maybe even forget about being an *interracial couple* for a day. On the ship everything reminded her of the latter.

They had an immensely action-packed and gratifying day. They went scuba-diving and to a water park with the tallest slides Tara had ever seen. Finally, they even had some time to swim and sunbathe on the beach. They

joked that Tara finally traveled beyond the American South, although, ironically, she had to travel even more South for that. As it turned out, Marcus had been to Jamaica, Mexico, Canada, England, Germany, and France before. Traveling might not have been a novelty for him, but traveling with Tara was, and he was engrossed in every moment of their first vacation together.

When back on the ship, they collapsed into each other's arms. They were tired, but not too tired to make love. After a quick shower they dressed up for dinner. Tara was hoping for a dinner for two this time, but Marcus had other plans. He insisted that he was ravenous and eager to meet another couple at a table for four. Tara sighed and acquiesced. Marcus was a textbook extrovert, and Tara didn't want to spoil his fun. She also sensed that this was important for him; probably it hadn't been a coincidence that he had selected this cruise.

They were led to a table where two men had already been seated. They seemed to be absorbed in conversation.

"Hi," Marcus said hesitantly, "We don't mean to interrupt, but we were guided to this table."

"Please, you're not interrupting. In fact, please interrupt," exclaimed one of the men. "You don't have to be so polite, dear. Not that we don't enjoy each other's company, but we've been together for 14 years. Probably we've talked about every single topic on Earth already. We can use some new blood. I'm Antoine, and this is my partner, Eric. Don't let the name and his looks fool you; he's not an actual Viking. His ancestors came from Norway, though. Back in the day. Please don't be intimidated, dears, take a seat. I might talk a lot, but in exchange, Eric will hardly make a sound. Do I detect a slight southern accent?"

Tara glanced at Marcus. She knew that he was proud that his southern accent was almost imperceptible and sometimes deliberately didn't use southern expressions. His parents were the same way. So she jumped in to answer, "Yeah, we're from North Carolina. I'm Tara, and this is Marcus."

"Nice to meet y'all," Antoine joked. "Originally I'm from Alabama, but I've lived away from the South for about 18 years, so I'm not such a southern boy anymore."

"Sometimes you are," Eric inserted quietly.

"Yeah, I am," Antoine admitted. "*Sometimes*. Now, tell us all about you dears. Where did y'all meet? Are you really-really in love? I remember that phase; it's such a nice one. Do you wanna have each other's babies? I don't recall that phase, though, but I hear that's a thing."

Tara laughed exuberantly, and Marcus chuckled gently. Antoine was a character, for sure. Tara told them about themselves, while Marcus and Eric were listening intently. Antoine often interrupted her with more questions and puns. Finally, he asked, "So, how do you

like being a caffe latte? That's what I call me and Eric. Sometimes coffee with whipped cream. When you add milk to coffee, or whipped cream, for that matter, they mix so well together, and you get something that's much yummier than either one separately. That's us. And that's how I hope you see yourselves."

Marcus smiled and didn't look reserved anymore, "I like that, man. Yes, that's us, too. That's what I want to be," he added, glimpsing at Tara.

"That's what I'm talking about," Antoine burst out, high-fiving both Marcus and Tara. "Some people might not want to mix coffee with milk or whipped cream. They might not realize or acknowledge that it actually makes both of them better. But you know that taste, and you know it's a good mix. Never let others tell you otherwise. I did in the past a couple of times and ended up regretting it. But what can I say? I was just a scared little black boy in Alabama. I didn't always have such a big mouth. When I realized I was gay, gay was a taboo word in my small town, in my family, and especially in my church. It was kind of like, don't ask, don't tell, so I did that; I never said anything. I just quietly left my hometown and moved up North. How ironic that Eric and I actually met at church. Can you believe that? Of course, it's not the kind of church I used to attend as a child. And I do take him home when I visit, which is not too much these days, maybe once a year. My folks still call him 'my friend,' but whatever, I don't care. I know what's going on, and they know what's going on anyway. Do you know how much shit we've gotten over the years from so many different people? Interracial, gay, and Eric being 25 years older than me? Yeah, I know, he looks so good for his age. Oh, and he has a ton more money than I do, too. *And*? Who cares? What does it matter? Some people think they know better what a good relationship is, and they doubt we can be it. And look at us. We've been together for *14 years*. It works. It just works."

Tara glanced at Marcus, who seemed to be drinking in Antoine's every word. Tara was impressed as well. She had had some skepticism about the special-themed cruise, but she had to admit that they had learned a lot from fellow travelers. Yes, they were a couple, and for them it truly didn't matter that they were born with different skin colors. So, for them being members of an interracial couple was insignificant. However, until or unless the world changed, some people would continue to see them as an *interracial couple*, and they couldn't be in denial about that. At least, Tara had to stop being in denial about that. In addition, she and Marcus had to begin to engage in more talks and more open talks about the issue, at least among themselves. Tara was ready to start tonight.

Discussion Questions

1. Continue the story of Tara and Marcus. What do you think will happen next? How do you envision their relationship in the future?

2. Discuss the role of gender in the various relationships in the story.

3. Based on the story, how do perceptions of different couples vary depending on the specific racial and ethnic combination each couple represents? Could they encounter different reactions if the race of the participants was switched (e.g., if Marcus was white and Tara black, and so on)? Why/why not? That is, do you think there is a combined effect of race and gender in this case?

4. A stereotype is a simplified, exaggerated, generalized idea about members of a group of people. Prejudice is a biased judgment (either positive or negative) and/or amplified feelings (likes or dislikes) about an individual based on his/her belonging to a specific group. Stigma is a salient, persistent, negative label that people apply to individuals who diverge from social norms (Goffman, 1986). Discrimination is treating someone differently because he/she belongs to a specific group. Give some examples for stereotyping, prejudice, stigma, and/or discrimination from the story.

5. Some racial or ethnic minorities in the United States are often viewed as "model minorities" and/or "honorary whites." What do these terms mean? Give an example from the story. Do these labels exemplify prejudice (either positive or negative)? Why/why not? Could these labels be harmful in any way? Why/why not?

6. The Bogardus social distance scale (Bogardus, 1933) measures levels of prejudice toward different groups. The highest level of prejudice occurs when people would not even allow a person from a specific group to enter their country. Prejudice gradually declines on the scale as people would allow a person belonging to a specific group as a visitor to their country, a citizen, coworker, neighbor, and close friend. The lowest level of prejudice (or virtually no prejudice) materializes when people would not mind becoming relatives with a person of a specific group through marriage (e.g., that person marrying their daughter or son). Select some characters from the story and discuss which level of the social distance scale they seem to be on. Do you think there is a more exaggerated mental, conceptual distance between any of the categories than the others (e.g., a greater perceived difference between "friend" and "relative" than "co-worker" and "neighbor") that might almost require a "mental quantum leap" to bridge (Zerubavel, 1991)? Why/why not?

7. Bonilla-Silva (2013), who coined the term "color-blind racism," argued that covert racism had mostly substituted overt racism in American society, but color-blindness could involve dangers as well, because pretending that race has lost all of its relevance in this society could easily perpetuate racial inequalities instead of mitigating them. Can you apply color-blind racism to any aspects of the story? Why/why not?

8. Brekhus (1996) highlighted that marked categories tend to be perceived as less natural or potentially more problematic than unmarked categories. Do you think that marking interracial relationships by placing the term "interracial" in front of them suggests that they are different from other relationships? Why/why not? Discuss Tara's opinion on this and yours.

9. Sociologists define race as a social construct—that is, it is not perceived as biological, essential, or universal, but a concept that is shaped by societies, in particular, by cultural, economic, and political forces (Omi & Winant, 2014). Therefore, racial classifications vary over time and across cultures. How do you think the increasing number and acceptance of interracial relationships and marriages, as well as the surge in multiracial children, might modify racial classifications and the meaning of race in the United States?

Find the Answers

Go to http://www.gallup.com/poll/163697/approve-marriage-blacks-whites.aspx to find answers to the following questions.

1. How have approval rates of black-white marriages changed from 1958 until recent years?

2. How do approval rates of black-white marriages vary by race? How do you explain the difference? How is this represented in the story of Tara, Marcus, and the other couples?

3. How do approval rates of black-white marriages vary by age? How do you explain this variation?

4. How do approval rates of black-white marriages vary by region? What do you see as the main reasons for this variation?

Mini Research Assignments

1. Find and watch a documentary on the *Loving v. Virginia* case. Also, research anti-miscegenation laws. Summarize what anti-miscegenation laws stood for and describe the *Loving v. Virginia* case. Compare this case with Marcus, Tara, and the other couples in the story and analyze the role of history, region, gender, and age in the differences between the stories.

2. Watch a movie, documentary, and/or episode of a TV show on a heterosexual interracial couple and another one on a gay interracial couple. Compare and contrast the portrayal of the two relationships. Is there any prejudice or stigma in either case? Is there more in one case than the other? Discuss the intersection of race, gender, and sexual orientation. Select another factor (such as social class, age, region) and analyze its intersection with the other factors. Draw parallels with the stories of Tara, Marcus, and the other couples.

3. Study at least two interracial dating sites and a third site that does not specifically cater to interracial couples only. Compare and contrast the three sites. How do they portray relationships in general? How do they depict interracial relationships? What kind of dating trends, messages, and clients do you observe for each site? Do you find a difference between two people meeting and establishing a relationship, which is coincidentally interracial, versus deliberately seeking out an interracial relationship? Why/why not?

4. Survey at least seven individuals, asking them to rate their agreement with the following statements on a scale of 1–10 (1 meaning complete disagreement and 10 indicating full agreement): 1. "I have either dated someone from a different race or wouldn't object to doing so if I were single and the opportunity presented itself." 2. "I wouldn't mind it if my child or another close relative married someone from a different race." 3. "I see absolutely no difference between interracial couples and couples who are the same race." Summarize your results and discuss why you might have received these answers. Analyze the potential role of race, gender, age, region, and so on. Draw parallels with the story of Marcus, Tara, and the others.

References

Bogardus, E. (1933). *Social problems and social processes. Selected papers from the Proceedings of the American Sociological Society 1932.* Chicago, IL: University of Chicago Press.

Bonilla-Silva, E. (2013). *Racism without racists: Color-blind racism and the persistence of racial inequality in America* (4th ed.). Lanham, MD: Rowman & Littlefield.

Brekhus, W. (1996). Social marking and the mental coloring of identity: Sexual identity construction and maintenance in the United States." *Sociological Forum, 11,* 497–522.

Goffman, E. (1986). *Stigma: Notes on the management of spoiled identity.* New York, NY: Touchstone. (Original published 1963)

Newport, F. (2013). In U.S., 87% approve of black-white marriage, vs. 4% in 1958. Washington, DC: Pew Research Center. Retrieved from http://www.gallup.com/poll/163697/approve-marriage-blacks-whites.aspx

Omi, M., & Winant, H. (2014). *Racial formation in the United States* (3rd ed.). New York, NY: Routledge.

Zerubavel, E. (1991). *The fine line: Making distinctions in everyday life.* New York, NY: Free Press.

CHAPTER

"He didn't mean it."
DOMESTIC ABUSE

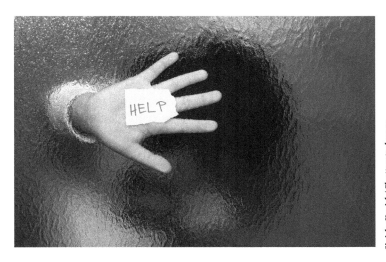

Sinisha Karich/ Shutterstock.com

Violet Larsen looked around vigilantly, confirming that she was alone. She took a small pill and washed it down quickly with some tap water, drinking straight from the bathroom faucet. Her heart was beating rapidly, her mouth was dry, and she felt as if there was a lump in her throat, so it was difficult to swallow the pill, and she had to take another gulp of water to force it down. She glanced behind her back and shoved the rest of the pills back to where she was hiding them. She was relieved to have managed to take the pill without being caught, but, at the same time, a familiar sense of guilt started to set in. She knew that she was doing something wrong and betrayed her husband. She startled as she heard his voice from downstairs.

"Hey, honey," Violet's husband, Bradley called from downstairs. "Where are you?"

"I'm upstairs, I'll be right down," Violet responded, slightly out of breath.

"No, no, I'll be right up," Bradley countered, his voice sounding closer with every word. In less than a minute he entered the master bedroom, kicked off his shoes and embraced Violet tightly. "Whew, this was a long day at work. I've missed you so much. I could hardly wait to do this," he whispered, kissing her hard on the mouth. He grabbed her with both hands. Violet felt lethargic and not in the mood by any means, but she was reluctant to disappoint Bradley. As he made a certain move, her heart sank because she realized he also wanted her to do the thing that made her uncomfortable. She gulped and smiled, pretending that she was into it.

The first time he had asked her to do that, years ago, she had refused. He had looked extremely hurt and had been sullen for a while before blurting out, "What's wrong? I don't turn you on enough? I want every inch of your body, and you couldn't ask for something that I wouldn't be happy to do. Am I disgusting you now?"

"No, of course not," Violet protested. "I just… I just don't want to do *that*. You turn me on, of course, but that doesn't turn me on. Is that okay?"

"Yeah, sure it's okay," Bradley sighed with a long face. "I won't *make* you do anything you don't *want* to do. I'd want you to be into it. I just thought that you loved me so much you wanted to please me. Love is about compromise sometimes."

Violet was confused and quiet for a moment. She wasn't sure how it would be a *compromise* if she did what he wanted her to do, but she did love him and did wish to please him.

"You know, I thought you were adventurous," Bradley continued. "I've always loved that about you. I didn't think you were such a little prude. None of my girlfriends in the past had had an issue with this. In fact, they liked it. So, I don't understand what the big deal is. But you know I love you. I'm committed to you. And I love you so much that I guess this just won't be a part of my sex life anymore. Not that I won't miss it a whole lot, but I'm willing to give it up to be with you."

It had taken Violet a few more days and some more persuasion, but finally she had caved. This had happened 6 years ago. They had been married for 5.5 years now, and while she still didn't particularly enjoy *the thing*, she was used to it now. Bradley had been right, love involved compromise. There had to be a compromise about the frequency of their intimate encounters, too. Bradley seemed to want it almost every day, while Violet had a gradually decreasing desire. She was puzzled about her apathy, as in the beginning of their relationship she had used to want to sleep with Bradley just as much as he had with her. She blamed her hormones and exhaustion, and worriedy that her low libido indicated a problem with her. Bradley appeared to be concerned about that, too, and also that she was losing interest in him, so, in most cases, Violet pretended that she was consumed by passion. In body she was almost always prepared for sex, for example, she made sure that she was constantly freshly shaven, after he had complained that her legs felt stubbly and were a turn-off. She was nearly perpetually ready in body, but hardly ever in mind and emotion.

It had only happened about once in every 2 months that she said no to Bradley's advances, usually when she had had a severe headache or unbearable fatigue. He was normally sulking for a few hours and later informed Violet that he watched porn to release his tension, which she found very hurtful. As he explained it, "I'm so sorry, honey. I know that you don't like that. But you know I'm not doing that to hurt you. But I'm a man, I have needs. I understand that you have such a low sex drive and can't always be there for me, so I accommodate my needs. And it's not that I go out and cheat on you. No matter how many women flirt with me every day, I'm totally committed to you, you know that."

Violet was befuddled as to why she felt so numb sometimes. Occasionally it was as if all emotion was sucked out of her, and the only thing left was emptiness. Periodically it was hard to conjure up any emotion even when she was with Bradley, and that's how she knew that something was seriously wrong with her. How could she feel so numb with the person that she was so in love with and so dedicated to? Time after time, when she sensed emptiness engulfing her, she deliberately daydreamed about how she had met Bradley and the first few months of their relationship to cheer herself up.

Violet had met Bradley over 6 years ago. She had recently turned 32, with a few long-term relationships in her past, but mostly just a myriad of failed short-term attempts at romance. She had started to lose her confidence, especially as her last boyfriend had cheated on her with one of her friends, whom he ended up marrying. Somehow marriage proposals had avoided her in the past, and she started to doubt if she was marriage material. One of her colleagues had had a lot of success with online dating and recommended it to Violet. Violet had some reservations, but decided to give it a try. The first few weeks didn't offer high hopes. She exchanged some messages with a few guys and even went on a date with one, but they didn't click. One day Bradley sent her a message, which changed the game entirely. She couldn't believe how handsome he was. He was also highly educated, which impressed her, along with his job as a market risk analyst at a big firm. But what blew her away the most was the message he had sent her. It was the most romantic message she had ever received.

They began dating shortly afterwards. Bradley had taken her to five-star restaurants, to the opera, ice-skating, long walks, even a horse-driven carriage ride. Dating him felt like her favorite chick-flick movies all combined. She thought she was dreaming and didn't want to wake up. He incessantly complimented her hair, her eyes, her figure, her mind, her warmth, and virtually everything about her. He was so enthusiastic,

CHAPTER 4: "He didn't mean it." Domestic Abuse

75

caring, attentive, and so madly in love. He told her he loved her within 3 weeks of dating and proposed to her after 3 months. She was worried that they might be going too fast, but everything was so idyllic, and she could hardly wait for their life together. Also, she quietly reminded herself that her previous boyfriends had never proposed to her, and it was a great sign that Bradley was not afraid of commitment. So, they were married 7 months after their first date.

The first 6 months of their marriage felt like an enchanting dream to Violet. She never used to believe that marriage could be so fairytale-like. What she had experienced as a child in her parents' marriage had been immensely different. Her father had been a recovering alcoholic for most of his life, but he often relapsed and during those periods he didn't refrain from hitting Violet's mother and yelling at her for everything. He never laid a hand on Violet and her sister, but they couldn't escape his angry verbal outbursts. After marrying Bradley, Violet realized that she might have avoided marriage before because of fearing to repeat her parents' example.

In the beginning of their marriage Bradley brought her flowers almost every day. He read poetry to her and took her out to the most outlandish places. He never failed to praise her for everything she did. He treated her like a princess. Violet felt that life couldn't get any better, and they couldn't be any happier.

Six months into the marriage Bradley was offered an incredible promotion. The only catch was that it involved a cross-country move.

He never considered not taking the job and was surprised when Violet voiced her concerns.

"I know it's a great opportunity," Violet asserted. "I just... I like living here. I have my job here, we have our friends. Your parents." Not that she spent a lot of time with her friends anymore. She and Bradley spent virtually all of their free time together, and for some reason, Bradley wasn't very keen on her friends. He was very observant and noticed some flaws in them that Violet never had. He pointed it out how jealous they seemed to be of the happiness he and Violet had found. Violet hadn't recognized that, but now that Bradley called her attention to it, she was cognizant of that, too.

As far as Bradley's parents, she had grown fond of them, and they saw much more of them than her own parents, which she didn't mind. Since she had become an adult, she had visited her parents two or three times a year, but with Bradley it was once a year, if that. He was protective of Violet and always accompanied her to ensure that she felt safe enough when her father was around. When he heard that Violet's mother made a negative comment about him, he didn't leave Violet alone with her so that she couldn't hurt Violet with such destructive remarks. He offered to be on the other line when Violet talked to her parents on the phone to provide her with safety. She didn't feel comfortable with that, but didn't want to offend Bradley, so she just ended up calling her parents less. She was somehow afraid to call them and visit them now, and she was amazed to realize that probably she was more scared of them, especially her father, than she had ever known.

"I know, honey, I'm so sorry," Bradley's voice pulled her back to their discussion on the move. "I hate to leave my parents, but we'll visit. And as far as your job, I hate to say it, but you're too good for them. They're exploiting you."

Violet worked as a paralegal at the time, and she used to like her job. However, Bradley opened her eyes to not being treated right at her workplace. Thankfully, he also made her understand that maybe part of the reason why they might not have taken her seriously at work was because of the way she dressed. He gently called her attention to some blouses that showed slightly too much cleavage and a few skirts that were a tad bit too short. She gradually changed her outfits, but still not gained a higher level of respect at work. She did at home, though, as Bradley was proud of her for standing up for herself.

Bradley painted a glamorous picture of their new life after the move, just the two of them, and she eventually caved and agreed to the move. They had a second honeymoon at their new place. And Bradley was right; it was indeed just the two of them. They spent all of their free time together, and Bradley needed her more than ever as he was adjusting to his new job, so Violet didn't get to make new friends. Bradley often emphasized that they had their own world, and they were enough for each other, and Violet began to agree. She had become disappointed in her former friends anyway. Most had pulled away from her and stopped calling, and one of them told her that maybe it wasn't the best idea to move with Bradley. Violet was outraged and finally it dawned on her that Bradley had been right; her friends had turned out to be jealous of their happiness and went as far as trying to ruin it. After all of this, she wasn't too eager to make new friends.

About 6 months after their move, when she felt she had helped Bradley enough to settle in, and she had made a great home for the two of them, she brought up the issue of going back to work, finding a new job near their new home. Bradley was partly supportive, but he wasn't sold on the idea, "I understand how important your job is, honey," he proclaimed. "Some men might say that being a paralegal is not such an important job, it's not like being a lawyer, or a risk analyst, for that matter, but I'm not one of them. You know that. I've always supported you. I've always been fine with me making a lot more money than you, too. I don't mind supporting you in that way either. So, you can do whatever you want. You can find a job, or you can stay home. I'm just worried about you. I know how exhausted you used to be when you worked so much. All that work put a strain on you, and sometimes I thought you might not be able to take it any longer. You remember how tired you used to be? And how frustrated because of not being appreciated enough? They never took you seriously. And I hate to tell you, but those guys at those law firms, they never take paralegals seriously. That'd be the same at a new job, at any job you'd find. Not that you're not great, you are, of course, but they'd never appreciate that. I'm the only one that can see you for who you are, the only one that can really appreciate you. And I need you. You can give me so much. I've been so much more productive with you being home and cheering me on. You're my greatest cheerleader. You're the best little cheerleader; that's your real strength; that's what you're really good at. I don't know what I'd do without you. You know, I thought you cared about *us* the most. I didn't think you'd be so selfish and only focus on *you*. We're a team now, and I thought you wanted to be a good team player and do what's best for the team."

"I didn't think I was being selfish for wanting to go back to work," Violet mused. "I haven't looked at it from this perspective. But maybe you're right. I wasn't too happy at work in the last year or so, and maybe there's a reason for that. Maybe I'm on a new path now."

"There you go," Bradley beamed. "I like that thinking. Maybe being a wife is what you've always been cut out to do, you just haven't had the chance to practice it, as no one had offered you that chance before me. It's their loss. I don't care that no one had ever wanted to marry you. In fact, that makes me happy because I could have the honor to do that. And you know what else I think you're really cut out to be? A mother. And now, that's an honorable job if I've ever known one. My mother did a fine job of that. And she has never wanted to do anything else because she loved my father and me enough for that."

Violet understood the implications and didn't want Bradley to believe that she didn't love him enough. She knew she needed to prove it to him. Still, she was reluctant to have a baby at that point. Something held her back, although she didn't know what. She gently asked Bradley to give her some more time. He was hurt, of course, and from then on, he was unwilling to use a condom when they made love. Violet tried to affectionately guide him to use one, but he pushed her hand aside, along with her concerns. He firmly entered her without a condom and with a smile.

Violet began to worry that she might get pregnant against her will, and she was aware that she wasn't ready, but she didn't know how to stop Bradley's sexual advances and how to make him understand that she didn't want a baby yet. The more she protested, the more sex he wanted to have. She knew better than to raise objections against the sex itself by then, but she at least tried to stand up for having protected sex. Bradley brushed her requests aside and kept telling her that she really wanted a child, too; she was just scared, and she would be grateful to him one day for helping her ease her concerns and prompting her to jump into motherhood. Violet usually accepted Bradley's viewpoints almost unconditionally, but she had a visceral feeling that he wasn't right this time. She felt entirely helpless and finally went to an OBGYN out of town and had him prescribe birth control pills for her. She felt like a traitor and was terrified that Bradley might find it out, but there didn't seem to be another choice left. She thought that she could gain some time, and in the meantime would probably eventually become ready herself, and then, she could just stop taking the pill and wait for getting pregnant. The only problem was that she had been taking the pill for nearly 4 years and still didn't feel any closer to being ready for a baby.

In the last 3 years Bradley periodically expressed his disappointment in not having a baby yet. Two years ago he got suspicious, burst out, and accused Violet of doing something to prevent it. He grabbed her purse and poured out its contents to the living room floor, hoping to discover birth control pills that she might be hiding. He searched all the medicine cabinets as well. Violet was terrified that he might find the pills, but apparently she

CHAPTER 4: "He didn't mean it." Domestic Abuse

79

had hid them better. He warned her that if he found out that she was using them, he would throw them away and make her sign something to have access to all her medical records. He would accompany her to all doctor's visits from then on, not only to OBGYNs, but to a family doctor as well. He informed her that he would be incredibly disappointed in her as a result of such a severe betrayal, and she would have to face the consequences. A year ago he had made her visit a gynecologist he had selected and undergo some testing to figure out if something might be wrong with her. He articulated that he hoped she wasn't damaged goods. Violet passed the tests, and the gynecologist suggested more rest and less stress. For a while, Bradley had been noticeably relieved and very gentle and attentive with Violet. However, lately he started to become restless and impatient again.

Some days Violet was almost suffocating under the heavy weight of the guilt she was carrying. There had to be something wrong with her, she knew that. She felt like a pathological liar and a traitor. She was often filled with self-hatred. How can she deceive her husband like that, and also, how can she not want a child to begin with? In her youth she had always envisioned having at least two children. It wasn't just about a baby; there was something amiss with her in general. She was frequently plagued by anxiety attacks, filled with dark, unexplainable fears. Other days she was simply numb and empty. Her mind was regularly cloudy, having trouble remembering small details. She was bordering on being constantly tired. She had recurrent headaches, backaches, and bouts of nausea. She had trouble sleeping and had a decreased appetite. She had lost about 15 pounds in the last few years and was on the edge of becoming underweight. Bradley blamed her thinness for not getting pregnant as well. Also, he simply didn't find it attractive and claimed that she looked flat and boyish. At the same time, he reassured her that he still loved her and wanted to be with her, even if other men would turn their back on her at this point. Nevertheless, he cooked substantial meals time after time and urged her to eat them. Sometimes she was full after a few bites, but he didn't let her leave the table until she ate what he had served on her plate. He proudly smiled when she ate it all.

Violet knew that she needed a doctor. Not an OBGYN and not a family doctor, either, who hadn't found anything physically wrong with her. She started to suspect that she might have developed a mental disorder. She was filled with shame and self-loathing and realized that Bradley couldn't find it out. He would really think she was damaged goods then and might even leave her. He might have noticed the psychosomatic symptoms, but she had managed to keep her anxieties, numbness, and memory troubles a secret. She needed to get herself fixed because Bradley deserved a better wife than this. Who knows, if her mental disorder was treated, she might become ready for motherhood as well.

At first, she thought she might go to a psychiatrist, but finally settled on starting with a psychologist. The first roadblock was finding the money for it. She was under Bradley's health insurance plan, which might have covered this, but, of course, he would learn about it then. As she wasn't working, she didn't have any money of her own. Bradley gave her $300 for food, $30 for gas, $100 for clothes, especially sexy underwear, and $100 for beauty salon treatments every month. Violet couldn't skimp on the food or gas because he would notice if she suddenly bought cheaper foods, and she already had to be frugal with the gas money to get to places she needed to go to. One time she had run out of gas before the end of the month, but Bradley was unwilling to give her more money for it and suggested that maybe she had been running around too much or too far. She decided to buy some cheaper lingerie and pass it as more expensive and skip beauty salon treatments for the month to have enough for therapy. It was risky, especially because he had called the beauty salon a few times before when she had been there, just to say hi, but she thought she needed to take that chance.

A week later Violet was sitting in Dr. Alba's office. The doctor was a short, plump, middle-aged woman with benevolent eyes and a soothing voice. It occurred to Violet that "alba" meant "dawn" it Italian, which she took as a sign and trusted that Dr. Alba could shine a bright light on the darkness engulfing her. As the doctor heard about Violet's financial dilemma, she offered the first session for free as a new patient discount. The first session would take 2 hours and all subsequent ones 1 hour. Violet was tremendously relieved, and she calmly listed all the symptoms that had been plaguing her. Dr. Alba listened attentively, inserting pertinent questions where necessary. She asked Violet a myriad of questions about her parents and her current life. As she carefully absorbed the answers, she was gradually turning somewhat somber.

Violet grew concerned that Dr. Alba had discovered something gravely wrong with her and blurted out, "Please tell me. Something *is* wrong with me, isn't it? You don't need to be tactful with me. Just tell me. I'm willing to work on it and want to get better. I need to do it, for Bradley's sake."

"As far as I can see, you have gone through a lot, but you're doing fine, at least as expected, regarding the circumstances," Dr. Alba began slowly. "I know you don't *feel* fine, and we'll work on that. But I believe ultimately you're healthy. You're experiencing healthy responses to unhealthy situations. I'm glad you have the determination to want to get better. But let me point out something: this isn't for Bradley's sake; this is for you. Right now you might feel like you're not important, or even that it's selfish to want to do it for you. I understand you might feel that, but neither of those statements is correct, and by the end of our work together you'll realize that."

Violet felt a wave of relief by being pronounced healthy, but also some discomfort about focusing on her own importance. And what did Dr. Alba mean by "unhealthy situations"?

"Violet, how would you describe the dynamics of your relationship with your husband?" Dr. Alba inquired gently.

"Well… we're very close. Very close. We have our own world, just the two of us, and we don't need others. He loves me so much. I know he couldn't live without me; he's told me that several times. He said that if I died or left, he would die, too. He's committed to me. Maybe others wouldn't stick by me or would find me unattractive and weak, but he reassures me that he's always by my side. He's protective of me and makes sure that others can't hurt me, like my parents or old friends. He protects me from the whole world. When I'm unsure about something, he helps me decide. He knows what's best for me. He knows it better than I do. He takes care of me. He supports me. He gives me so much even when I can't give him anything in return. He puts up with me when I have nothing to offer. He could have anyone, any woman, and he still wants me. That's a husband to cherish, isn't it?"

"Violet, based on everything that you've told me, I see your relationship a little bit differently," Dr. Alba responded. "Do you want me to tell you what I see? This might be difficult to grasp at first, but I think it's essential for you to know sooner or later. It doesn't have to happen today, but one day it does. So, do you want me to tell you now?"

Violet hesitated for a second, then whispered yes.

"What I see is control. Your husband is controlling you in any way he can. He controls your body, your clothing, your eating habits, your finances, your decisions, your thoughts, your feelings, your relationship with your parents and others. Yes, you have your own world, but it's because he has systematically isolated you from everyone. Unfortunately, he has isolated and alienated you even from yourself. He makes decisions for you. He checks up on you. He minimizes your feelings. He puts you down, and you feel bad about yourself as a result. He manipulates you and applies emotional blackmail and hidden little threats to achieve what he wants. I'm sorry to tell you this, but this is all classic. Everything that I've just listed is classic abusive behavior. This is emotional or psychological abuse. I know this is a lot to take, and it's understandable if you feel shocked, but this is a safe space. I want what's best for you. I want you to get better, but that can't happen until you realize what you've been dealing with. You're not weak. In fact, you're very strong for holding yourself up as much as you have. I applaud you. And I applaud you for coming here. This is the best thing you could have done. I know things don't feel right at this moment, but they eventually will. Just trust me and work with me. Let me help you."

"I... I don't understand," Violet stuttered incredulously. "*Abuse?* I've seen abuse, remember? My father abused my mother. He beat her up. *That's abuse.* Bradley has never laid a hand on me."

"I know. At least he hasn't done that," Dr. Alba confirmed. "But there are many different kinds of abuse. Physical abuse is just one of them. Of course, that's the most obvious. Then there's sexual abuse. I'm afraid Bradley has crossed the line there because I believe there are some things he has done without your full consent. It might look like you ultimately gave permission for everything, but for some things it was a result of emotional blackmail, manipulation, and latent threats, not out of your free will. Another type of abuse is economic or financial. That constitutes depriving someone of their own source of income and making her financially dependent on the abuser. That's about control as well. And this is something Bradley has done, too. For instance, by not giving you enough money for gas, he can control where and how far you're going. You could have your own income, you could work, but he made sure you don't have that. And then emotional, psychological abuse, what I described to you before, that's the most insidious, the hardest to notice. There might not be physical bruises, but there are emotional ones. I believe that's what you're suffering from. All of the

CHAPTER 4: "He didn't mean it." Domestic Abuse

83

symptoms you told me about can be explained by systematic and persistent abuse. Those are natural reactions to abuse. And, unfortunately, your denial, minimizing, and excuses for him are a part of this picture as well. He's managed to convince you that he's perfect, and you're flawed. Victims often believe it's all their fault, and something is wrong with them. As victims are usually isolated from others, they don't have any other feedback but that of the abuser, and that might seemingly become the ultimate truth. And just because you have seen and experienced abuse with your father, that's not a guarantee that you'll recognize other forms of it. Unfortunately, actually exactly because you have experienced abuse before, you could be more vul-

nerable to it. People often subconsciously repeat patterns that they have brought from home. Based on what you told me, I suspect Bradley might have at least partly learned his behavior from his father."

"But Bradley can be so caring and treat me like a princess," Violet countered.

"Yes, I know," Dr. Alba sighed compassionately. "That's often the case. They tend to seemingly start out as the most caring guys, and then they might suddenly or gradually turn. That's usually after trust is established. And periods of warmth and abuse frequently come in cycles. There's an episode of abuse. For example, emotional blackmail. Until you give in, they raise the pressure. After you have given in, and they have gotten what they wanted, the pressure will stop, and they'll appear more loving than ever. This is typically referred to as a honeymoon phase. It can be confusing, especially if it lasts a while because then everything might look perfect again. Until the next incident of abuse. Look, let's work together on this, and let me also refer you to group therapy, which can be extremely beneficial. It's people in the same situation. I'll assign you to a group that has worked together for a little while because I think at this point you can learn a lot from them."

"I don't know how I can make the time," Violet protested. "Bradley might notice if I'm away from home too long."

"I know you're scared," Dr. Alba validated her fears. "But exactly because you're so scared is why you need to make the time. Fear of your partner is a telling sign of abuse. If you feel like you are walking on eggshells and need to be careful in terms of what you say and what you do, it's because you have experienced abuse in that relationship. Your husband works at least 8 hours a day, doesn't he?"

"Yes," Violet whispered.

"Perfect," Dr. Alba responded. "We'll schedule the individual and group therapy sessions for when he's at work."

Three days later Violet walked into the room where group therapy was held. In the last few days she had felt as if in slow motion or underwater. She was in shock and unconvinced. At the same time, she had started to see herself and Bradley from the outside, from a slightly different perspective. She noticed some things, where she began to wonder if they constituted abuse. She still quickly found excuses for Bradley, but then actually caught herself making excuses and recognized a few times that she was giving him an easy pass. She also observed fear being the most dominant underlying emotion when with Bradley. Her predominant feeling was not love, not excitement, not warmth, not peace, not satisfaction, but fear. She tried her best to justify to herself why this might have been the case if Bradley was actually *not* abusing her. She didn't have an answer for that. She couldn't explain it either why her anxieties, fears, and feelings of numbness were the strongest around Bradley if they had nothing to do with him.

At the group therapy, Dr. Alba introduced Violet and another new member, and the older members introduced themselves. Dr. Alba asked the members to raise their hand if they had ever found it difficult to admit that their partner abused them. Everyone put up their hand, including Violet. Dr. Alba asked them why this was difficult.

"Because you're in denial. I used to be in denial for so long," a thin woman began. "It wasn't a shove, it was just a vehement touch. He just grabbed my arm so hard because I made him mad. I spoke back. The kids made him mad. He's stressed because of work. He just drank a little bit too much. He didn't really hit me. He didn't mean it; it was an accident."

"Yes, denial and excuses," another woman added. "It's all familiar. I used to tell myself my husband was just jealous because he loved me so much. So what if he looked through my phone, emails, and mail? What if he called to check up on me eight times a day? What if he dropped by my workplace almost every day just to say hi? What if he didn't let me go out with friends? I told myself it was all normal. It wasn't."

"You love him," a petite, young woman interjected. "You assume the best. You want to see him in the best light. He shows himself in the best light—in the beginning and many times after. You hope he'll change. You hope that it was the last time, and he'll really change this time."

"Yes," another woman echoed. "Plus, you're scared. You feel helpless. OK, maybe you admit it that he's an abuser. And then what? What can you do? Where can you go? You don't have any money. You don't have anyone close to you at this point. You have children together."

"Talking about children," a middle-aged redhead inserted. "He's always been a good father. Not a good husband, oh no, but a good father. Can I take him away from my kids? And what if he takes the kids away from me? He's threatened me to do that a few times."

"Me, too," a couple of the members agreed.

"Shame," a somber man whispered. "I'm a man, how can I not stand up to her? How can I let her beat me up with words and even beat me up physically? But how could I hit back? I can't hit back exactly because she's a woman. I won't hit a woman even if she keeps jumping up and down on my stomach. And how could I have admitted that several times I was so afraid to make her mad that I just went along with sex although I really didn't want it and hated myself for it? Sometimes I said no, and she still went ahead until she was satisfied. But whom could I have told that? That my wife practically raped me? That she beats me up? I'd have been ridiculed. I've felt so ashamed, so emasculated."

"I can see that," the thin woman, who had spoken first, contended. "Women are more likely victims, but exactly because we are, when the victim is a man, no one might even believe him. And yes, we're all ashamed. Or were at a point. But I can see how that aspect of it can be even more complicated with a male victim."

"I can attest to that, too," another man spoke. "You feel ashamed and emasculated by abuse as a male even if your abuser is a male as well. I've always thought that Stan and I had this egalitarian thing going, even more so because we're both male. But as he puts me to my place, as he's physically violent, it makes me feel like less of a person and less of a man."

"It's important to recognize that not all the victims are women," Dr. Alba affirmed. "Yes, women are much more likely victims. Women, children, the elderly. These groups are generally in a more vulnerable situation, and so, due to the power dynamics of abuse, they can become more likely victims. But men are not en-

altanaka/ Shutterstock.com

tirely unaffected either. Now, Selma," Dr. Alba addressed the other new member of the group. "I know you've just started out. I'm aware that you're not necessarily ready to call your husband an abuser. But let me ask if he's done something in the last, let's say few months, that resulted in you feeling ashamed, helpless, scared, or angry?"

"Well," Selma began hesitantly. "He just used to tell me some stuff that made me feel ashamed. He kept telling me that I was so flat, that I didn't look like a woman, that my breasts were so small. I knew they were; I had always felt self-conscious about them. But when he told me, I started to feel worse and worse. He began to suggest breast implants. I really didn't want them, but finally I gave in. I wanted him to find me beautiful. After the surgery, he admired my new breasts for a while. I felt proud, but still ashamed a bit. I haven't felt like me since then. It's like my body isn't my body anymore. He keeps buying me new bras and low-cut shirts, which make me really uncomfortable. He says he won't go out with me unless I wear those. So, we're not going anywhere these days. I've even missed work a few times—when he told me how horrible I looked in my old turtlenecks, and I shouldn't even be seen that way by people who have any taste, I just couldn't go. Now I feel more ugly than ever, and I just don't want to go anywhere. Now he tells me that I probably have agoraphobia, which is a fear of open spaces and reluctance to go outside as a result. He's told me that so many times, and one day I even found my computer opened up at a site that described agoraphobia. I don't even know how he got into my computer. He says he never did and that probably I opened up the site myself because I know that this is what's wrong with me, but now I deny it. I know I never opened up that site, but I'm starting to doubt myself now. Maybe there *is* something wrong with me. Maybe I *am* agoraphobic. I really don't feel like going anywhere anymore. I could hardly make myself come here. He says that the only way to prove that I'm OK is to go out with him; he'll keep me safe if I'm scared, but in exchange for him keeping me safe and helping with my agoraphobia, I should please him by wearing the low-cut clothes he got for me."

"He's trying to make you think you're losing it," one of the women exclaimed. "He's blackmailing you. That's so twisted. I say he's the one who has lost it."

"I don't know anything anymore," Selma continued. "I'm just so scared and ashamed. What is wrong with me?"

"There's nothing wrong with you," Dr. Alba retorted firmly. "This is a manipulative mind game. He's trying to take over your body and mind, but you know what's going on now and have the option to not let him achieve that."

Violet felt anger boiling in her. It was sudden and rapidly bubbling up to the surface, bursting out like a volcano. She had never experienced such rage before, "How dare he? How dare he do that to you?" she screamed at the top of her lungs. "How dare he claim he's concerned about you, that he loves you and do this to you at the same time? Don't you see? Don't you see what this is all about? Please open your eyes and see it before it's too late. It's not you. It's never been about you. You're fine. It's him. It's been him all along. Oh, my God, yes, it's been him all along."

Violet was shaking and sobbing uncontrollably. She sensed some surprised glances, but even more so, Dr. Alba's compassionate, reassuring, and proud look. She felt that something had broken in her, but strangely, she didn't feel weak. In fact, she felt strong and undefeatable. The clouds in her mind had begun to clear, and she caught a glimpse of light beyond them.

Discussion Questions

1. What do you think Violet will do next? Do you see her staying with Bradley or leaving him? Why?

2. Which types of abuse do you detect in the story: emotional/psychological, sexual, physical, financial/economic? Mention a few specific examples and discuss what made it abuse.

3. Why is emotional/psychological abuse often difficult to recognize? Why is it so difficult to leave an emotionally abusive relationship (or a relationship with other types of abuse)?

4. Discuss the role of gender and power in abusive relationships.

5. Learned helplessness is an attitude and resulting behavior that tends to occur when someone has faced several instances of a negative experience, where they have felt a lack of control over the situation (Petersen, Maier, & Seligman, 1995; Seligman, 1992; Walker, 1979, 2009). The individual might end up generalizing those negative feelings of lack of control to other similar situations and feel helpless even when they could have other options that they do not realize. Mention examples for learned helplessness from the story.

6. The battered woman syndrome is a psychological condition, similar to posttraumatic stress disorder, which frequently plagues victims of domestic abuse. Walker (2009) listed the main symptoms as follows: high levels of anxiety; emotional numbing (often expressed in minimizing, denial, repression); intrusive recollections of trauma events; disrupted relationships due to the abuser's control measures; body image distortion and/or somatic, physical complaints; and sexual intimacy issues. Which of these symptoms (if any) do you recognize in Violet or any other victims in the story?

CHAPTER 4: "He didn't mean it." Domestic Abuse

91

7. Domestic abuse often occurs in cycles: tension building, abusive incident, and a honeymoon period, an idealized, romantic period of apologies and/or peace (Walker, 1979). Discuss examples for this from the story.

8. Scott and Lyman (1968) defined accounts as linguistic devices or statements to explain unanticipated or disturbing behavior. There are two main types of accounts: excuses and justifications. Excuses recognize that a behavior was bad, but deny responsibility. Justifications acknowledge responsibility, but deny that the behavior was wrong, often by suggesting that the victim deserved the behavior, or that there was actually no harm done. What is the role of excuses and justifications in domestic abuse, both from abusers and victims? Mention at least one specific example, too.

9. Blumer (1969) identified three premises of symbolic interactionism. The first is that humans act toward things based on the meanings those things have for them. The second is that meanings are created through social interaction. The third is that meanings are understood and potentially transformed through an interpretative process. Apply this theory to definitions of domestic violence.

10. Through his concept of the looking-glass self, Cooley (1998) explained how our sense of self is shaped by how others view us. Apply this theory to Violet's story and explore the role of isolation and limited feedback from others in developing a distorted looking-glass self.

Find the Answers

Go to https://www.cdc.gov/violenceprevention/datasources/nisvs/2015NISVSdatabrief.html?C-DC_AA_refVal=https%3A%2F%2Fwww.cdc.gov%2Fviolenceprevention%2Fnisvs%2F2015NIS-VSdatabrief.html to find answers to the following questions. Scroll down and click on Intimate Partner Violence.

1. List some gender differences in intimate partner violence.

2. List four different types of intimate partner violence.

3. What are some of the impacts of intimate partner violence?

4. Discuss the role of age in intimate partner violence.

Mini Research Assignments

1. Survey at least seven individuals, asking them to rate their agreement with the following statements on a scale of 1–10 (1 meaning complete disagreement and 10 indicating full agreement): 1. "Verbal abuse can be just as harmful as physical abuse." 2. "Women are much more likely victims of abuse than men." 3. "Domestic violence is always obvious and easy to recognize." 4. "All of the following exemplify abuse: name-calling; constantly checking up on someone; humiliating someone; denying someone's access to money or other necessities; stalking; emotional blackmail; isolating someone from family and/or friends; undermining someone's self-esteem by constant criticism; forcing or coercing someone to have sex." Summarize your results and draw parallels with Violet's story.
2. Watch a movie or TV show that depicts domestic violence. Describe which type(s) of abuse occur and the background of the victim and perpetrator. Draw parallels with Violet's story. Discuss the role of gender and whether you detect learned helplessness, the cycles of abuse, battered woman syndrome, the looking-glass self, and/or accounts (see definitions under Discussion Questions).
3. Search and select at least two domestic violence tests online. Analyze the questions and draw parallels with Violet's story. Discuss which type of abuse each question refers to. Explore potential examples for learned helplessness, the cycles of abuse, battered woman syndrome, the looking-glass self, and/or accounts in the questions (see definitions under Discussion Questions).
4. Conduct an online search for domestic violence hotlines or any other form of help in your area. Summarize what kind of help is available. Discuss if any groups might have easier access to help than others (based on sex, sexual orientation, type of abuse, social class, education, place of residence, age, disability, immigration status, or any other similar factors).

References

Blumer, H. (1969). *Symbolic interactionism: Perspective and method.* Englewood Cliffs, NJ: Prentice-Hall.

Cooley, C. H. (1998). *On self and social organization.* Chicago, IL: University of Chicago Press. (Originally published 1902)

Petersen, C., Maier, S. F., & Seligman, M. E. P. (1995). *Learned helplessness: A theory for the age of personal control.* New York, NY: Oxford University Press.

Scott, M. B., & Lyman, S. M. (1968). Accounts. *American Sociological Review, 33*(1), 46–62.

Seligman, M. E. P. (1992). *Helplessness: On depression, development, and death.* New York, NY: W. H. Freeman & Company.

Smith, Sharon G. et al. (2015). National intimate partner and sexual violence survey. Atlanta, GA: CDC. Retrieved from https://www.cdc.gov/violenceprevention/datasources/nisvs/2015NISVSdatabrief.html?CDC_AA_refVal=https%3A%2F%2Fwww.cdc.gov%2Fviolenceprevention%2Fnisvs%2F2015NISVSdatabrief.html

Walker, L. E. (1979). *Battered woman.* New York, NY: Harper & Row.

_____. (2009). *The battered woman syndrome* (3rd ed.). New York, NY: Springer.

CHAPTER

"I really want a child;
I really don't want a child."
VOLUNTARY AND
INVOLUNTARY CHILDLESSNESS

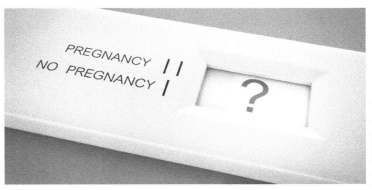

Dabarti CGI/ Shutterstock.com

olly Hansen dejectedly stared at the pregnancy test she was holding. She was waiting for a second pink line to appear, indicating pregnancy, as if she could materialize it by the sheer force of her will. There was only one line that stubbornly remained. She checked the instructions again, hoping that she misread them. Maybe one line meant pregnant, not the other way around. As she scanned the instructions again, they clearly confirmed that she wasn't pregnant. Tears slowly began to roll down her face. Although her tears blurred her vision, she didn't want to see the negative test, either, so she carefully wrapped it up and shoved it in the garbage. She left the restroom and sank into her favorite armchair in the bedroom. Her period had only been 2 days late, but she had allowed herself to dream that it was finally due to pregnancy. A slimmer of optimism lifted her spirit for a second. Maybe it was just too early for the test to pick up the pregnancy hormones; maybe in a few days the result would change. Deep down, however, she sensed that this wasn't the case.

Molly had always wanted children; the possibility of not having them had never even crossed her mind. Her parents had raised her in a very gender-specific way, giving her a lot of dolls, including baby dolls, to play with. Dolls were her favorite toys, and she had spent endless hours rocking and cuddling them. Her parents and grandparents used to smile, praise her, compliment her for her gentleness, and reassure her that she would become the most wonderful mother one day. When she had been asked as a child how many children she would want when she grew up, she responded at least two, preferably three, without any hesitation. Her sister was born when Molly was 7, and she cared for her in a very nurturing and responsible way whenever her parents asked her to babysit. As a teenager she often babysat for neighbors as well. She had been groomed for motherhood by her family, her peers, church, and the media. She had subconsciously absorbed those messages, and they had become ingrained in her mind. She had been preparing for the role of mother since early childhood.

Yuri Shevtsov/ Shutterstock.com

Besides her warm and caring nature, Molly had also turned out to be a very bright child, so her parents and teachers encouraged her to focus on studying and develop her talents. She earned straight As throughout her schooling. Studying had become her passion, and she had also fostered a zeal for travel, languages, and foreign cultures. By age 25, Molly had become fluent in four languages. She had earned a bachelor's degree in two languages and a master's degree in international relations. She had completed two study-abroad opportunities on two different continents. After graduation she returned to her beloved native Minnesota and took a job as Assistant Director of International Programs at a local university. She was soon promoted to director. She worked long hours and frequently traveled all across four continents to maintain and develop international exchange programs and collaborations between her own university and dozens of others across the globe.

Her job was incredibly rewarding, but didn't leave her too much time for anything else. Around the age of 30, her parents, her grandmother, a few other relatives, and even a couple of friends from high school began asking her when she would get married and have children. It was always a "when," never an "if." Everyone assumed that she would eventually marry and have children, including Molly herself. Her mother and an old friend from high school occasionally set her up with blind dates. She protested at first, but soon realized that the people caring about her meant well, and she had to admit that she struggled to find promising dates on her own. Molly was aware that her appearance wasn't extraordinary: dark blond hair; small, deep-set blue eyes; a round face; a slightly large, round nose; smooth skin with some red spots; a height of 5.3 feet; and weight of 163 pounds. At the same time, her intelligence and warm personality made her outstanding. Still, she had a difficult time to date, possibly because many men were deterred by her high level of education and demanding job.

Molly was 34 when she met Ryan. He wasn't a blind date; their meeting was entirely unexpected, almost unbelievable. Molly was walking by Lake Como, a quaint lake in Saint Paul, Minnesota, one of her favorite spots. Ryan suddenly zipped by on a bike and inadvertently scared her, as he seemed to have come out of the blue. She gave a small yelp, and Ryan turned back and got off his bike to make sure she was okay. It might not have been love at first sight, but it was undeniably a strong attraction at first sight, which soon increased in intensity, deepened, and developed into love.

Molly and Ryan got married a year later and bought a house near Lake Como. They often walked or biked around the lake and recalled memories of their first meeting, which invariably stirred a wide smile on their faces. They started discussing children shortly after their wedding. Ryan seemed to want them as much as Molly. They started trying for a baby almost right away. After a year, when nothing happened, Molly began to worry. Ryan reassured her that they might simply have to give it more time. As the months kept passing, Molly's concern amplified. Whenever her period was a few days late, she purchased a pregnancy test and was filled with hope. The test was always negative, and she got her period a couple of days later.

When they had been married for 1.5 years, questions started flooding in, all addressed to Molly. Her parents, grandmother, sister, uncles and aunts, cousins, Ryan's family, friends, and even a few colleagues periodically asked her when they would have a baby. Some were very tactful, only hinting at the possibility; others were more direct, even blunt. Hardly anyone ever posed those questions to Ryan; most people targeted Molly. A few people gently reminded her that she wasn't getting any younger, which, of course, didn't help. Molly began to feel like a lifesize, ticking biological clock. Her sister, 7 years younger than her, had had two children by now.

Also, up to this point, she had succeeded in anything she had set her mind to. She hadn't been used to failure and feeling out of control. In addition, she began to be plagued by guilt. She wondered if she might have placed too much emphasis on her education and career, and if it might be too late now to turn toward motherhood. She didn't want to let Ryan down,

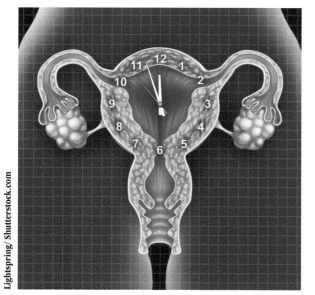

either, as she was cognizant of how much he wished for a baby, too.

Although Molly had thrown away the most recent failed pregnancy test, she still saw it when she closed her eyes. She had a visceral feeling that she couldn't simply wait around any longer. She was ready to undergo some tests to figure out if there might be a problem preventing pregnancy. She knew it would take some effort to convince Ryan, the relentless optimist, but she suspected this was the necessary next step.

A month later Molly and Ryan were sitting in the office of Dr. Echler, her OBGYN. Molly needed Ryan there, in case they were about to learn something upsetting. They had both undergone some tests that had been recommended. Ryan had been very reluctant to do the test that he needed to do. He had missed an appointment and almost didn't show up for the next one. After some prodding, he admitted it to Molly that the idea of the test made him immensely uncomfortable and that he couldn't face Molly if his test came back abnormal. He couldn't bear the responsibility of not being able to give her the child she had so desired. Molly reassured him, affirming that she would never blame him for that and would love him the same. She wondered, however, if Ryan would believe *her* to be responsible if a problem turned up on her side, which became more likely now, as Ryan's tests had come back normal about a week ago.

Dr. Echler cleared his throat and somberly looked at Molly and Ryan, "Molly, we've done several tests, as you know. I believe we've found what the problem is."

As the doctor went into some medical jargon to explain her condition, Molly tuned out and couldn't comprehend his words. The only word she heard and understood was "problem." That word was flashing in her mind, squeezing out everything else. She felt Ryan stroking her back and noticed his anxious, tender look. Under other circumstances, Molly would have had no problem whatsoever grasping any kind of medical terminology, but at this moment, for now, she had ceased to be a bright, highly educated, confident professional. She was simply a scared, vulnerable woman. She appreciated Ryan's presence and reassuring touch, but she still felt that he could never fully understand what she was going through.

Suddenly, Dr. Echler said something that burst into Molly's consciousness, "So, Molly, I'm afraid it's highly unlikely for you to become pregnant spontaneously."

"*Highly unlikely*?" Molly asked, stressing each syllable. "What do you mean? Is it a subtle way to say there's zero chance? Or is there some? 5%, 10%, what?"

"I don't feel comfortable speculating like that," Dr. Echler stated.

"Please, speculate. I insist," Molly countered.

"It's hard to say," Dr. Echler asserted. "But it's a very, very small percentage, almost negligible."

Molly sank into the chair, disheartened. She heard Ryan take a sharp breath. As Dr. Echler's words echoed over and over in her head, she zoomed in on another word in his statement, which suddenly seemed like a lifeline on extremely rough seas: "What do you mean by *spontaneously*?" she inquired. "If it's highly unlikely spontaneously, maybe it's not as long as it's non-spontaneous?"

"Right," Dr. Echler confirmed. "In your particular case, and considering your age..., you're 36, correct?"

"Almost 37," Molly whispered.

"Yes, I see," Dr. Echler mused. "Considering your age, we have no time to lose. I'd go right to IVF."

"In vitro fertilization?" Ryan queried.

"Yes," Dr Echler affirmed. "It's a relatively common process now, and it could be an option in your case. I can recommend a great clinic that specializes in this."

"It could be an option," Molly repeated. "Is it pretty much guaranteed success, or is it just an option, which or might not work? Don't get me wrong, I want to try anything that could help, but I need to know what to expect."

"Right," Dr. Echler began slowly. "There's no guarantee, but success rates are pretty good these days. Your age is a factor, as success rates decline with age, but they're still not bad in your case. This is a good option."

A few months later Molly was ready for her embryo transfer appointment at the fertility clinic. These months had been a rollercoaster ride emotionally. Right after their talk with Dr. Echler, she was dispirited. If Ryan was upset as well, he didn't show it and was back at his optimistic self in less than a day, and he cheered Molly on. Molly took longer to recover from the shock, but the option of IVF gave her hope and a concrete goal to work toward. She read everything she found online about IVF, as well as the brochures she was offered at the fertility clinic. She learned that success rates in her age were around 33% to 36%. While that didn't sound superb, it was much higher than "negligible," which her chances would be without IVF. She had taken the fertility medications prescribed for her to stimulate egg production. There were some side effects, but she ignored them as much as she could, keeping the main purpose of the process in mind. There were some blood tests and ultrasounds. Then, some eggs were retrieved through minor surgery and fertilized with Ryan's sperm. They were closely monitored, the most viable ones selected, and today they would be transferred to Molly's uterus. It was recommended to transfer more than one to elevate the odds of at least one surviving and resulting in a live birth.

Molly and Ryan considered carefully what would happen to the other fertilized eggs. They could choose for the not implanted embryos to be discarded, donated to other couples, or frozen for later use, in case the first IVF attempt is not successful. This was a considerable ethical and moral dilemma for Molly and Ryan. Based on her upbringing, she was aware that her parents, and especially her grandmother, would be uncomfortable with the mere idea of IVF. They might think it was not natural, and if God really wanted them to have a child, he would bless them with one. So, although Molly felt guilty about it, she decided to keep the IVF a secret from her family, which put an additional burden on her. She didn't fully share her family's religious beliefs anymore, but she did struggle with the idea of discarding unused embryos. So, she and Ryan opted for freezing them for later use. If she ended up needing them, it would mean that the first transfer was unsuccessful, and she didn't want to entertain that idea at this point.

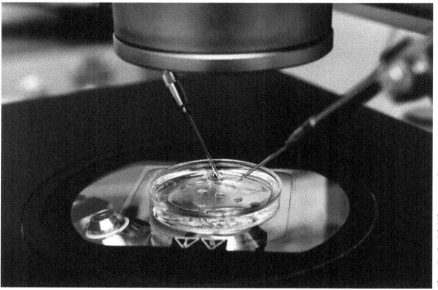

Elena Pavlovich/ Shutterstock.com

The embryo transfer itself turned out to be relatively quick and un-eventful. However, the waiting period that was about to follow seemed like torture. It would take about 2 weeks until Molly and Ryan would know the results. Molly was advised to take it easy for a few days and avoid travel. Although it had only been a few months since she had started the IVF pro-cess, it had already impacted her job to a small extent. She had had to miss a few days of work for medical appointments and cancel a work-related trip right after the embryo transfer. Her whole life had begun to revolve around her cycle and getting pregnant. She didn't mind it, but it was an unusual experience after years of prioritizing her job.

During the 2 weeks of waiting Molly was carefully scrutinizing herself physically, mentally, and emotionally to try to speculate if she was pregnant. She didn't feel any different; she sort of felt as if she was about to get her period, but she did her best not to draw any conclusions from that, as she had been warned she might experience that whether or not the transfer was successful. Ryan turned out to be an incredible support; his humor and opti-mism helped her through some anxiety-ridden days during the waiting pe-riod. Molly could hardly restrain herself from doing a home pregnancy test after about a week, but she resisted, as her doctor explained it that a series of blood tests would be more reliable after such a procedure. They would begin with a blood test after 10 days, then there would be a few blood tests at 2- to 3-day intervals before pregnancy could be confirmed, so, overall, it would be more than 2 weeks before they would know anything for sure.

After the last blood test, Molly's doctor confirmed it that they should be able to determine the results. He was firm on not giving her any results beforehand. After a relaxed day at work, taking it easy, Molly decided to take a brief walk in Como Zoo, right near where they lived. Ryan was still at work, so she went on her own. There were several families with kids in the zoo this afternoon. She gazed at a few of them and smiled as she imag-ined that soon their family, complete with a child, could visit the zoo. She was dreaming of a bright future as her phone buzzed, "Hello, this is Molly Hansen," she answered it wistfully.

"Hi, this is Brenda from Dr. Klein's office," a nurse from the fertility clinic announced. "We have your results. Would you like to come in, or are you ready to hear them over the phone?"

"Please, don't make me wait any longer," Molly blurted out. "I'm ready."

"I'm so sorry to have to tell you this, but it looks like the procedure wasn't successful this time. You're not pregnant."

Molly felt as if a heavy stone fell on her chest, squeezing out all her dreams and hopes. She drew a deep breath and a few more right after, as

it seemed as if she suddenly couldn't get enough air into her lungs. Tears started to burn her eyes, but she collected herself and didn't release them—at least not yet.

"Are you sure?" she asked, her voice quivering.

"Unfortunately, yes," the nurse confirmed. "Your hCG levels remain low; they should be elevated by now in case of a pregnancy. The implantation was not successful."

"What do we do now?" Molly inquired, visibly shaking.

"Let's set up an appointment to go through your options with Dr. Klein," the nurse suggested.

Molly finished the phone call mechanically, in a daze. She sank down on a bench, suddenly weak and dejected. Her legs didn't seem to be able to hold her up any longer. She felt as if her whole body was failing her and turning against her: her legs, her fallopian tubes, her uterus, maybe even her brain, the one organ she had always been immensely proud of. Before this she could figure out and achieve anything with the help of her sharp mind. She looked around, and the sight of families that had offered an exciting sense of anticipation a few minutes ago turned into torture. She began to sob and ran out of the zoo, outpacing the concerned glances that followed her. She couldn't outrun her tumultuous thoughts and grief, however.

Once home, she collapsed into bed and cried for the rest of the afternoon and evening. When Ryan came home, she couldn't say anything. Her voice stopped working, and she was desperately riding the wild rivers of disappointment and helplessness that overwhelmed her. Of course, Ryan realized right away what had happened and embraced her tightly, whispering to her, stroking her hair, and he, himself quietly weeping for a few minutes, carefully hiding it from Molly. Finally, Molly regained her voice and kept tearfully repeating, "I really want a child. Please, Ryan, I really want a child."

It took Molly 3 days to strengthen herself, go back to work, and continue on with her life. Although she had been informed of the statistics and the chances of the embryos implanting, versus not implanting, she still took it extremely hard when the procedure turned out to have failed. After her discussion with her doctor at the fertility clinic, she regained some hope, and she and Ryan decided to give the procedure another chance. She now knew what to expect and was somewhat wary going through the steps of the whole process again. A couple of weeks after the second embryo transfer, they learned that it failed this time as well. The same scenario unfolded that they had experienced after the first one: Molly was devastated, while Ryan was gently trying to soothe her, quietly grieving on his own.

After the third unsuccessful procedure, Molly wanted to take a break, as she felt she couldn't bear more heartache in such close succession. Ryan cheered her on, and Dr. Klein reminded her that time was a crucial factor, and he didn't recommend taking a several months' break that she was considering. So, Molly strengthened herself and went through the fourth round of IVF mechanically, deliberately trying to numb herself to potential failure and grief.

In the meantime, she stopped socializing almost entirely and avoided her family, being unable to tolerate their questions and keep secrets from them. She and Ryan ran into financial problems as well. She had good health insurance, which covered some costs of the IVF treatments, but a sizable portion still remained their responsibility, and each round of IVF cost thousands of dollars. As Molly was advised against intercontinental travel after each embryo transfer, she had to make the very difficult decision of voluntarily reducing her work hours and salary and requesting an assistant to do the bulk of traveling. She missed travel and the gratification she used to find in her job, but this was a price of motherhood she was willing to pay at this point. She was cognizant that she and Ryan should consider themselves lucky because couples without health insurance and/ or relatively high incomes could never afford these procedures.

After the fourth failed attempt, Dr. Klein asked both Molly and Ryan into his office.

"Look," the doctor began slowly. "We've tried this four times. Some doctors might have stopped and had this discussion with you after three in your circumstances, but I wanted to give it just one more try, as I was pretty optimistic of success. I'm sorry it hasn't worked out so far. We've tried fresh embryos and frozen, we followed every protocol, and you, Molly, you followed every protocol and did everything beautifully. We've done what we could, and you have done what you could. We could keep trying; sometimes there is success at the fifth or sixth try, or even more. But, in the meantime, time is passing, and also, I realize this is a substantial financial investment as well. So, it might be time to try something else instead and see if that works better."

"Something else? What else is there?" Molly asked, with a hint of sarcasm and fatigue in her voice. Ryan looked at her slightly taken aback. He hadn't been used to her using such a tone, and he was worried that hopelessness and bitterness might begin to take root in her.

"There are other options, Molly; we're still far from running out of options," Dr. Klein asserted with a compassionate look. "We can try more IVF, but I'd suggest to do it with donor eggs."

"Donor eggs?" Ryan asked hesitantly. "You mean…?"

"As in not my own eggs? Someone else's eggs who donates them?" Molly asked with a rising volume and pitch.

"Yes," the doctor affirmed. "Sometimes there's more success with donor eggs because the donors tend to be young, healthy women in their twenties with great quality eggs."

"Young and healthy, huh?" Molly asked brusquely. "Because I'm *not* healthy. And more importantly, I'm *not* young. If I had a dollar for how many times I've heard references to *my age* being a factor in the last several months, we wouldn't be going into debt paying for these procedures. Am I really that *old*? I'm still under 38. But I feel ancient now. When I was promoted to international director, I was told how young I was to have achieved that. And now I'm suddenly almost *too old* for *this*. And what about Ryan? He's 4 years older than me, but his age has never been a factor. I'm sorry, but that's so unfair."

"I know, Molly," Dr. Klein sighed, while Ryan stared at Molly with empathy, bordering on pity. "I know you're upset. You're very young, of course, for many things. But this is one area where even with our medical advances we can't entirely overpass age. Age is a *factor*, but it's just one factor; it doesn't have to be the sole determinant in the outcome here."

Molly took a deep breath, endeavoring to calm herself, "Look, I'm sorry, I know it's not your fault; you're trying to help us. I'm just… I just feel so helpless, sad, and angry. With donor eggs… They come from another woman, so if we use donor eggs, the child wouldn't be my biological child?"

"Technically, no, the child wouldn't be your biological child," Dr. Klein confirmed.

"So, at this point…," Molly hesitated, her voice shaking. "At this point I can't have a biological child, not even with IVF?"

"It's not impossible; you still might," Dr. Klein countered. "I just don't think it's the best solution in this case to keep trying that when we might have better, quicker success with donor eggs. And they may be donor eggs from family members if you prefer."

"Yeah, sure," Molly sighed gloomily. "My family doesn't even know we're doing IVF, and I don't intend to inform them. So, I just ask my sister or a cousin to give me some eggs and have a biological child with my husband? That's just… I don't know, that's just odd to me."

"The donor could be a stranger if you prefer," Dr. Klein explained. "Look, the point is that you still have options. You could keep trying IVF with your eggs and hope for the best. Or, for better success, we could go with donor eggs. Or, you could opt for a surrogate mother even, but that's a discussion further down the road, only if IVF is unsuccessful even with donor eggs. A surrogate costs much more than IVF, though, just so you're aware, at least if it's done in this country. And you wouldn't carry the child then, either. You don't have to consider that yet, though. I'm just throwing it out there so you see that this is not the end of the road. And then there's always adoption, too. Even if it turns out that you are not able to have a biological child, there are other options. It doesn't mean that you'll remain childless."

The last word, "childless," left a mournful echo in Molly. Even through the failed attempts and sorrow of the last several months, she hadn't considered that she might ultimately end up childless. This still wasn't the end of the road, though, as Dr. Klein attested. She exchanged a glance with Ryan, knowing that they had a lot to discuss in the upcoming weeks and months. She was willing to march on and continue the fight for a child. At the same time, the word "childless" lingered in the back of her mind.

*

Rhea Sullivan fought hard to catch her breath. She had just finished a brutal tennis match, but she enjoyed it immensely. She had always been athletic, vibrant, and in some ways larger than life. She was tall and had broad shoulders, D-cup breasts, large hands and feet, and an almost untamable mane of hair. She was a very attractive woman, who commanded attention not only because of her looks, but because of her exuberant personality. Whatever she did, she attacked with full force, whether it was a tennis match or work. She was a successful interior designer, and her creativity and energy had no limits. At 37 she seemed to be at her prime, both as a woman and as a professional.

Rhea took a quick shower and jumped into her stylish convertible, hastily, but efficiently applying makeup when she had to stop at traffic lights. She pushed the gas and savored the light breeze that stroked her hair. She loved living in Miami. She had moved from Chicago 3 years ago, and had never regretted it. The climate and the city's vibe fit her better than Chicago. As she was considerably talented and popular, she had no difficulty establishing a client base and a network of friends in a new city. She loved her life as much as she admired Miami. She had everything she had ever desired. She had a fulfilling career, fueled by an endless flow of creativity, a successful business of her own, fascinating friends, an intense social life, a beautiful condo in a Miami Beach high-rise, abundant resources for entertainment, travel, designer clothes, and jewelry.

She hadn't always been fortunate with men, but for a long time she hadn't been looking for a very serious commitment, either, and she had had no trouble finding dates. She had doubted if she was capable of, ready for, or even interested in settling down with a man, but in the last couple of years she had reevaluated that. When she had met Drake Ferrell, she was immediately drawn to him. He had a magnetic personality and looks, matching her own. His level of success and lifestyle were very similar to hers, too. First, they had been casually dating, agreeing on an open relationship, not closing themselves off from the possibility of meeting and dating others. After about a year they had mutually realized that they didn't wish to date others anymore and agreed to be exclusive. They both used to be reluctant to commit because of fearing that a long-term partner would impede on their freedom and independence. They were surprised and delighted to discover that this was never an issue in their relationship. In fact, they felt even more free and independent in their individual lives by sharing a close romantic, emotional, and physical bond with each other.

Rhea glanced at the clock in her car and pushed the gas a little bit more. She was almost late for her work appointment, but just almost. As she devoured life and constantly endeavored to squeeze as much into her time as humanly possible, she was often cutting it close to tardiness. But eventually she usually managed to get everywhere just on time. She pulled into the driveway of her next client's home exactly at 9 a.m. It was an impressive, expansive, lavish home in an upscale neighborhood. Rhea was assigned with designing and decorating a nursery. She had visited the home already to assess the space, and now she returned with some designs to show the client.

Rhea and the client, Alice, walked to the nursery together. They had agreed to go on a first-name basis during their first meeting. Alice was an attractive woman in her early thirties. She was 5 months pregnant, but hardy showing yet. She was glowing and immeasurably excited about her baby. She promptly fell in love with the designs Rhea showed her.

"Oh, my God, this is so cute. I love it," Alice exclaimed, her voice filled with enthusiasm. "Look at that. I'm sure Elizabeth is going to love it."

Elizabeth was the baby Alice was expecting. Alice was over the moon when she had learned that she expected a girl and insisted on a girly design for the nursery. Pink, frills, and ribbons weren't Rhea's style, but she didn't reveal that to Alice. She had a special talent in grasping a client's needs and wants and making their dreams come true. She came up with a creative design that didn't compromise her own taste and fully satisfied each client.

Alice kept raving about every small detail of the design and suddenly added, "It shows that you have a knack for children. You must love children to design a room like this. Do you have any children of your own?"

"No," Rhea responded with a slightly forced smile.

Alice looked at Rhea expectantly, but when Rhea didn't elaborate on the answer, she continued, "Well, when you have them they'll be so lucky to have you as their mom. They'll have the most awesome room ever."

Rhea gulped and warned herself that she should let the remark go and keep her mouth shut, but she just couldn't because she was honest, and she vowed to always be true to herself, "Actually, I'm not planning on having children," she stated firmly.

"Oh? Oh, I'm sorry, I'm so insensitive," Alice apologized. "I didn't know you had fertility issues. That must be so hard. I'm so sorry. One of my friends is struggling with that."

Rhea was aware that she didn't owe this woman an explanation, just as she didn't think she owed *anyone* an explanation. However, she could never let an opportunity pass to expand people's horizons, even if it was a client, "I don't have fertility issues, at least not that I know of. I simply don't want to have children."

"I understand," Alice chirped. "I wanted to go to college and have a career first, too. You're so successful, but still so young; you'll feel differently later and can still have children then."

"I won't feel any different later," Rhea countered quietly. "I was raised in the assumption that I would have children. I have always been told that I *should* have children. I've been told that maternal instincts would kick in eventually. Well, I was waiting for them for a while, but they never kicked in, and now I know that they never will. I realize now that I don't *have to* have children. Motherhood is not for everyone, and I know that it's not for me. I really don't want a child."

Alice could hardly hide her incredulity and pity, "You know, it's none of my business. It's your choice, of course. It's just… Now that I'm expecting a baby, I can't believe how incredible that feels. It took a while for me to decide that I'm ready for a child, but it was the greatest decision of my life. Even greater than I would have ever imagined. To think that I could have missed this experience… I wouldn't want to miss it for the world. I realize now that my life hadn't been complete before the baby, and now it absolutely is."

"Well, I'm glad to hear this is working out so well for you and you're happy," Rhea began slowly. "But I'm happy, too. My life is complete the way it is. In fact, it couldn't feel more complete."

"But, if you don't mind me asking, don't you like children?" Alice queried curiously.

"I like children just fine," Rhea sighed. "I just know myself and my life enough to realize that they don't fit into my life."

"I see," Alice mused. "Look, I don't want to pry; I just find this so interesting, and I'd truly like to understand. Aren't you concerned that you might change your mind when it's too late? Aren't you concerned that there may not be anyone there for you when you get old? I'm just asking because that's a concern I'd personally have."

"No, I'm not concerned about any of that," Rhea said unshakably. "Look, I had thought about this long and hard before I came to this decision. I probably thought about this decision much more than many parents who decide to *have* children. I considered many factors, but frankly, being worried that no one would be there for me when I get old wasn't one of them. I plan on putting money aside and staying healthy and independent as long as I can. Also, I have a lot of friends and a partner who could take care of me if need be. Even if I had children, I wouldn't count on them or expect them to take care of me. You know, it's funny how I have heard some people say that people who don't want children are selfish. I beg to differ. I think it can be more selfish to want children for your own benefit, only to satisfy your own desires and emotional needs, to try to secure a caretaker for your golden years. Some people know that they are not fit to be parents, or that their circumstances are really unfit, and they still choose to have children. That's selfish in my opinion."

"Oh, I agree with that part," Alice nodded. "Look, I'm sorry. I hope I haven't offended you."

"No, you're fine," Rhea smiled, although she was slightly bothered by Alice's comments. "I know it can be difficult to understand for some. That's why I try to explain it. I try to explain it so that maybe eventually enough people understand that it's a choice, not an obligation, and others after me won't have to explain it any longer. I've never asked anyone why they have chosen to have children, nor have I tried to persuade them to change their minds. Because it's none of my business. Just as it should not be anyone's business what I'm doing or not doing."

Alice mumbled an apology, but she looked unconvinced. Rhea turned the conversation back to the nursery design, and they soon wrapped up the appointment. Rhea was slightly annoyed, and as she walked to her car, she stopped in her track, suddenly realizing that this is a topic she and Drake had not discussed. She doubted that he did want to have children, but what if he did? Their relationship was going so smoothly, and she could see a future with him. She didn't want that possibility to crumble to pieces if they turned out to disagree on such a crucial issue. She did not consider herself selfish. She knew that if Drake wanted to have children one day, she would have to let him go. She decided to bring up the issue today after dinner. She was hoping that she could have the future that she had envisioned—life with a fulfilling career, a network of friends, and a partner who loved and respected her and offered independence besides closeness. Her dream life was childfree, and she wouldn't compromise on that. She smiled at the word "childfree." Someone had once told her that she might come to regret remaining childless. Rhea had corrected her and stated that she wouldn't be *childless*; she would be *childfree*. She felt that this statement rang more true now than ever.

Discussion Questions

1. What do you think Molly and Ryan will decide to do? Do you see them with at least one child in the end? Why/why not?

2. Do you think Rhea will have the life she has envisioned? Why/why not?

3. Discuss the role of gender in the two stories. What is the relationship between femininity and motherhood? What about masculinity and fatherhood?

4. Discuss the role of socioeconomic background in voluntary and involuntary childlessness, as well as in attempts and opportunities to remedy involuntary childlessness.

5. Discuss the role of modern medicine and technology in avenues to combat involuntary childlessness. Also, address any potential ethical, moral, and/or religious concerns in the use of technology in conceiving and carrying a child.

6. West and Zimmerman (1987) explained that gender was a routine, everyday accomplishment, something that we do in interaction with others, as opposed to something that we are. Discuss a few examples of how characters in the two stories do gender (or fail to do gender in conventional ways).

7. A stereotype is a simplified, exaggerated, generalized idea about members of a group of people. Prejudice is a biased judgment (either positive or negative) and/or amplified feelings (likes or dislikes) about an individual based on his/her belonging to a specific group. Stigma is a salient, persistent, negative label that people apply to individuals who do not follow social norms (Goffman, 1986). Do you believe that there are any stereotypes, prejudice, and/or stigma surrounding voluntary and/or involuntary childlessness? Why/why not? Do they vary by gender? Are men or women any more affected by such stereotypes, prejudice, or stigma? Why/why not?

8. There are many reasons for not having children (Scott, 2009). Do stereotypes, prejudice, and/or stigma vary based on the reason for not having children? If yes, list a few examples/reasons that involve more stereotypes, prejudice, and/or stigma and discuss why.

9. Based on the two stories, use an ethnomethodological approach to discuss whether having children is still a social norm in society, especially for a married or committed couple. Ethnomethodology is the study of how norms of the social world are created and understood (Garfinkel, 1984). Ethnomethodologists intentionally break social norms to explore whether those norms are flexible or inflexible.

10. Lumping is emphasizing similarities between certain groups and neglecting their potential differences, whereas splitting is focusing on, or even exaggerating, differences between certain groups (Zerubavel, 1991, 1996). Do most people tend to apply more lumping or splitting in discussions of childlessness? Do they tend to lump all childless people together (regardless of gender and/or reasons for childlessness), or is there more splitting—that is, focusing on differences between various groups of childless individuals? Why?

11. Do you see any difference between the terms *childless* and *childfree*? If yes, how so? What does each express?

Find the Answers

Go to http://www.pewresearch.org/fact-tank/2018/07/17/a-third-of-u-s-adults-say-they-have-used-fertility-treatments-or-know-someone-who-has/ to find answers to the following questions.

1. How do fertility treatments vary by education?

2. How do fertility treatments vary by income?

3. How do fertility treatments vary by race/ethnicity?

4. How do fertility treatments vary by geographical area within the United States?

Mini Research Assignments

1. Research and study some websites and/or blogs advocating a childfree/childless by choice lifestyle. What kind of messages do they convey about childless/childfree living? What do those messages seem to do with gender, age, social class, education, and other similar factors? What kinds of stereotypes/prejudice/stigma are discussed (if any)? Draw parallels with Rhea's story as well.

2. Survey at least seven individuals, asking them to rate their agreement with the following statements on a scale of 1–10 (1 meaning complete disagreement and 10 indicating full agreement): 1. "It is perfectly fine for individuals and couples, struggling with infertility, to use modern medicine and technology to assist them." 2. "There are absolutely no ethical, moral, or religious dilemmas with the use of modern assistive reproductive technologies, such as in vitro fertilization." 3. "It is a perfectly valid choice for individuals or couples to decide not to have children." 4. "Women who decide not to have children are still judged more than men who choose the same." Summarize your results, analyze the role of gender, age, education, and other similar factors, and draw parallels with the two stories.

3. Watch a movie and/or a documentary and/or a news story depicting an individual or couple facing voluntary or involuntary childlessness. How is he/she, or how are they portrayed? What kinds of messages are conveyed about childless/childfree living? What do those messages seem to do with gender, age, social class, education, and other similar factors? What kinds of stereotypes/prejudice/stigma are discussed (if any)? Draw parallels with the two stories as well.

4. Interview an individual or couple who has struggled with infertility or has decided on voluntary childlessness/childfreeness. Summarize their narratives. Discuss the role of gender, age, education, social class, and other similar factors. What kinds of messages are conveyed about childless/childfree living? What kinds of stereotypes/prejudice/stigma are discussed (if any)? Draw parallels with the two stories as well.

References

Garfinkel, H. (1984). *Studies in ethnomethodology*. Malden, MA: Polity.

Goffman, E. (1986). *Stigma: Notes on the management of spoiled identity*. New York, NY: Touchstone. (Originally published 1963)

Livingston, G. (2018). A third of U.S. adults say they have used fertility treatments or know someone who has. Washington, DC: Pew Research Center. Retrieved from http://www.pewresearch.org/fact-tank/2018/07/17/a-third-of-u-s-adults-say-they-have-used-fertility-treatments-or-know-someone-who-has/

Scott, L. (2009). *Two is enough: A couple's guide to living childless by choice*. Berkeley, CA: Seal Press.

West, C., & Zimmerman, D. H. (1987). Doing gender. *Gender & Society, 1,* 125–151.

Zerubavel, E. (1991). *The fine line: Making distinctions in everyday life*. New York, NY: Free Press.

_____. (1996). Lumping and splitting: Notes on social classification. *Sociological Forum, 11,* 421–433.

CHAPTER 6

"I like my own space."
LIVING ALONE AS A GROWING "FAMILY FORM"

Mackenzie Grant leisurely stretched on her brand new beige couch. She closed her eyes and thoroughly enjoyed the silence that wrapped her like a cozy blanket. She loved peace and quiet, and the relaxation and fulfillment she gained from it. Sunday mornings were her favorite time of the week these days. She didn't have anywhere to rush and any obligations to complete. She could immerse herself in some well-deserved rest after a long workweek.

Mackenzie worked as a technical writer at a prestigious firm in Atlanta. She loved her job and put in an extraordinary amount of hours. She often had to work weeknights and sometimes Saturdays, but usually not Sundays. She was well qualified for the job, and had studied and worked years for it. She was immensely proud to have accomplished so much already, as she had just recently turned 29.

Mackenzie was the first in her family to have earned a college degree, which she found an admirable feat. She was from rural Arkansas, and had undeniably come a long way. Her parents had barely finished high school and had had very modest incomes. In fact, her mother stopped working after her second child. Mackenzie was the third child to come along, after two older sisters, and she had a younger brother later. Their family had a small house, and Mackenzie had to share a room with her two sisters. The room was cramped, and Mackenzie frequently felt confined in it, as well as in the entire house. They had one and a half bathrooms, which tended to get extremely crowded with six people. Mackenzie liked to play outside, where there was a little more room. She didn't remember ever spending time alone as a child or teenager, at least not in the house. She often craved more space and time on her own and vowed to attain it when she grew up.

Mackenzie turned out to be bright and very diligent, working hard to get into college. She could hardly wait to leave the packed family home. Although she wasn't lucky with her roommate in her first year of college, it still felt like a breath of fresh air to have to share a room with only one person. While concentrating her energies mostly on studying, Mackenzie got a part-time job to be able to afford moving out of the dorm. She managed to rent a tiny house with two other girls in her sophomore year, where she could finally have a room to herself. It was one of the greatest joys she had ever obtained. By her senior year she could have her own bathroom as well, in addition to a separate room.

When she landed her first job as a technical writer in Atlanta, one of her must-haves was renting an apartment by herself. She was done with roommates and housemates. In the beginning, she had to spend a sizable portion of her salary on rent, especially to be able to afford an apartment in a neighborhood that was not only attractive but safe for a single woman. However, it was all worth it. A year later she changed jobs and negotiated a higher salary, which made renting on her own more feasible. It even allowed her to put some money aside every month, so 3 years later she had enough for a down payment for her own place.

She decided to buy a small condo in Buckhead, a highly coveted area in Atlanta. Buying her own place was the greatest achievement of her life. It was a symbol of success and independence, especially as she was barely 27 at the time. Her parents, especially her mother and siblings, had a difficult time understanding why purchasing a home was so crucial for her. They wondered why she didn't simply wait until she was married to buy a home, one that was suitable for a family. Her mother was often concerned about her safety living alone in a big city and that Mackenzie was settling down for a long-term, or even permanent, single lifestyle, relinquishing any desire and opportunity to get married and have a family, complete with a family home.

What was a source of angst for her mother was a fountain of pride for Mackenzie. She loved owning something and having her own space. The neighborhood and building were safe, so she was never afraid alone. The condo was cozy and decorated in her own taste. It felt like home and generated a sense of having arrived. She could go to bed and get up whenever

she wanted or needed to, without having to accommodate other people's schedules. She knew that what she put in the fridge would remain there unless she ate it herself. She could walk around naked or stay in her pajamas all day on a Sunday. She could watch whatever she wanted on TV and listen to loud music. She didn't have to worry about a mess and could clean up when she saw fit.

Mackenzie rarely felt lonely. Occasionally, there was an evening or night when she couldn't sleep, and loneliness sneaked into her consciousness and grabbed hold of her heart. However, she mostly enjoyed being alone, and it didn't mean that she wasn't social. First of all, she had Sophie, her 2-year-old white terrier, a constant, loyal companion. She had never been able to have a dog before. Her family had been cat people, and she normally couldn't keep animals when she was renting. Sophie stirred her social life not only by her presence, but also through being very friendly and frequently approaching other dogs when Mackenzie walked her. It gave Mackenzie opportunities to meet and chat with other dog owners. In fact, she had acquired a few close friends by walking Sophie.

Mackenzie also had an active social life with friends. She knew some through work; she met others in the yoga studio she frequented. They often had coffee, did yoga together, walked in Piedmont Park, visited museums, watched shows in the theater, or just had a girls' night in. Occasionally, they went to a club, but that wasn't Mackenzie's favorite ways to spend her free time. Sometimes people had assumed that as a single girl in her twenties living alone she must be a party-girl, but that was far from the truth.

Mackenzie also had a vivid social life online, so on some evenings or weekends when she was home alone, she was still connected and definitely not lonely. She had several hundred friends on social media and an active presence on those sites herself. She had some friends on online poetry fan sites as well. She didn't mind going to places on her own, either. As none of her friends in Atlanta were too much into poetry, she tended to go to poetry readings on her own. Sometimes she went to the movies, theater, and exhibitions alone as well. The High Museum of Art was one of her favorite places, and when she visited without the distraction of others, she could immerse herself in art much better. A few times she had traveled on her own, too, which really recharged her.

Living alone had taught Mackenzie a lot about herself that she had not been cognizant of before. She had only known herself as a daughter, sister, roommate, girlfriend, and friend, always in relation to others. She had seen herself as a reflection in other people's eyes. She was very adaptable and easy-going, so she had tended to go along with other people's wishes, lifestyles, and preferences. She hadn't had opportunities to dig deep within and get to know herself, figuring out her own wishes and preferences. Now she felt more secure about herself than ever before. Now she was simply Mackenzie, and she had no doubts about who that person was, which she found a privilege, as she knew that so many people went through their entire lives without that level of self-awareness.

Mackenzie realized that her mother was sometimes worried about her, often along with her sisters. She wished she could help them understand that she was fine and happy. Yes, living alone had its incidental drawbacks, like everything else, such as random bouts of loneliness, being solely responsible for every chore, mortgage, and bill, and being asked to do overtime at work because she was the one without family obligations. However, for Mackenzie the advantages still surpassed the impediments. Although her family tended to warn her that she might become antisocial and unsuitable for future family life by living alone, Mackenzie disagreed. She firmly believed that by procuring so much in-depth knowledge of herself she would become more capable of harmonious social existence and co-residence with others. She didn't view living alone as a permanent state. For her, it was an essential, but temporary, stage of obtaining independence, confidence, maturity, self-reliance, and self-awareness, which could prepare her for a blissful family life in the future.

*

Janet Bosco looked around her garden contentedly. She had just finished watering her plants and admired the lush, colorful landscape that her blooming flowers offered. Gardening was a relatively new pursuit that she had embraced, but she turned out to be an ardent fan of every aspect of it. The only thing she regretted was not having started this relaxing hobby decades ago. She wiped sweat from her forehead and sank into her soft, comfortable outdoor couch. She took a gulp of fresh lemonade that she had squeezed that morning. She delighted in watching some butterflies dance around her flowers. She loved nature, but she didn't use to have sufficient time or opportunity to be so engrossed in it.

In another life, Janet had been swallowed by conflicting expectations and obligations. She used to work as a psychiatrist at a hospital in Columbus, Ohio. Her work had been demanding and her schedule relentless. She had done her best to be a spotless wife and mother as well. She used to sleep an average of 5 hours every night, then work, take care of her daughter, Amy, her husband, Tom, and their household. Her strong sense of duty and her love for her family and job kept her going, even when she was suffocating under her heavy responsibilities. Tom had left Janet when Amy was 6 for a woman who was 13 years younger, 20 pounds lighter, much less educated, and significantly less overworked than Janet. Janet had been devastated for almost a year, but hadn't showed it to remain strong for Amy. She raised Amy on her own to the best of her abilities, and she seemed to have done a good job, as Amy was 25 now, a happy and content college graduate with a lucrative career and a doting significant other.

A year after Amy had left Columbus to attend college in another state, Janet had begun to sense some restlessness overtaking her. Her role as a mother had been winding down, as Amy didn't need her on an everyday basis anymore. She grew dissatisfied with her job at the hospital as well. She was suddenly yearning for something new and challenging. After watching a series of interviews with doctors who volunteered in Africa, she unexpectedly realized that it could be a novel goal for her, too. As a psychiatrist, she had a medical degree, and after a brief training, she found herself in Uganda, helping the sick. It turned out to be the most eye-opening and fulfilling experience she had ever had. Amy was slightly surprised and concerned, but mostly proud of her mother. In the last 6 years Janet had returned to Africa four more times, usually for a month, but her longest stay was 3 months. She had developed a new passion, and she couldn't stop anymore, discovering the need for doctors there and the inconceivable gratification she had obtained from the trips.

Janet had resigned from her job at the hospital in Ohio before her first visit to Africa. After that first journey she realized that Ohio was becoming too restrictive for her, and she needed a more permanent change of scenery beyond her temporary travels. So, she decided to sell her house in Columbus and buy a new one in southwest Florida, at an unforgettable spot of past vacations. This house was her dream home. She had made numerous compromises when having bought their house together with her ex-husband in Ohio. She made it her own to some extent after they had got a divorce, but the changes predominantly revolved around Amy's needs and tastes. This house in Florida was the first to have been entirely her own. Amy liked to visit on school breaks and holidays, but she didn't have her own room here; she stayed in the guestroom like other guests.

Janet finally had a white kitchen, which she had always dreamed of, but her ex-husband, and later Amy, disliked, so in the house in Ohio the kitchen cabinets had been dark wood. White felt more airy and homey to Janet. She had all-white sofas and pastel armchairs, too, which would have been impractical when Amy was a child. Janet even got a white cat, Priscilla, who didn't only fit the décor of the new house, but she made it considerably cozier. Janet loved her private patio and garden the most, which always cheered her up with its kaleidoscope of bright colors.

When not in Africa, Janet did private counseling sessions, which gave her more flexibility and fulfillment than her prior job at the hospital. It allowed her time for more volunteering as well, which she had grown immensely fond of. She regularly volunteered at a children's shelter and a nursing home. At 59, she felt that her life was more complete, productive, content, and satisfying than ever. She even had time for some travel for leisure; she visited many cities in the United States and Europe, including Italy, where her grandparents had come from. She started learning some Italian and changed her name back to her maiden name, Bosco, to honor her ancestors.

The buzz of her phone jerked Janet out of her daydreaming. She smiled hearing the melodious tone, which was solely assigned to her boyfriend, Clint. As the word "boyfriend" crossed her mind, her smile widened, as it sounded so liberating, pure, and simple and made her feel extremely young. After her divorce, as a single mother Janet had rarely had time and energy to date, so she had mostly been alone, only dating once in a while. After Amy had left for college, and Janet had moved to Florida, she became more open to the possibility of romance. She had dated a divorced man for nearly 3 years, but the relationship ended abruptly when the man moved to Seattle for his job. He asked Janet to go with him or continue their relationship long-distance, but Janet wasn't interested in either option. She loved Florida and her new life and home too much to leave, and a long-distance relationship of that scale wouldn't have met her companionship needs at this point of her life.

She had met Clint online, on a 55+ dating site. He was a widow, 9 years her senior. He was intelligent, polite, gentle, and a good listener. Janet found all of these qualities essential in a man. He often traveled to New England to visit his adult children and small grandchildren, but he still spent the bulk of his time in Florida, so this relationship was not long-distance, except for short periods of time when she was in Africa or he in the Northeast. He was an avid gardener, so he could offer Janet great tips on that. They both loved old movies, which they frequently watched together. They took up golf as a new sport that they pursued together. They enjoyed long walks on the beach or in parks when the weather wasn't too hot. They traveled together domestically and once in Europe as well. Clint was retired, so his schedule tended to be flexible. Normally they spent three weekends together every month and two or three afternoons or evenings per week, occasionally a weeknight with Janet going over to his house or Clint coming over to hers. This relationship was very exciting and satisfying for Janet. She couldn't have imagined it becoming any better than it already was.

After her musings about Clint, Janet answered the phone with a grin, "Hello, darling. How are you?"

"I'm just great," Clint responded with an audible smile. "So, are you almost ready for our date tonight?"

"Um, yes, almost," Janet said, quickly glancing at her watch. She didn't realize that she had spent so much time in her garden, nearly missing their date. "I'll be ready in half an hour."

"Splendid," Clint grinned. "I'll pick you up soon then."

Janet hurried into the house and took a quick shower. She normally preferred long baths in her jetted tub these days, but there was no time for that now. After the shower she fixed her hair and applied a touch of makeup. While the woman in the mirror had marked wrinkles and a few grey hairs, Janet liked her reflection immeasurably more than she did in her twenties, thirties, or forties. This woman was more peaceful, fulfilled, and wiser than her younger selves, which made her more beautiful. By now she had learned what was important in life and that appearance wasn't a top priority.

Clint picked her up in his beloved convertible in half an hour, as promised, and they drove to the beach. They had found a relatively secluded spot over a year ago, and it had become their favorite place to walk. They walked hand-in-hand while Janet enthusiastically talked about her flowers. She was aware that this topic usually interested Clint, and he generally had some useful tips about gardening. However, today he was quieter than

expected. He almost looked embarrassed, which surprised Janet because he tended to be so comfortable around her.

"Is something bothering you?" Janet asked gently.

"No, everything is fine," Clint countered absentmindedly. "Could we maybe just sit down for a while?"

"Sure," Janet said with some concern. Clint could routinely walk at least 4 miles without any problems, even at a fast pace, so Janet was wondering if he might feel sick or tired today. They hadn't even walked a mile at this point. However, she found it easier to simply sit down, and if there was anything wrong, it would turn out sooner or later.

Clint hugged her with one arm and took her hand in his other hand. "Janet, darling," he began carefully with an almost imperceptible tremble in his voice. "You know you mean a lot to me, don't you?"

"Yes," Janet affirmed. Clint was definitely acting odd. Why did he seem so awkward? An unpleasant thought crossed her mind: was he trying to break up with her? That would inevitably sadden her, as she loved him and profoundly enjoyed his company.

"I enjoy your company very much," Clint said, inadvertently echoing her thoughts. "In fact, I enjoy it so much that I would like more of it."

He let go of her hand, reached into his pocket, took out a small box, and opened it. "Would you marry me?" he asked, beaming.

Janet was astonished and speechless. This was the most unexpected thing Clint could have done. She tried to force her mouth to work, but even her mind seemed to be unable to function properly, let alone her lips. A heavy silence followed, and the smile slowly disappeared from Clint's face.

"I see that I might have surprised you," he said faintly, lowering his hand that was holding up the box.

"Um…, I guess so," Janet stammered. "I just thought… We were having such a wonderful time… I thought you enjoyed it. That you enjoyed it just the way it was. I didn't realize that you'd want more."

"Of course, I would want more," Clint sighed resignedly. "It has been a very nice courtship, and I *have* enjoyed it. But if it works well, courtship moves toward marriage, doesn't it? And it's been 2 years. Or is it still too early? Did I ask too early?"

"No, I'm glad you asked," Janet contended softly. "I'm glad you did because I had never realized before what your intentions were. I'm sorry. Maybe we should have discussed this before."

"Maybe," Clint agreed. "As now that we're discussing it, it's clear that you don't want to marry me."

"It's not that I don't want to marry *you*," Janet protested. "It's just… it's just that I don't want to marry anybody."

"I'm not sure I follow," Clint said, confused. "I thought women wanted to get married. Not necessarily the young women these days, but our generation. We grew up with those values."

"Yes, we did," Janet confirmed. "And I followed those norms for most of my life. I got married, I raised my daughter. I'm not saying I would've done that differently. No, I don't have any regrets. But I've been married before. I have a grown daughter. I have my own life and my own home. I can't give all of that up. I've fought too hard for it, and I love it too much. I like my own space."

"Oh, Janet, you don't have to be afraid," Clint breathed. "I respect you and your life. I would never ask you to give it up. I know your home is important to you. If we got married, we could live there if you wanted."

"You're sweet," Janet said, stroking his hand. "But it wouldn't be *my* home then, would it? My life would change completely, and I'm not ready for that.

I don't want it to change. I like it just the way it is. I like it with you in it, the way we have been, and I hope that doesn't have to change, but I have to say no to your proposal. I'm so sorry, but I have to say no now, and I'd have to say no in the future because that is the only way I can say yes to *me*."

Janet felt sadness squeezing her heart, especially when she looked at Clint's crestfallen face. She didn't know if this was the beginning of the end for them, if Clint could only envision a future together with marriage in it, or if he could ultimately come to terms with continuing the affectionate companionship-style relationship they had been sharing. Janet didn't want to hold him back or push him to compromise, but she knew that she couldn't compromise either and give up her own privacy, space, and independence.

*

KUCO / Shutterstock.com

Earl Kowalski gloomily stared at a picture of his late wife, Eva. Eva had barely been 20 when the picture had been taken, 60 years ago. She had been a radiant, energetic woman, and her beauty seemed almost ethereal to Earl after all these decades. Her personality and love for Earl shone through the photo, touching his aching heart. They had spent 60 years together, and today was the first anniversary of her passing away.

Earl and Eva had met in the mid-1950s. She was 19 at the time, and he was 21. Eva was Earl's best friend's cousin, and they had run into each other by chance at a family gathering. They instantly fell in love and got married within a year. They had a son, Richard, 2 years later and another son, Raymond, who was born 4 years after Richard. Eva stayed at home with the children as long as she could, but when they were both in school, she had to go back to work at a factory because they couldn't make ends meet on Earl's wages as a warehouse worker. With two incomes and the types of jobs they were engaged in, they were considered a working-class family. They managed to buy a two-bedroom house, which they were immensely proud of. They could provide the basics for their family, but couldn't afford any luxuries. Eva was dreaming about having a third child, a daughter that she would have named Rita, but Earl, worried about finances, dissuaded her. Over 50 years later, in the late stages of Alzheimer's, Eva often talked about Rita, her daughter, so in the end, in her mind, she got the daughter she had always dreamed of.

Richard died in a car accident in his late twenties, which left Earl and Eva devastated. Fortunately, they had each other and could provide incredible support for one another in their shared grief. Raymond moved from their native Pittsburgh to California and hardly looked back. Although he didn't go to college either, like his parents, he managed to obtain a relatively stable job and a respectable income. He moved up on the social ladder by a little bit; compared to his parents' working-class status, he shifted to the lower-middle class. He got married and had three daughters, Amanda, Nicole, and Stacy, within 5 years in the late 1980s. At first, he visited home about once a year, then it was once every 2 or 3 years, and in the last decade, he only visited once. He invited Earl and Eva to California no more than a few times, but they couldn't have afforded to regularly travel there anyway. Eva was heartbroken not only due to the loss of Richard to death, but also because of the loss of Raymond to California and his wife, who wanted him for herself.

The last 8 years of her life that Eva spent with Alzheimer's proved to be very difficult for her and Earl, but, in a strange way, the late stages of forgetting painful memories of her past might have provided a kind of relief for her as well. Earl cared for her at home for the most part. It was pure agony for him to watch her deterioration, and in the last year of her life he often felt extremely lonely. Her passing ushered in the most excruciating pain he had ever felt, even worse than what he had experienced after Richard's death, most likely because during that other grief he had still had Eva. After her passing, he had no one. He knew that he couldn't count on Raymond, and he didn't have any other relatives, and all of his friends had passed away.

Raymond did come for the funeral and to make sure that his father sold the house, half of which he had inherited through his mother's passing. Earl desperately wanted to stay in the house he had spent most of his adulthood and married life in, but Raymond didn't budge; he insisted that he needed the money. As the house was small, old, and run down, and it was a buyer's market at the time, half of the sale price that Earl ended up with was a meager sum. It was instantly obvious that he couldn't buy another house. He looked into some options and finally moved into a low-income apartment building for seniors.

The building was ancient and dilapidated, and the apartment itself an efficiency with outdated appliances (no dishwasher or washer and dryer), leaky faucets, and peeling paint. Some cockroaches and other bugs easily found their way into the apartment. The apartment was located on the second floor, without an elevator, and because of his knees Earl found it difficult to manage the stairs, so he rarely left the apartment unless it became absolutely necessary. He frequently skipped meals to save some money and a

burdensome trip to the grocery store. When he couldn't go to the laundromat, he wore the same clothes for weeks. He tended to skip baths as well to conserve water and energy. His physical, mental, and emotional condition quickly deteriorated after Eva's death and his move. He nearly incessantly felt lethargic, sleepy, irritable, sorrowful, and achy all over. He had been prescribed some medicine for some health conditions that he had, but sometimes he couldn't go to the doctor to renew the prescriptions or the pharmacy to fill them. Even when he had enough pills, he took them intermittently, often forgetting or not caring whether he took them or not. Occasionally, he felt that he didn't have the strength to go on and wished that he could follow Eva. He suspected it wouldn't be too long before he did, but he wouldn't have gone as far as taking matters into his own hands.

It could have been beneficial to have some company once in a while. He had a landline, and he sometimes wondered if that might be a luxury, but it could have been important in case of an emergency, and also, it provided a connection to the outside world. He was occasionally called by telemarketers, and he always enjoyed chatting with them. It felt nice to hear a human voice. He could have tried to make friends with some of the other residents in the apartment building, but they tended to keep to themselves and seemed cautious, or even distrustful. As it wasn't a very safe neighborhood, they had a good reason for vigilance. The neighborhood also discouraged Earl from leaving the apartment too much and venturing out. He knew that as an elderly, fragile man he could become an easy target.

He unavailingly wished for a dog that could offer some company and ease his loneliness. However, he was cognizant of not being able to take care of it, especially walking it every day. Also, he probably wouldn't be able to afford food and medical treatments that a dog might require. Eva had been scared of dogs, so they never had one during their marriage, but Earl often mused these days about the dog he used to have as a boy. If he could have a dog, he might have a reason to get up in the morning and the motivation to go on.

He glanced back at Eva's photo that he was holding. Her face was illuminated by a smile that she had reserved for him. Earl laid down on his 25-year-old couch, tightening his grip on the picture. He hoped to drift to sleep, entering a better world, where dreams were attainable. He yearned for Eva to appear in his dreams. At least she would be there with him in his dreams, and finally he wouldn't be so desperately, utterly alone.

Discussion Questions

1. What do you think will happen to Mackenzie, Janet, and Earl? Continue their stories.

2. What is the role of age in living alone? How can living alone be influenced by age, health, different life stages, and family statuses?

3. More women than men now live alone in the United States (Klinenberg, 2013). What is the role of gender in living alone?

4. What is the role of social class, socioeconomic background in living alone?

5. Living alone is one of the most prominent and fastest growing household arrangements (Klinenberg, 2013). Do you see it increasing further in the future? Why/why not? Could the rise of living alone affect families in some way? Why/why not?

6. Multiperson families are more likely to own pets than individuals living alone (Klinenberg, 2013). Is this surprising? Why/why not? How can pets be beneficial when someone lives alone?

7. Some theorists argue that today people have responsibilities primarily to themselves, more so than to spouses, partners, or children (Cherlin, 2010; Klinenberg, 2013). Do you agree with this? Why/why not? Does this suggest that we live in a culture that puts more emphasis on the individual than the social or collective? Why/why not?

8. A stereotype is a simplified, generalized idea about members of a group of people that is usually taken to the extreme. Prejudice is a biased judgment (either positive or negative) and/or exaggerated feelings (likes or dislikes) about an individual based on his/her belonging to a specific group. Stigma is a significant, persistent, negative label that people apply to individuals who do not follow social norms (Goffman, 1986). Do you believe that there are any stereotypes, prejudice, and/or stigma surrounding living alone? Why/why not? Do they vary by gender? Are men or women more affected by such stereotypes, prejudice, or stigma? Why/why not?

9. Through his concept of the looking-glass self, Cooley (1998) underlined how our sense of self is shaped by how others perceive us. If someone lives alone, how do you think his/her looking-glass self might develop?

10. Goffman (1959) explained in his theory of dramaturgical analysis that we all played roles as if we were actors in a theater. We prepare for roles on the backstage, whereas the frontstage is where our performances take place. Do people still play roles when they live alone? Why/why not? Do you think the line between backstage and frontstage might blur in their performances, or does it become even more rigid when alone? Why?

Find the Answers

Go to http://www.pewsocialtrends.org/2016/02/18/1-gender-gap-in-share-of-older-adults-living-alone-narrows/ to find answers to the following questions.

1. Among adults over the age of 65 are men or women more likely to live alone? How has the gap between elderly men and women living alone changed in the last 100 years?

2. How has the marital status of adults over the age of 65 changed since 1990?

3. Do more elderly men or women remarry if they are divorced or widowed? Why?

4. How has solo living among individuals over the age of 85 changed since 1990?

Mini Research Assignments

1. Read the following article: http://www.pewsocialtrends.org/2016/02/18/2-living-arrange-ments-of-older-americans-by-gender/
   Summarize the main findings, paying attention to variations by gender. Then research hous-ing options for seniors in your area. Discuss the options and what you see as their key advan-tages and drawbacks. Draw parallels with the stories you read in this chapter and describe the role of age in living alone.
2. Watch a movie, documentary, or TV show that depicts at least one character living alone. How is the character portrayed? If there is more than one, how are they depicted? Compare them as well. What seem to be the advantages and disadvantages of living alone in the movie, documentary, or TV show that you watched? Discuss the role of gender, age, social class, and geographical location. Draw parallels with the stories you read in this chapter.
3. Interview at least two people living alone. How do they describe their experience? What do they see as the main advantages and drawbacks of living alone? Compare and contrast their experience. Discuss the role of gender, age, social class, and geographical location. Draw parallels with the stories you read in this chapter.
4. Survey at least seven individuals, asking them to rate their agreement with the following statements on a scale of 1–10 (1 meaning complete disagreement and 10 indicating full agreement): 1. "Living alone has more drawbacks than advantages." 2. "Living alone can be easier for men than women." 3. "Living alone is easier for the young than for the elderly." 4. "If many people live alone in a society, it might indicate the decline of families in that society." Summarize your results and analyze the potential role of gender and age in the responses. Draw parallels with the stories you read in this chapter.

References

Cherlin, A. J. (2010). *The marriage-go-round: The state of marriage and the family in America today.* New York, NY: Vintage.

Cooley, C. H. (1998). *On self and social organization.* Chicago, IL: University of Chicago Press. (Originally published 1902)

Goffman, E. (1959). *The presentation of self in everyday life.* New York, NY: Anchor.

_____. (1986). *Stigma: Notes on the management of spoiled identity.* New York, NY: Touchstone. (Originally published 1963)

Klinenberg, E. (2013). *Going solo: The extraordinary rise and surprising appeal of living alone.* New York, NY: Penguin.

Stepler, R. (2016). Gender gap in share of older adults living alone narrows. Washington, DC: Pew Research Center. Retrieved from http://www.pewsocialtrends.org/2016/02/18/1-gender-gap-in-share-of-older-adults-living-alone-narrows/

_____. (2016). Living arrangements of older Americans by gender. Washington, DC: Pew Research Center. Retrieved from http://www.pewsocialtrends.org/2016/02/18/2-living-arrangements-of-older-americans-by-gender/

CHAPTER

"He just disappeared"
GHOSTING AND OTHER BREAKUP STRATEGIES

©Antonio Guillem/shutterstock.com

K acie Drummer opened a popular dating app on her phone. Her heart was beating rapidly as she was expecting a message from Laz. When she caught a glimpse of the new message icon, her mouth instantly turned dry with excitement. She was dazed to notice her strong reaction to a few typed-up sentences from a man she had yet to meet in person.

Kacie had signed up to this particular dating app three weeks ago, about a couple of months after her significant other of five years had broken up with her. She just recently turned 30 and had spent half of her twenties with Luke. They lived together for nearly three years, and Kacie had been hoping that they would grow old together. At one point, Luke even proposed, but took it back the next day, apologizing that he was drunk and not thinking clearly, arguing that they should simply continue to share a home without committing to a piece of paper just yet. Kacie was somewhat disappointed but decided to be a good sport and go along with Luke's wishes. She convinced herself that she was too young to get married at 28 anyway.

In the last year of their relationship they broke up twice. The first time it was only for a day, and they both regretted it right away. The second time Luke actually moved out, but he returned a week later. They remained a couple for another four months, but it turned out to be mere torture for both of them, as the relationship deteriorated fast. They were constantly fighting and stopped having sex. Kacie tried to hold on to the relationship both because a part of her still loved Luke, but also because she was abhorred by the idea of becoming single at 30. All her friends had been married for a couple of years, and that had always been her plan as well.

One day, Luke came home, sat her down, and told her that he just could not go on any longer. He spoke the words softly. They had been yelling so much already, and all the passion to be together, or to hate each other and fight, had just evaporated. There was nothing left, certainly not anything to build a life on. After he left, Kacie wept for a little bit, but soon she realized that all her tears were gone. She had cried them all in the previous months. She felt empty and recognized that Luke was history, and he had been for a while. She had just been struggling to hang on to a beautiful past with him and dreams of a future that would never come to pass.

Shortly after their break-up Kacie sensed a desire for a new relationship stir in her. She was concerned that she couldn't just wait around to meet someone one day, especially as she didn't intend to postpone her plans to get married indefinitely. She decided to take control of her fate by giving dating apps a chance. She knew that she wasn't looking for hook-ups, so she refrained from the use of the apps that were renowned for being more likely to deliver romantic adventures and fun than potentially more serious relationships. She vowed not to make her own choice of partner based on looks only either. After researching some dating apps, she settled on one that offered a personality test and compatible matches based on that.

She was thrilled to first sign in, then disappointed to scroll through the initial matches. She caught herself excluding some men based on their unfavorable appearance, then she was slightly ashamed for judging so quickly and forced herself to study the profiles of those men, hoping to find a diamond in the rough. She went to bed defeated that night, realizing that finding an incredible match will not come easy.

By the next day, she had fifteen messages in her inbox. Her mood improved immediately, especially when she came across a message from a man named Laz. She loved his name instantly; it sounded unique and cool. He was pretty handsome as well – good-looking not in a movie-star kind of way, but more in a wholesome, nice-guy sort of way, which Kacie preferred anyway. He looked trustworthy, and Kacie's fears of potentially being catfished that had plagued her before signing up for the app suddenly dissipated. Many other characteristics matched, too, such as their age, level of education, hobbies and interests.

They began to exchange messages, first just one a day, then two, three, or four. Now they had been texting back and forth through the app for over a week, and in the message that she just received and that made her mouth dry with elation, Laz suggested a first meeting. Kacie smiled at how thrilled she was and could hardly believe she felt this way about a stranger. Then she reminded herself that he was not a stranger by now; some of the conversations they had had through texts were more meaningful and intimate than what she had experienced with Luke for a long time.

When the day of their first meeting finally arrived, Kacie was a wreck. She was fired up, but also on edge and anxious. Her legs felt weak as she walked up to Laz, who had been waiting for her.

"Hi," she whispered, as she held out her hand to him. "I'm Kacie."

"Hey, Kacie, I'm Laz. Actually Lazarus, but please never call me that" he said, and a smile brightened his clean-shaven face.

Kacie loved his gentle voice, and it reached right into her heart. The expression "he had me at Hello" gained a whole new meaning for her, and, for the first time in her life, she accepted the possibility of love at first sight. Maybe in her case, it had happened even before then, however inconceivable that seemed.

Their first date lasted almost six hours. They talked incessantly, they laughed and discovered more things in common than they had thought imaginable. Fifteen minutes after they said good-bye Laz already texted her, thanking her for a beautiful evening, which had only been outshined by her own beauty. A few days later he proposed a second date.

Their second date turned out to be even longer than the first. Three hours into the date Laz asked if Kacie received messages from a lot of guys through the app.

"Yes," she admitted slowly.

"Yeah, I would have bet," Laz sighed. "No wonder you do. You're a special girl. I just knew that right when I saw your profile picture."

"Thanks," Kacie blushed a little, his compliment warming her face.

"So...?" Laz breathed.

"So... what?" Kacie echoed.

"I mean...," he stammered. "I know there are other guys interested, of course, there are. But... do I have a reason to hope that you have made up your mind yet?"

"We're here, aren't we?" Kacie said softly.

"Yes, we are," Laz grinned, pulling her closer and planting an unforgettable first kiss on her lips. "Wow, I'm a lucky bastard," he murmured later.

Kacie couldn't agree more; she felt extremely fortunate as well. She was aware that many people struggled with online and phone dating apps, so she could hardly believe her luck that she found someone so incredible after only a few short weeks on the app. She wondered if this might be a karmic compensation for the difficult last year and all the agony with Luke.

In the next month, sparks continued to fly, texts were flowing, now through their regular phones and messaging apps, not through the dating app, and the relationship seemed to blossom. After their first date Kacie stopped checking her messages on the dating app. She simply didn't care who might be attempting to get in touch with her because she gradually grew more and more convinced that she had found the One. She felt faintly guilty because after meeting Laz, as she didn't go back to the app, she probably failed to respond to some guys she had been in contact with. They may have messaged her or may not have, but if they did, she unintentionally left them hanging. Still, she felt that she owed it to her feelings for Laz to focus on him and not be looking at the profiles of other men and not be in contact with anyone else.

Kacie and Laz met at least twice a week, as their schedules allowed. They both yearned for as much time together as possible. Laz often told her that he was really into her and that time without her was almost unbearable because all he could think of was her. They enjoyed the unparalleled emotional, intellectual, and physical connection they shared. Laz could look into her eyes so deeply that she felt his gaze pierce into her soul and leave an indelible mark. As their closeness was so palpable, Kacie didn't sense a need for them to define their relationship and put a label on it. Laz never initiated a conversation like that either, but it didn't occur to Kacie to worry about that, as his devotion to her seemed so obvious.

After about five weeks of dating Kacie noticed one afternoon that she had received no text from Laz that day. For a moment she was taken aback by that realization because Laz usually texted either in the morning or by lunchtime the latest. She felt some concern starting to rise in her, but she quickly dismissed it. He must be busier at work than usual or something came up. She could have texted him but didn't want to cause any interruptions if he was indeed having a remarkably tough day. By 8 pm that evening, she began to be truly uneasy, so she shot him a text, "Hey, what's up? U OK?"

When there was no response by 10 pm, she called one of her best friends, Ivy to distract herself from her increasingly perturbed thoughts.

"Hey," Ivy answered the phone. "Great timing. Timmy is finally in bed, and we're just hanging with Dex," Ivy added, referring to her toddler son and husband.

"Hey," Kacie sighed.

"What's going on? You sound weird," Ivy claimed.

Kacie sighed again, "Yeah, I feel kind of weird, I guess. Laz hasn't checked in all day, and he hasn't even answered the text I sent a couple of hours ago."

"That's odd," Ivy said, frowning. "Have you tried calling him?"

"No. I mean, we so rarely call each other. We usually text. But he texts every day. Normally several times a day, actually."

"Probably something came up," Ivy asserted. "A deadline at work, some kind of emergency. Maybe he's sick."

"Yeah, I guess," Kacie said slowly. "I was thinking the same. I'm just still a little worried."

"Worried about what?" Ivy queried. "Him dumping you or something? No way, he's so into you," she laughed.

"*Dumping* me?" Kacie asked with genuine astonishment. "No, that's not what I meant. What made you even say that?"

"Sorry, bad joke," Ivy apologized. "He's so smitten that it's just funny to imagine him dumping you because it's so unlikely. Even him lying unconscious in a hospital bed is more likely."

"You see?" Kacie said, frightened. "That's why I'm worried. What if there really is something wrong with him? What if something happened to him?"

"Come on, the chances of that are slim. I'm sure there's an explanation, and he'll tell you when he gets back in touch. I wouldn't worry about it."

"I'll try not to, you're right," Kacie exhaled.

She decided to shoot Laz another text, "Rough day? Hope u OK : / . A little worried." She stayed up until 1 am, checking her phone every five minutes, just to make sure she didn't miss a text notification. She was wondering if there may be a technical issue with the cell phone provider, delaying his messages to come through. After she finally fell asleep, she was tossing and turning all night, dreaming about Laz. In one dream they were making love, in the next she saw him in a hospital bed, pale, unresponsive. She woke up with a massive headache, reaching for her phone immediately. The screen was still blank, the opposite of how she felt. Her mind was bursting with racing thoughts and a myriad of questions. She was tempted to send another text, but if Laz had a strong reason for not getting in touch, if he really was busy or struggling with an emergency, she didn't want to be a nuisance and bombard him with texts.

During the day Kacie endeavored to distract herself with work, but her mind frequently wandered to Laz. "*Where* is he? *How* is he?" The same questions kept reverberating in her. When she got a text from him around 9 pm that evening she literally jumped, and the heaviness that had started to grow around her heart lifted. However, her relief waned when she read his text, "Sorry. Was sent on a business trip unexpectedly. Work hectic here." The text was so dry, so devoid of warmth, the usual emoticons, and terms of endearment that Kacie shivered for a moment. Then she shook off her discomfort and convinced herself that he had to hurry and was probably too exhausted from travel and work to go beyond the essentials.

Kacie texted back promptly, praying to catch him and obtain a little more information, "Oh.? That must suck. Would have been nice to know, though. Was worried."

"I know. Couldn't write sooner," Laz's response read.

"When will u be back?" Kacie typed quickly.

"Couple of days. Maybe more. Depends on how fast we get done."

"Miss u," Kacie wrote, adding a kiss emoji and holding her breath while waiting for his response. She stared at the screen, willing it to show her the favorable image she yearned to see.

Laz sent back a couple of kissing emojis. Kacie slowly exhaled the breath she had been holding, taking the emojis as the first promising sign of their exchange. The emojis might have seemed trivial, but they were an integral part of their everyday communication and intimacy and thus gave her some reassurance. At least there was an explanation now. Somehow the business trip and how and when he communicated it didn't sit right with her, but she pushed her doubts aside. She didn't have a reason to distrust him. "At least until now you didn't," a small voice resounded in her. She stifled it before it could add anything else.

The next time Laz got in touch with Kacie was two days later. During those couple of days Kacie restricted herself from sending him a text. She didn't want to seem pushy or needy and was curious to see when *he* would seek her out. She always prided herself on giving men sufficient space and not making any demands on their time and affections. It is just that she had never needed to do that either because the boyfriends she had been involved with so far had checked in and texted her or called her at least once a day, which is what Laz had done up to this point as well. She imposed patience on herself and reminded herself to give him a break. Maybe this business trip was indeed such a burden, and things would go back to normal once he returned. She immersed herself in work more and exercised more than usual. She also went out with one of her friends – anything to draw her attention away from the deafening silence emanating from her phone.

Laz broke the two-day absence of any communication with the following text, "Hey, still away on business. Hate it : / . Hope u are well." When Kacie responded, he took another 24 hours to get back to her. His text was succinct, and there were no emojis. For some reason, the lack of emojis bothered Kacie even more than his spotty communication. She would have tolerated less frequent texts as a result of the business trip if he at least expressed more tenderness in them.

Another two days later Kacie was positive that he had to be back from the trip. There was no way it would last this long. And even if it did, how could he be so busy the whole time that he couldn't find the time to text her something short and sweet at least daily? Or could he be somewhere with sporadic cell phone reception or no WiFi? But where? What kind of *business trip* is in the middle of nowhere? She alternated between escalating annoyance with him and almost debilitating bouts of fear. And an underlying sense of doom and confusion was nearly omnipresent.

It still seemed inconceivable that he might be growing distant from her or not interested in her anymore, after everything they went through and how close they were the last time they saw each other, but she had her moments when his sudden indifference was the only possible explanation that made sense. But if he felt that way, wouldn't he say so? Or might he want to sort out his feelings and wait to tell her face-to-face instead of texting something like that from a business trip? By now, while she strove to keep her cool at least to some extent, she felt that even the phrase *business trip* made her skin crawl, and she would scream if she heard it one more time, especially in the context of an excuse. All the while she suspected that she was making even more excuses for him than he made for himself.

Eventually, she feverishly typed up this text, "Back from the trip yet? Look, it seems like something is off. Is it *us*? U can tell me." As she stared at her own words, she burst into tears and felt like a pathetic loser. It seemed like she was talking to a brick wall instead of a person, and definitely not the person that has caressed her, kissed her, and smiled at her lovingly just over a week ago. That time felt so close, but also lightyears away at the same time. Is it even the same guy? Is this an alternate universe? Sure, someone can grow distant during the span of weeks, months, or years, depending on the length of the relationship, like she did with Luke. But in a few *days* and so *unexpectedly*? What happened? She wanted and explanation. She *needed* an explanation. But as she stared at the blank phone screen, it glared back at her, not offering a response. She felt a sudden rush of animosity toward her phone, as if it was the source of her pain. She experienced an urge to shake it and demand it to supply an answer. Helplessness about the whole situation was devouring her.

After 24 hours of exasperating silence from Laz she called Ivy.

"I can't take this anymore," Kacie cried into the phone as Ivy picked up. "I'm going crazy."

"I know," Ivy sighed, aggravation and empathy radiating from her voice. She didn't need to ask if Laz showed up, as it was obvious that he didn't. "I'm coming over," Ivy added.

When Ivy got to Kacie's apartment, she hugged her and let her cry on her shoulder. As much as she had liked Laz and used to think he was an unbelievable match for Kacie, she truly despised him right now.

When Kacie's sobs subsided, Ivy cleared her throat and began to talk, "Honey, I'm sorry to have to tell you this, but he's a goner. I know that's not what you want to hear, but I know you, and that's exactly why I'm telling you. I'm sure you might still cherish some hope that he might be back. You need to give up on him, Kace. I'm sorry."

"I know," Kacie said, her voice trembling. "But maybe he just…"

"No, Kacie," Ivy said firmly. "No more excuses. I have done this with you, and I gave him the benefit of the doubt, too, but not anymore. No way."

"But maybe he just needs time to think," Kacie interjected. "Just needs to figure things out. If he wanted to break up with me for good, he would have broken up with me. He didn't."

"No, but he might as well have," Ivy asserted. "His silence speaks louder than any words could. Please don't do this, Kace. You're smarter than this. And he's not worth it. I used to think he might be, but if he's doing this to you, he's not. Apparently, he didn't have the decency to tell you what's going on. He's ghosting you instead."

"*Ghosting* me?" Kacie repeated incredulously.

"He just disappeared, didn't he?" Ivy pointed out. He did the *slow fade*, then some *breadcrumbing* with those brief, sporadic texts, and eventually a full-on *ghosting*."

"Since when are you an expert on non-break-up breakups?" Kacie asked bitterly.

"Since I read up on this last night. And my cousin told me about it. A girl did the same thing to him," Ivy explained. "Look, I don't pretend to know how you feel. I'm just saying it's pretty common stuff."

"It hasn't happened to you...," Kacie trailed off.

"No, not to me," Ivy acknowledged. "But it has to many people. Women and men. And I have been with Dex since ... since forever. Dating is different now. Especially online and on the phone. I know you haven't been single for years either, but this is what's out there, so you might need to brace yourself for next time."

"Next time?" Kacie exclaimed. "I hope there's no more ghosting for me. One is more than enough. It hurts like hell."

"You have never done it?" Ivy queried.

"Of course not," Kacie protested. She had a sudden flash of the guys that she stopped responding to on the dating app after she got involved with Laz. But that was different, wasn't it? They weren't in a *relationship*. But was she in a relationship with Laz after all? If he didn't bother breaking it off, maybe he thought that there was *nothing* to break off. The end of their relationship broke her heart, but the invalidation of the entire relationship, as if it had never existed, as if she didn't exist, shattered it to a million more pieces. She had no idea how to recover from this blow, how to even begin.

She would never get closure, at least not from Laz. She would eventually have to find her own closure.

As weeks went by, Kacie started to slowly heal. But the mending of her broken heart was a slow-moving process. She often felt confusion, indignation at Laz and the whole world, distrust in men, and, above all, a heart-wrenching, nearly constant pain. When she read up on ghosting herself, she realized that it could have pretty severe emotional consequences, like the ones she experienced. It was difficult to digest something when she wasn't even aware what she was digesting, what actually happened and how to react accordingly. Did he simply get bored with her? Did she do something that he didn't like? Did he get scared of them getting more serious? Was there another woman? Other *women* in plural even? Did he need to go under the witness protection program? Was he abducted by aliens? Was he eaten by a bear (maybe at the secluded location of the business trip where there was no cell reception or WiFi…)? Some days she almost wished for one of the pretty ridiculous and unlikely explanations to be true, except the ones involving his death or physical harm, of course, because in a way even some of those would be more bearable and understandable than the more probable reasons. Especially because it wouldn't be his *choice* then.

Ivy asked Kacie at one point if it really mattered whether he ghosted her and why or actually broke up with her face-to-face, via phone, or text, as the end result was the same: he was gone. Kacie was adamant that it did make a difference and that ghosting made the loss and rejection so much more complicated to work through. She thought back to her break-up with Luke, for example. Yes, it still hurt, but if he had just walked out, without a word or any explanation, it would have been worse. Kacie tried to illustrate how ghosting felt by telling Ivy that it was as if you were in the same room with someone, or even the same bed, having a lively conversation, and then the person next to you suddenly and unexpectedly left the room (or the shared bed) without breathing a word, and never returning. When she put it like that, doing that in a face-to-face conversation did seem kind of absurd and very rude. She couldn't grasp why norms would be so different online and on the phone, which would make ghosting there more acceptable than in person.

After a couple of months of grieving Kacie logged into the dating app again. She felt more cautious and vulnerable than she had before Laz. For a few weeks she couldn't find anyone she was even remotely interested in. Then, two guys contacted her who were both somewhat attractive and intriguing. She started exchanging messages with them both, and when one of them began to text her more often, and she got a little more interested in him than the other one, she stopped responding to the less captivating guy. For days, she was composing a good-bye message in her head, but she was procrastinating, and eventually too many days passed, so she never sent it despite feeling guilty about it.

When she met the guy that looked more promising, they didn't click. She was slightly disappointed, and it just reminded her of Laz again, how vastly different their first meeting was. She and the guy went their separate ways, never writing to each other again. A similar scenario was repeated a couple of weeks later, but in that case the guy did text her a day later and expressed that she was great, but he just didn't feel a spark. As she didn't like him that much either, she didn't particularly care one way or the other, but it still felt kind of nice to be given some sort of feedback and closure. At the same time, she was aggravated to think that this near-stranger had the guts and decency to tell her straight-up what was going on, while Laz did not.

One day, out of the blue, the following text appeared on Kacie's phone, "Hey, how are u? Thinking about u a lot." It was from Laz. For a moment she thought she went crazy. Was she imagining things now? Was the message really from Laz? She double-checked it, and it was still there, and still showing Laz as sender. The entire scenario felt so surreal. Was it possible that Laz wrote this text back in the day, and, due to some technical glitch, it just got to her now? Or was he really messaging her like this, as if nothing had happened, almost three months after he disappeared? Or did he send her the text *by accident*, meaning to send it to another woman?

Kacie felt like a shaken snow-globe, as if all the shattered pieces of her heart were suddenly up in the air, rattled, crashing down, and who knew where they would land, or if they would ever really settle. She blindly reached for her phone and called Ivy.

"Guess who just texted me?" Kacie blurted out without even saying hi.

"Who?" Ivy asked, alert and ready to jump into the middle of a conversation.

"Laz," Kacie exclaimed.

"*Laz?*" Ivy inquired in disbelief. "*Lazarus?* He's back from the dead? I mean, bad joke, I know, but seriously? What did he say?"

Kacie read the text.

"Hmm," Ivy began. "I don't know, Kace. That's it? After so long? What is he thinking? What does he want?"

"I don't know. I haven't replied."

"But you want to?" Ivy posed the question slowly. "I mean, think about it, Kacie. He fell off the face of the Earth and just waltzes back like that? Could you even *trust* him?"

"Don't know," Kacie sighed.

"You know, you could just ghost him back right now," Ivy suggested. "Give him a taste of his own medicine."

"No," Kacie said firmly. "I won't be like that. Plus, I want to see what he wants. I may even get some answers."

"I seriously doubt that," Ivy proclaimed.

After they hung up, Kacie texted Laz, "Hey, nice to hear from u. Little confused, though. Had no idea what happened or where u went." Ten minutes later Laz messaged her back, ignoring the implied questions, "Nice to hear from u, too. I wanna see you. Bad."

Kacie's heart did a summersault, but the pain of him disappearing on her also came back at full force. He wanted to see her *now*? What about the last few months? He didn't want to see her *then*? Was he really trying to pretend that nothing had happened? She felt a mix of indignation, heartache, and some futile hope that maybe he would explain it all, he really was missing her, and they may even get back together. If she could forgive him and trust him again, of course.

"I *have* wanted to see u," Kacie typed. "But it seemed like u didn't. Do u wanna start over, is that what this is?"

She waited for an answer. Ten minutes passed. Then twenty, thirty, an hour. After two days of stubborn silence Kacie knew with absolute certainty that she would never get a response. Not to her last text, nor to any of her lingering questions. This was merely a brief sighting, and the ghost vanished into thin air, once more, never to be heard from again. Or…?

Discussion Questions

1. Do you think Laz might ever show up again? Why/why not? How do you envision Kacie's romantic life in the future?

2. What do you believe the role of technology is in ghosting (if any)? Draw examples from the story, as well.

3. Do you see any gender or age dynamics in ghosting versus face-to-face or other verbal break-up styles? Why/why not?

4. Ending a relationship on social media, by texting, or by NOTHING has become more common (Ansari, 2016; Collins & Gillath, 2012; Turkle, 2016). Have you seen or experienced this around you, too? Refer to the story as well.

5. Collins & Gillath (2012) found in their study of breakups that people found open confrontational style as the most ideal and avoiding a partner and withdrawing from contact as the least ideal form of ending a relationship. Do you agree or disagree with this? Why? How does this relate to ghosting, the slow fade, and similar strategies?

6. Use an ethnomethodological perspective to describe norms regarding breakups and particularly ghosting. Ethnomethodology studies how norms of the social world are created and understood (Garfinkel, 1984). Usually we see what norms are when they are broken. Accordingly, do you find ghosting a norm today or a deviance from a social norm?

7. Emile Durkheim (1998) defines *anomie* as an absence of clearly delineated social norms, a state when norms in society are unclear, confusing, or confused, lacking consensus, and rapidly changing, therefore, too fast to follow. Do you think that a state of anomie characterizes modern dating and breakup styles? Why/why not?

8. Coupling, that is, becoming a couple and *uncoupling*, that is, the end of couplehood have both been described mostly as a *process*, a series of transitions and changes leading to a final outcome (Vaughan, 1990). Does this still seem to apply to the *slow fade* from a relationship or *ghosting*? Why/why not? Do you think that it is more ideal when uncoupling is a process than when it is seemingly very unexpected and abrupt? Why/why not? Relate this to the story, too.

9. Through his concept of the looking-glass self, Cooley (1998) elucidated how our sense of self was shaped by how others around us see us and the feedback they provide us about ourselves. Based on this, when someone is ghosted, how do you think it could affect their sense of self, their self-esteem (if at all)?

10. In twenty years from now how do you think most relationships will end (face-to-face talk, by the phone, by text, on social media, ghosting, or some other, novel way)? Why do you believe that? Do you think relationships will break more easily or last longer and be more durable? Why?

Find the Answers

Go to the following article to find the answers to the questions below:
https://www.bankmycell.com/blog/what-is-ghosting-someone

1. Who ghosts more, men or women, or there is no difference? Include some specific numbers.

2. Why do men versus women ghost?

3. What are the most common dating app lies? Is there a difference between what men and women tend to lie about?

4. What are the most frequent lies for a delayed message response? Is there a gender difference?

Mini Research Assignments

1. Survey at least 7 individuals, asking them to rate their agreement with the following statements on a scale of 1-10 (1 meaning complete disagreement and 10 indicating full agreement): 1. "There is nothing wrong with ghosting as a way to end a romantic relationship." 2. "I would be hurt if someone I was interested in ghosted me." 3. "Women ghost men just as often as the other way around." Summarize your results. Draw parallels with the story in this chapter, too and refer to the gender and age composition of your sample, and if that may have influenced your results.
2. Watch a movie, TV show, or documentary depicting ghosting or a similar way of ending a relationship. How is ghosting portrayed there? Who does the ghosting? Who is ghosted? How are the participants depicted? Draw parallels with the story in this chapter as well. Then, watch another movie, TV show, or documentary with a face-to-face breakup. Compare and contrast the portrayal of the two.
3. Go online and read at least three brief articles on ghosting. How is ghosting characterized in each article? What new information do they offer about ghosting that the story in this chapter did not? Compare and contrast the articles and draw parallels with our story, too.

References

Ansari, A. (2016). *Modern romance*. New York: Penguin Books.

Collins, T. J. & Gillath, O. (2012). Attachment, breakup strategies, and associated outcomes: The effects of security enhancement on the selection of breakup strategies. *Journal of Research on Personality*, 46, 210-222.

Cooley, C. H. (1998). *On self and social organization*. Chicago, IL: University of Chicago Press. (Originally published 1902)

Durkheim, E. (1998). *Suicide*. New York: Free Press. (Originally published 1897)

Garfinkel, H. (1984). *Studies in ethnomethodology*. Malden MA: Polity.

Turkle, S. (2016). *Reclaiming conversation: The power of talk in a digital age*. New York: Penguin Books.

Vaughan, D. (1990). *Uncoupling: Turning points in intimate relationships*. New York: Vintage Books.

CHAPTER

8

"Is that too much?"
GENDER, CULTURE, AND SOCIAL CLASS IN WEDDINGS

Sophia Whitmore was very eager to try on the first wedding dress of her lifetime. She was in the dressing room of an elegant bridal boutique in Jacksonville, Florida, while her entourage was expectantly waiting outside, on the floor of the shop. She had brought her mother, father, sister, best friend, and future mother in-law. She was slightly concerned about a difference in opinions, but she was optimistic about managing to please everyone, including herself, or at least come to a reasonable compromise.

While the wedding consultant squeezed Sophia into the first dress, her mind wandered back to the numerous times in her childhood when she and her sister, Carissa, had put on their mother's wedding dress. Their mother also owned an ivory evening gown, which they used as well to play bride. They switched back and forth which one of them got to wear the wedding dress. As they both preferred it to the evening gown, they often fought about whose turn it was to put it on. They both posed in front of the mirror and argued who looked more spectacular as a bride. The one wearing the wedding gown generally won. Of course, they had to do this in secret and very carefully, as their mother was not keen on them playing with her wedding dress.

Sophia could hardly believe that the time of selecting a wedding gown for real had finally arrived. She had imagined choosing a dress and her entire wedding multiple times throughout the years. Interestingly, in her dreams the gown and various details of the wedding had looked crystal-clear, but the image of a potential groom had remained foggy. The fact that now she had her fiancé, Cody, and she could envision him on her side, made the wedding much more realistic than it had ever been in her childhood fantasies.

She and Cody had met in graduate school. As a teenager and young adult Sophia had often visualized running into the One randomly, under highly romantic circumstances and instantly realizing that they had been made for each other. These fantasies had undeniably been fueled by the movies and TV shows she tended to watch. In reality she had known Cody for over a year before she got involved with him and used to think that he was kind of cute, but nothing special.

Then, one day, after celebrating the success of an especially difficult exam, they hooked up. Even after that Sophia didn't really consider dating him; if anything, she was sort of embarrassed and endeavored to avoid him, and he seemed to be on the same page. Then, in another course they were thrown together as study partners. Sophia normally preferred to study alone and was resistant to the idea of study partners, but somehow the project with Cody went very smoothly. They complemented each other, and through working with him Sophia discovered how smart, reliable, creative, hard-working, and encouraging he was. One day, as he was explaining a tricky concept to her, she stopped paying attention and stared at his moving lips, which suddenly appeared immensely enticing to her. She leaned closer and planted a kiss on those lips. He looked slightly surprised for a moment, then grinned and kissed her back.

"About time," he whispered, stroking her hair. Sophia moved into his apartment a few days later, and they had been together ever since. After about two years of cohabitation Sophia began to hope that he would propose. When they vacationed in Europe that summer, Sophia was convinced that he would finally ask. Every time they visited a romantic spot, like the Eiffel Tower in Paris, the Dome in Florence, took a wine tasting tour in Tuscany, a gondola ride in Venice, strolled on the banks of the Seine in Paris and Arno in Florence, Sophia was expecting a picturesque proposal. It didn't happen, and on the plane back she was frustrated with him to some degree. How could he miss an abundance of perfect opportunities to propose? Did he *not* want to marry her? She didn't reveal her disappointment to him because she didn't want to push him into something that he wasn't ready for or might not even desire at all.

Three days after arriving home Cody took her to the library where they used to study together and led her to the desk where they always sat, in a hidden corner.

"Do you remember what happened here?" he asked with a wide smile.

"Yes," she responded. "Tons of studying, that's what happened here."

"And nothing else?" His grin broadened. "What about our first kiss? Do you recall that?"

"Yeah, I guess," she finally smiled, too despite still feeling faintly agitated with him for not taking their relationship further during their vacation. "But you know, technically that wasn't our first kiss. We had hooked up before. Don't you remember?"

"Um, sure," he laughed. "But I'm trying to be romantic here. Help me a little, okay? So, I was saying, here is where our *very memorable first kiss* happened. I just knew then. I knew I wanted to spend the rest of my life with you. So, here I am, asking if you want the same." He sank to his knees and took out a box from his pocket, with a sparkling engagement ring in it. "Will you marry me, Sophie?"

She teared up immediately. "Yes," she whispered. She was incredibly moved and thankful that he had come up with a proposal that was much more personal and sweeter than anything he could have devised in Europe. She realized this would become a memory to be cherished forever, illumined by their deep love for each other.

The next day, after an unforgettable night of celebration, she was admiring her engagement ring. She had always obsessed about having a princess cut ring, and the one shining on her finger was a round cut diamond in platinum. She was aware that this cut could cost even more than a princess one, especially because it was a sizable diamond, but she still wished for a princess cut for a moment. Then she immediately reminded herself that she wanted a ring that Cody chose for her. Knowing him, she was positive that he must have agonized over this decision and strove to choose the best.

The ring was truly exquisite, and Sophia was cognizant that it must have cost somewhere around $9,000-10,000. She quickly googled the average cost of engagement rings and found close to $6,000, but also that most American men spent more in the neighborhood of $1,000-5,000. She also read that the recommended spending was as much as the groom's salary in 1-3 months. Spending 3 months' worth of income seemed excessive to Sophia, but she also had to admit that she might have been offended if Cody gave her a ring that cost less than $5,000-6,000, mostly because she was aware that he could easily afford more than that. A fleeting thought crossed her mind that some people had cars that were worth less than her engagement ring, what's more, some individuals *made less* in a year than that, but she didn't dwell on that. She grew up in an upper-middle class family and had always been surrounded by material comfort. Having both earned a graduate degree in a lucrative field, with Cody, their household income climbed to upper-class level. She didn't feel part of the upper-class, as she usually envisioned the top 1% when she thought about the upper-class, but based on their wealth, income, and education, their socioeconomic status was actually upper-class, even if closer to the lower end of it and far from the top 1%.

Sophia laughed when Cody suggested to get married three months after the proposal. How could he be so naïve? Organizing a proper wedding would take much longer than that. The most coveted reception venues alone were booked almost a year in advance. He tried to argue for a simpler wedding and less lengthy preparations, but both Sophia and his mother convinced him otherwise. Sophia didn't necessarily want a huge wedding either, but she dreamed about it being an elegant and romantic occasion. Eventually they settled on a wedding date in ten months, at the end of April.

The next point of contention was hiring a wedding planner or not. Cody's mother was adamant about it, and Sophia's mother was leaning toward it as well, but Sophia and Cody decided that they would prefer to organize it themselves. Cody had no idea what he signed up for, whereas Sophia was battling increasing levels of anxiety because she was actually aware of what it would involve. Nevertheless, she didn't want to deal with a wedding planner.

Selecting the wedding and reception venue turned out to be a huge hurdle, too. Cody's family was lobbying for an indoor location with an ocean view, and Cody himself was mostly sold on the idea. Sophia loved the ocean, but living so close to it and having a wedding there seemed like a cliché to her. Everybody she knew had had a wedding on the beach or at a fancy hotel by the ocean. She didn't aim to have a repeat of someone else's wedding as her own. She dreamed of an outdoor wedding, saying their vows under majestic oak trees, draped with Spanish moss. Her family and future in-laws warned her about the weather – in Florida it could get hot in late April, or there may be a storm. However, Sophia was relentless about an outdoor wedding. To be reasonable, she agreed to look for a venue that offered a covered patio at least in case of unfavorable weather. Cody could be swayed from the beach, but he was insistent on getting married near some body of water. After checking out several possibilities, they opted for a location that combined their wish-lists. It had a charming, chic hotel with a large patio overlooking a river and towering oak trees with Spanish moss. The venue seemed magical to Sophia, and she could somehow sense eternity there, making it very suitable for the inception of their everlasting union as a married couple.

When they finally chose the location, Sophia was relieved to some extent because she knew it would set the tone for the entire wedding. Still, there were a million more details to arrange. Beside the venue, Sophia felt that the wedding dress was the other key element in the process of planning their wedding. If she had the dress, she could breathe. At this moment, though, as the bridal consultant pulled on

the gown to make it tighter, Sophia could do anything but breathe normally.

"Isn't this a little too tight?" she asked, struggling to get some more air into her lungs.

"Um, no," the consultant said politely, but firmly. "This is what it's supposed to look like. If I let it out even just a little more, we lose the shape. We're trying to create a dramatic waistline here."

"Dramatic, huh?" Sophia exhaled. "We don't want to create a dramatic effect by me passing out in the dress, though."

"You'll get used to it," the consultant asserted. "And I assume you'd lose a few pounds before the wedding anyway. Aren't you planning on that? Most brides are."

Sophia looked in the mirror, biting on her lower lip. She was cognizant of a couple of extra pounds on her, or maybe even 8-10 extra pounds, but she was mostly satisfied with her figure. More importantly, Cody preferred her this way. When she had lost some weight after an incident of food poisoning, Cody was complaining about it and wished for her curves back. Still, she already felt that she was buckling under pressure and would probably attempt to lose at least 2-3 pounds before the wedding. Everyone would be looking at her during the wedding and reception, and she didn't want people to talk behind her back and criticize her body. She vowed to give up ice cream, or maybe *reduce* her consumption of ice cream. The way she exercised was sometimes sporadic; perhaps she could make that more regular.

Sophia's musings were interrupted by the wedding planner clearing her throat, "Shall we get out there?"

"Oh, sure," Sophia said, returning to the present.

She felt regal as she walked out to the floor of the bridal boutique. She saw her mother tearing up when she caught a glimpse of her.

"Wow, honey, you're so beautiful," Sophia's mother murmured.

"You look great," her best friend, Lila announced.

"I don't know," her sister, Carissa contended. "I mean, it's a very nice dress. And it does make your waist look pretty skinny. But I'm not sure I like it being sleeveless. Your arms… I mean, I'd prefer a dress with sleeves on you."

"Sleeves?" Sophia asked in disbelief. "In late spring in Florida? Should we add a coat, too, or something?"

"No, it's just…," Carissa trailed off. "Never mind."

"It's not the lack of sleeves," Sophia's future mother-in-law inserted. "That's fine. It's more that sweetheart neckline I'm not so sure about. Isn't that a little too much cleavage maybe?"

"I think she might be right, honey," Sophia's father chimed in.

"I chose this ball gown for her partly because it accentuates her waist, but also because it creates a nice cleavage," the bridal consultant interjected. "Do *you* like this style?" she stared at Sophia.

Sophia was suddenly confused. She had thought her breasts looked pretty spectacular in the dress, but now she felt slightly self-conscious, almost as if she were naked.

"I thought I did," she said hesitantly. "My waist does look much skinnier in this than it actually is. But it's really uncomfortable because of how tight it is. The ball gown is very elegant, but it's hard to walk in it, let alone sit. So, I don't know."

"Maybe a mermaid style?" the consultant suggested.

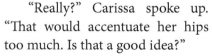

"Really?" Carissa spoke up. "That would accentuate her hips too much. Is that a good idea?"

"Cody would like that," Sophia affirmed. "He *likes* my hips. But I'm not sure a mermaid style would really fit the venue."

She felt herself getting aggravated at Carissa and her critical comments. At the same time, she reminded herself to go easy on her sister. Sophia knew Carissa was struggling with envy, as she had been together with her boyfriend

© LightField Studios/shutterstock.com

twice as long as Sophia with Cody, and he hadn't shown the slightest inclination to propose in the near future, or maybe ever. Carissa was disappointed, as she was more than ready for marriage.

Sophia tried on eight more dresses before finding the One. All of those were criticized by one or more members of her bridal party, and she wasn't fully satisfied with any of them either. When she was put in this particular gown she teared up, and her heart started to race. She sensed that no one could dissuade her from this dress. It was an A-line with an illusion neckline, beaded top and tulle skirt. Sophia looked stunning in it. When she walked out to the floor, everyone in her entourage was thoroughly impressed. Tears were shed, compliments were flowing.

When her father gathered himself, he asked an essential question, "How much?"

"$4,500," the consultant said without batting an eye.

"That's reasonable," Sophia's future mother-in-law piped up, while Sophia's father gulped.

"Is that too much, Dad?" Sophia queried with some concern rising in her voice.

"No," he confirmed. "I was surprised for a moment, that's all. I had no idea how much these things were. But no, nothing is too much for my darling daughter."

"$4,500 is the dress alone," the consultant added. "You'll also need to factor in alterations, the veil, accessories."

Sophia was aware that Cody had bought a tuxedo, accessories, and shoes for the wedding a couple of days ago, for $800, in under an hour, while her father would spend several thousand dollars, and they had been in the salon for over three hours. But no one would really care what the *groom* would wear at the wedding, and everybody would scrutinize the bride's attire. She was too exhausted to shop for shoes today, but a few days later she returned to the boutique and purchased a pair of shoes for $225. Later that day she googled the regular cost of wedding attires, just for fun and found that the average cost of a wedding dress was around $1,600 last year, and grooms, on average, spent a little under $300 on their formalwear. Apparently, their spending was over the average, but the proportion of the bride's spending compared to the groom's was similar in their case as well.

The next step was selecting bridesmaid dresses. Sophia refrained from having a final say in those; she let her sister, Carissa, the maid-of-honor make that selection, along with the other bridesmaids, her best friend, Lila, and another friend, Sasmita. Sophia had known Lila since high school, and they had been friends ever since. She had met Sasmita in graduate school, and the three of them with Cody had several classes together, so it seemed fitting to invite Sasmita as a bridesmaid, as she had been present at the budding of Sophia's and Cody's romance in grad school. Sasmita had been born in India and immigrated to the United States at the age of six with her family. Her name meant always smiling, which perfectly encapsulated her character.

Taking the color scheme of the wedding into account, as well as the complexion of each woman and what looked good on them, they decided on navy dresses. They all insisted that they didn't wish to wear the exact same style for a gown, so eventually only the color and length of the dresses were identical. Carissa opted for a V-neck, Lila chose an off-the-shoulder one and Sasmita went for a halter. They each paid $250-325 depending on the particular style. The advantage was that these were dresses that could be worn as evening gowns later.

After settling on the bridesmaid dresses the four women headed to a spa for the afternoon. Trying on dresses was exhausting, and they also viewed this occasion as a sort of pre-bachelorette party. In-between facial treatments and pedicures, they started to chat.

"So, you absolutely sure Cody is the One?" Lila asked teasingly. "Still not too late to change your mind."

"I knew you didn't want to be a bridesmaid," Sophia returned the joke. "And not shying away from any means to get out of it." They all laughed heartily. "Okay, kidding aside, of course, he's the One," Sophia continued.

"How do you know?" Lila challenged.

"I just do," Sophia sighed dreamily. "He's my soul mate. He's my best friend, my lover, and a great one at that," she smirked. "We have the same values. We like the same things. We have the same goals for the future. He lifts me up when I'm down. He makes me laugh. He complements me. Really, he's my better half."

"And with that you're almost done with your vows," Lila grinned. "Okay, maybe leave the part out about him being a great lover. You'll have two sets of parents and a couple of grandparents at your wedding after all."

"Isn't that how you feel about Ashley?" Sophia asked Lila.

"Of course, it is," Lila confirmed. "You just need to substitute she wherever you said he. But the rest is exactly the same," she chuckled.

"But you were still hesitant about marrying her, weren't you?" Carissa interjected.

"Yeah, thanks for the reminder," Lila remarked slightly sarcastically. "Anyway, yeah, I guess it took me a while. I mean, we have been together for almost ten years, and until 2015 we couldn't have got married officially anyway. At least in Florida we couldn't have. But that piece of paper wasn't that important to me anyway."

"But it was to Ashley," Sophia added.

"Yeah, it was," Lila affirmed. "She had been talking about marriage since like 2013. Even before it was legalized. But we were pretty young, too, and she was practically my first girlfriend. Okay, almost first. But then I realized that we were just extremely lucky to have found each other so young, and we're happy."

"So, you're happy you got married?" Carissa inquired quietly.

"Yes, most definitely," Lila asserted. "Somehow our love has deepened even more since then."

"So, you didn't mind her nudging you a little bit? And in the end, it was the best decision for both of you?" Carissa asked curiously.

"Well, I did mind her pushing me a little when I wasn't ready," Lila admitted. "But overall I'm happy she did it. And even happier that she was patient enough to wait for me until I was ready."

"Don't encourage her," Sophia inserted. "Carissa, I know you love Sam, and I know you want to get married. But I'm not sure it'd be a good idea to push him. With that, you might actually push him *away*."

"I don't know," Lila disagreed. "Maybe he does need a little push. I mean, you'd know where he stands at least. When Ashley talked so much about marriage, I realized that it's not that I didn't want it eventually; it's just that I needed some time, and we clarified that, and eventually we were on the same page. But if he doesn't *ever* want to get married, and you do… the sooner you recognize that, the better."

"I have the feeling that he doesn't want to get married," Carissa said, her voice shaking. "Due to his parents' divorce he has become pretty disillusioned about marriage. I think he prefers to just cohabit."

"Then you need to decide if you're okay with that," Lila concluded. "Is marriage more important to you, or do you want to be with him no matter what?"

"I don't know," Carissa sighed. "I've always wanted to get married. But I love him, and I'm not ready to let him go."

"Then maybe you can just give him and *yourself* some time to figure it out," Lila mused.

"How about you, Sasmita?" Sophia turned to her friend. She endeavored to involve Sasmita who had been pretty quiet, in addition, she felt that it was best to distract Carissa from her own problems before she had a meltdown, right in the middle of the spa. "Where do you stand on marriage? I just realized I don't think we have ever talked about that."

"I know I will get married one day," Sasmita said thoughtfully. "It's not just up to me."

"What do you mean?" Lila asked curiously.

"I mean, it's up to my parents, too," Sasmita responded.

"Are you for real?" Lila asked, surprised. "I'm glad it wasn't up to *my* parents. I'm afraid they wouldn't have chosen a *girl* for me to marry. You mean you're doing the arranged marriage thing?"

"Not quite like that," Sasmita smiled. "It's not that my parents will choose someone for me. We live in the U.S. now, after all, and times have changed. I can choose my own spouse, but my parents will need to approve. I could never marry someone my parents wouldn't approve of."

"But could it be anyone?" Lila inquired. "Young, old, Indian, American, Chinese, black, Native American? Could it even be a *woman*?"

"No, not a woman," Sasmita explained. "But I'm straight, so I'd be looking for a man anyway. But he would have to be Indian. Even if not born in India, but both of his parents being from India at least. He and his family would have to be from our social class. He would have to be educated and have a good job. My parents would have to meet him and his family and like them."

"Wow, that really narrows it down," Lila exclaimed. "It's hard enough to date nowadays as it is. It'd be even harder to meet all those criteria. Where do you even meet guys like that?"

"In Indian communities, social events," Sasmita elucidated. "Or Indian dating sites."

"You have those?" Lila smiled. "That's amazing. Okay, I guess it's not that hard then."

"But what about love?" Carissa asked. "Wouldn't you want to be *in love* with him?"

"I would," Sasmita confirmed. "I've spent most of my life in America. I was socialized on romantic movies, too. But I wouldn't marry a guy who didn't meet the criteria I listed, even if I were in love with him. And I *might* marry a great Indian guy with the same background and values even if I weren't crazy in love with him. Love could come later, after the wedding. I've seen so many examples of that in my culture. My parents had an arranged marriage. They had met only a couple of times before their wedding. And they did develop a very strong bond and deep love for each other later. When you're crazy in love, you might make crazy choices you regret later. I dream about romantic love, too, but that may not always be the best foundation for a long-lasting marriage. If you think about it, even in Western cultures marrying for romantic love to your soul mate is a pretty new development in history. People used to marry to become an economic, reproductive unit, providing for each other and raising children."

"That sounds so pragmatic and un-romantic," Sophia remarked.

"Yes, pragmatic, exactly," Sasmita echoed. "But it worked. Some people were happy with each other, others were not, but it did kind of work. And then everyone knew what they could expect from a partner. Women expected to be provided for, and men expected to be taken care of and have their wife bear children. Today, many people still expect that from a partner in a way, but also so much more, too. Like you said, Sophia, people want their partners to also be great lovers, best friends, counselors, encouragers, and so on. I read somewhere that people now expect their partner to fill all the needs that an *entire community* used to fill in the past. It's very hard for one *person* to do that. No wonder people have so many difficulties finding someone, settling down, and remaining satisfied with their spouse, and actually staying with them. Some are lucky and find that incredible partner, like you did, Sophia, or you, Lila, and I hope, you too, Carissa. But for many others, when the expectations are so high, it's easy to get disillusioned. And when people in most places in the world live longer, your *life partner* will stay with you longer than for people in the past. And in a very individualistic, not very community-based world, people tend to focus on their individual happiness and self-fulfillment. Their goals may change, and they may grow apart from their partner as a result. It's not easy to stay in synch for so many decades."

"Wow, I've never thought about that," Carissa whispered.

"So, you still sure about this marriage thing, Sophia?" Lila asked, grinning.

"Yes, more than ever," Sophia affirmed. "Cody is that person for me, and he will always be."

"And what about weddings?" Lila turned to Sasmita with curiosity. "Would you follow Indian traditions in your wedding?"

"Yes, to some extent for sure," Sasmita replied.

"What are some of those traditions?" Sophia queried.

"Well, it varies by which region in India you are from, too. Brides wear something colorful, usually red. It's grooms who tend to wear white,

sometimes gold, often with something red, too. Brides' hands and feet are decorated with henna. Brides wear a lot of jewelry, too. You'd look at the stars and planets and the couple's astrological sign to choose the best wedding date. The couple gets married under a mandap, a canopy with four pillars. The groom generally arrives there on a white horse. A symbolic fire is lit in the center of the mandap, and the couple walks around it four times. They exchange floral garlands. The groom gives the bride a special necklace. Red powder is applied on the bride's forehead. The groom takes off his shoes during the ceremony, and the bride's friends try to steal them. If they succeed, they ask for money to give them back. The ceremony normally takes hours, and with the pre-parties and pre-wedding rituals, weddings basically last for days. At the reception there is a ton of food and dancing. It's a huge party."

"Wow, it sounds like it," Sophia said enthusiastically. "Now I look forward to *your* wedding almost as much as mine. It's so interesting how wedding traditions vary by culture."

"They do," Lila burst out, grabbing her phone. "I've just googled some. Listen to this. In Congo you cannot smile at your own wedding. It'd mean you're not serious about marriage. In Greece the groomsmen give the groom a close shave, then his mother-in-law feeds him honey and almonds. In some parts of Kenya fathers spit on the bride to avoid jinxing their good fortune. In parts of Indonesia a couple needs to stay home for the first few days of their marriage and not use the restroom. In Romania guests "kidnap" the bride and demand a ransom from the groom. In Sweden, whenever the bride or groom leave the room, guest can kiss the one remaining in the room. In the Philippines doves are released after the ceremony. In Germany sometimes couples need to saw a log in half in front of the guests to show they can overcome obstacles. Or they have to clean up smashed porcelain for the same reason. In Poland and nearby countries guests buy a dance with the bride, and the donations often go toward their honeymoon. In Norway brides wear a crown with pendants to ward off evil spirits. In Australia couples collect a unity bowl made out of stones that the guests bring. In Jamaica the whole village gathers to criticize the bride's looks, and if they are not satisfied with her appearance, she has to go back and fix it.

"God," Sophia groaned. "I'm glad I don't have to do some of those. And this last one, the criticism one in Jamaica, people will do this anyway, even here. They might just do it behind my back and not *literally* send me back home to fix my appearance. It's such a pressure that you are expected to look your best on your wedding day. I mean, I *want* to look good. But I don't know if I can look my *absolute best*," she mused, dropping the piece of chocolate that she had just begun to lift to her mouth.

"You'll look great," Lila encouraged her. "And the most important thing is for you to *feel* great on that day. Don't let that be ruined by worrying about what others think, and if all the guests are enjoying your wedding, and all that stuff. It's *your* wedding."

In the upcoming weeks, to distract herself from all the small details of the wedding, Sophia started to focus more on organizing their honeymoon. This was one expense that they would cover (mostly Cody); the wedding would be predominantly paid for by their parents. She and Cody sat down one night and made separate lists of their dream honeymoon destinations. They both had Santorini, Greece on their wish-lists, so that's what they decided on. Sophia was very excited about the scenic island with its breathtaking views of the Aegean Sea, cliffs, and whitewashed houses. They would relax on a black sand beach, visit another beach with beautiful red cliffs, check out a volcano, sail, swim, hike, wine and dine, and catch incredible sunsets. Of course, most of all, they would enjoy each other. The hotel that they booked cost $400 per night, but it was worth it. The overseas flights to Athens would be close to $3,000 total for the both of them, plus domestic flights between Athens and Santorini. They yearned for an unforgettable honeymoon, so they didn't spare any expense.

Between the wedding and the honeymoon, there was another occasion to plan for: the wedding night. First, Sophia shopped for special wedding night lingerie. She found it difficult to find something unique, a sort of lingerie Cody hadn't seen on her. She thought it was even more tricky to come up with novel intimate ideas for the wedding night. Just as she felt pressure to look her best on her wedding day, she also felt compelled to have extraordinary sex during the wedding night. At the same time, she wasn't sure if they would end up having *any* kind of sex that night after an exhausting, stressful day of wedding festivities. Eventually she realized that it was best *not* to plan their wedding night at all, but let it unfold.

The night before their wedding Sophia laid awake for a while. She was thrilled, but also anxious. There were so many things that could go wrong. For example, it just dawned on her that she hadn't tried walking in her bridal shoes for more than ten minutes. What if they turned out to be impossible to wear for the whole ceremony? She at least had another pair of shoes she could change into for the reception, especially dancing, if the bridal ones got unbearably uncomfortable. Her mind also raced through a million small details of the wedding: flowers, decorations, food, music, photographs, and so on. She reassured herself that everything would go smoothly.

She thought about the cost of the entire wedding for a moment. It ended up being in the neighborhood of $50,000. She read that the national average cost of weddings was close to $30,000, in Northern Florida slightly higher. For a second, she felt guilty about how much they spent. There were some costs they could have lowered by making some compromises. However, she couldn't imagine planning a wedding on a very tight budget. Sure, one could have a backyard wedding, sparing the highest item cost of weddings, the venue. They could buy a wedding gown on sale, off the rack, or a used one online. Family members and friends could cook, do the catering, DJ, take photographs. You could forego flowers and use minimal decorations. Still, her heart ached for every bride who had to set limitations to their dreams due to a minuscule budget.

As she was finally drifting into sleep, she was fantasizing about Cody and their upcoming life together. She hoped that their wedding, wedding night, and honeymoon would turn out to be remarkably memorable. However, she had even higher aspirations for their marriage: that it would be strong, enduring, fulfilling, and blissful.

Discussion Questions

1. How do you envision Sophia's and Cody's wedding and marriage?

2. What is the role of social class in weddings? Refer to examples from the story as well.

3. What is the role of gender in weddings? How is this illustrated in the story?

4. What is the role of culture in weddings? How do customs vary by culture? What are some examples from the story?

5. What kind of social norms, pressures, and expectations are present in weddings, the wedding night, and honeymoons? Mention examples from the story and from what you have heard, read, or experienced.

6. Endogamy is when people marry someone from a similar social, cultural background (e.g. the same or similar level of education, social class, ethnicity, race, religion) and exogamy is marrying a person from a different background. Which one is illustrated in the story? Which one do you think is more common in real life?

7. In the past, until about the 1960s, people were more likely to marry for economic reasons and for having children than for romantic love, mostly establishing companionate marriages with clearly defined gender roles, while in recent decades people have tended to want to find and marry their soul mate (Ansari, 2016; Cherlin, 2010; Coontz, 2006). Identify some examples for this shift from the story and from families around you.

8. West and Zimmerman (1987) explained that gender was a routine, everyday accomplishment, something that we do in interaction with others, as opposed to something that we are. Discuss a few examples of how characters in the story do gender, and how gender is done in general in preparation for and during weddings.

9. Blumer (1969) identified three premises of symbolic interactionism. The first is that humans act toward things based on the meanings those things have for them. The second is that meanings are created through social interaction. The third is that meanings are understood and potentially transformed through an interpretative process. Apply this theory to weddings and marriage.

10. Same-sex marriage was legalized in all 50 states of the United States on June 26, 2015. Despite the legalization, have you heard or read about any instances of prejudice or even discrimination that same-sex couples have encountered when planning their wedding? As a reminder, prejudice is a biased judgment and/or feeling about members of a specific group, and discrimination is an action of treating them differently.

Find the Answers

Go to the following article to find the answers to the questions below:
https://www.worldatlas.com/articles/countries-with-the-oldest-average-marrying-age.html

1. List the 5 countries with the oldest average marrying age. Is the U.S. among the top 5 or even top 20?

2. What are the main reasons for an older average age at first marriage in the countries that lead these statistics?

3. Discuss the gender difference in the average age at first marriage.

4. What is the relationship between marriage and the economy?

Mini Research Assignments

1. Watch a TV show or a movie that features the wedding of an ethnic or religious minority couple in the United States. Discuss the role of gender, social class, sexual orientation, age, and culture in the wedding preparations and the depiction of the wedding itself. Mention how social norms and expectations play a role as well and compare and contrast those with "typical," mainstream American weddings. Describe if the marriage seems to be an endogamous or exogamous one and why. Draw parallels with the story in this chapter, too.
2. Think back to a wedding that you have attended (it could be your own if you are married). Discuss the role of gender, social class, sexual orientation, age, and culture in the wedding preparations and the wedding itself. Mention how social norms and expectations played a role as well. Describe if the marriage seemed to be an endogamous or exogamous one and why. Draw parallels with the story in this chapter, too.
3. Interview an engaged or married couple about their wedding preparations and wedding. You can come up with your own questions, but make sure you address the cost, who covered those costs, the role of bride and groom, customs, traditions, social norms, and expectations. Draw parallels with the story in this chapter as well.
4. Search the web for same-sex wedding discrimination cases and select at least three. Describe the cases and discuss why they constituted cases of discrimination.

References

Ansari, A. (2016). *Modern romance*. New York: Penguin Books.

Blumer, H. (1969). *Symbolic interactionism: perspective and method*. Englewood Cliffs, NJ: Prentice-Hall.

Cherlin, A. (2010). *The marriage-go-round: The state of marriage and the family in America today*. New York: Vintage.

Coontz, S. (2006). *Marriage, a history: How Love Conquered Marriage*. New York: Penguin Books.

West, C. & D. H. Zimmerman. (1987). Doing Gender. *Gender & Society* 1:125-151.

Part 2

Families with Children

CHAPTER

"That's not for you."
GENDER SOCIALIZATION OF GENDER-NONCONFORMING CHILDREN

Sudowoodo/ Shutterstock.com

Tessa Walker looked around with an escalating sense of panic at the boys' department of her favorite store. She was scrutinizing a dark blue shirt for boys when she noticed that one of her children was missing. A moment ago both her daughter, Kamryn, and her son, Kayden, had been standing right behind her, but now Kayden was nowhere to be seen.

"Have you seen Kayden?" Tessa asked Kamryn, her voice raised with alarm.

"He ran that way," Kamryn pointed toward the girls' department.

Tessa followed where Kamryn's index finger was pointing, grabbing Kamryn's hand and pulling her along in a rush. A minute later Tessa was relieved to spot Kayden, standing by clothes with Disney-figure prints on them.

"Kayden, what were you thinking?" Tessa exclaimed, letting go of Kamryn's hand and clutching Kayden's. "You can't just run off like that. You scared me."

"Sorry, mommy," Kayden said sheepishly.

"Why did you come to the girls' department anyway?" Tessa inquired. "We were getting clothes for you, but we would've come here later to get clothes for Kammie."

"Yeah, but it was so boring there," Kayden complained, pointing toward the boys' department. "There are prettier things here."

"Well, you're kind of right, I guess," Tessa broke into a smile. "Once we're here, we can get some things for Kammie and go back to the boys' department later."

"What about this, mommy?" Kayden blurted out excitedly, holding up a shirt with a Disney princess on it.

"Not bad," Tessa agreed. "What do you think, Kammie?"

Kamryn timidly smiled, but Kayden interjected before his sister could respond, "No, mommy, not for Kammie. For me."

"That's not for you, baby," Tessa sighed. "This is the girls' department. That's a shirt for girls."

"No," Kayden protested. "That's silly. It's a shirt for a person who wears it. Boy, girl, it doesn't matter. What matters is that it's pretty."

"Yes, it's so pretty," Kamryn inserted. "I want it. Not Kayden, it's for me."

"Why can't it be for both of us?" Kayden argued. "Look, they have two. We can both have one and look like twins. We're twins anyway."

"No, I don't want to have the same shirt," Kamryn wailed. "I want this for me."

"Kayden, Kammie is right," Tessa began, taking a deep breath. "That's nice of you to want to look like twins, but that's more fun for twins who are both boys or both girls. You're a boy, and she's a girl; you don't look the same anyway."

"That's silly," Kayden countered. "You said I could wear the same costume for Halloween as Asher. I can dress like my friend, but not like my sister? Why?"

"I don't know why," Tessa sighed, feeling drained. "I don't make the rules. It's just the way it is."

"So, I can't have this shirt? But this princess is my favorite," Kayden claimed, his voice quivering.

Tessa knew that he wouldn't give up easily, and as she was exhausted, she scrambled to find a compromise. After searching for a few minutes, she found a shirt with the same princess, but it also had other characters from the movie, and at least this shirt was navy. Kayden wasn't completely satisfied, but he was more or less placated. It was a solution that Kamryn could accept as well, especially because she got the original purple shirt with the princess. Tessa was slightly more worried about her husband, Sean. She doubted that he would approve of Kayden's shirt, but he worked so much as a mechanic and spent most of his free time with his friends, so he might not even see the shirt for a while, or at all.

Three hours later Tessa finished making dinner and called her family to eat. Sean was home tonight, nursing a beer and watching a game after a strenuous day at work. Kamryn was playing with a doll on the living room floor. Kayden was nowhere to be seen again. He finally showed up when Tessa had called out his name several times. He had a wide grin and Kamryn's new purple shirt on.

"What the hell?" Sean asked, lowering his beer.

"No," Kamryn wailed. "That's my shirt. Take it off. Mommy, make him take it off."

Kayden's smile disappeared as Tessa grabbed his hand and took him upstairs to change. He tried to protest, but eventually understood that it wasn't nice to take his sister's shirt. They came downstairs, Kayden dressed in a dark green striped shirt that said: "I love trucks."

"What the hell was that?" Sean asked, still outraged. "What were you doing in your sister's shirt?"

"Nothing," Kayden responded, shrugging his shoulder. "I was just having fun."

"You mean you were kidding? Was it a joke?" Sean queried.

Kayden shrugged his shoulder again.

"Don't shrug your shoulder at me," Sean raised his voice. "Look at me. Hey, Kayden, *look at me*. I am *not* joking. Was it a joke?"

"Yeah, I guess," Kayden said quietly. "Can we eat now?"

Tessa exhaled, not realizing that she had been holding her breath. She rushed to serve them dinner, and the meal was ultimately uneventful. After dinner, the kids were running around and screaming, and Sean finally had enough, not being able to hear his game.

"Hey, Kamryn, Kayden, stop," he yelled. "Sit down and play here quietly."

They did, but after a few minutes Kayden opened his mouth to talk, "We were loud, daddy, I know. I'm sorry. But you were loud, too, and not very nice."

"You're right," Sean sighed. "I could have told you more nicely, Kayden. I had a long day at work, and you were screaming really loud."

"It's OK, daddy," Kayden smiled. "But could you call me Kaydie? Kayden is not very nice, especially when you're mad."

"What the hell?" Sean snapped. "No, I won't call you Kaydie. It sounds like Katie. That's a girl's name. You're not a girl."

"But…," Kayden began, his voice trembling. "You call Kamryn Kammie a lot. You always just call me Kayden. Can't I have a nickname?"

"You don't need a nickname," Sean retorted. "You see, Tessa, you and your fancy names. Why did you have to push Kayden? Why couldn't we just name him Hunter or something?"

Kayden started to cry, huge teardrops trailing down his face.

"Oh, that's just great," Sean said sarcastically. "Man up, son. Boys don't cry."

Kayden began to howl louder until Tessa took him in her arms and carried him upstairs. She heard Sean grumbling, "That's just great. He'll never learn if you keep pampering him like that."

She tried to console Kayden, but it turned out to be more difficult than expected.

"Daddy doesn't like me," Kayden sobbed. "He would like a Hunter, but he doesn't like *me*. I don't get it. When Kammie does the same or wears the same, he says she's so pretty, and she's his princess. But he yells at me for the same."

Tessa was lost for words. She had run out of logical arguments and couldn't find the right thing to say. Sometimes she didn't know how to handle Kayden. Some days he behaved as a typical 4-year-old boy. He enjoyed playing outside and wearing his boyish clothes, which he often got dirty within 10 minutes of getting dressed. He often engaged in rough play with his friends, or even Kamryn. He played with trucks, hot wheels, power wheels, balls, LEGOs, and building blocks. Other times, he preferred Kamryn's baby dolls, kitchen sets, and Barbies and tried to put on one of her shirts or tights. One time he tried on Kamryn's tutu skirt that she wore for ballet. Kamryn was angry at first, but then she started to laugh and took a picture with Tessa's phone. Tessa made sure to delete it before Sean could catch a glimpse. Kayden's Halloween costume suggestions tended to be unpredictable, too, ranging from Spiderman to Little Mermaid, with a snail, cat, or dolphin in between. He insisted to keep his hair slightly long and passionately protested against haircuts. He had asked Tessa several times before to call him Kaydie, but most of the time, he didn't have any objections against Kayden.

There were three incidents that stuck out to Tessa and puzzled her the most. One time she was painting her nails and Kayden asked to have his nails painted, too. Tessa explained that boys didn't usually paint their nails, but Kayden pushed so much that she agreed to paint his nails as long as they removed the nail polish before Sean came home that night. Then, Kayden surprised her more by stating that he only wanted to paint his pinkies because that looked prettier to him than painting the nails on all the fingers. He chose a lavender color and, despite their former deal, he protested and cried when Tessa tried to remove the polish in a few hours. As only the nails on his pinkies were painted, and those nails were so small anyway, Tessa changed her mind, thinking that this was harmless. When Sean noticed later, he disagreed. He had some labels both for Kayden and Tessa for engaging in this experiment. Kayden was dejected, but he still

asked for painting his nails (including his toenails) a few more times. Tessa refused to let him from then on.

When Tessa took Kamryn to get her ears pierced, with Kayden in tow, Kayden wanted to get his ears pierced as well. Or rather, he wanted one ear pierced. He emphasized how great he would look with a dangling earring in one ear, a baseball cap, baseball shirt, and zebra-striped tights. Tessa wasn't sure whether to laugh at that or worry. She decided to laugh at the time, but in any case, she didn't let him pierce his ear. Later on that day, she found him in the bathroom with a paperclip, trying to pierce his own ear. Luckily, he couldn't do any harm with a paperclip, but the memory of that sight still left a chill in Tessa.

The third incident that touched Tessa the most involved shoe shopping. Kayden ran around the store and emerged with a pink tennis shoe with polka dots on one foot and a dark blue sneaker for boys on the other foot. He was very enthusiastic, "Look, mommy. Cool, huh?"

"Well, maybe," Tessa said cautiously. "Which one do you mean?"

"What do you mean which one?" Kayden asked, wringing his forehead, clearly confused. "I like both. I like them this way. One on one foot, and the other on my other foot. They look so nice!"

"But, baby," Tessa began, bewildered. "You can't wear two different kinds of shoes at the same time."

"Why not?" Kayden protested. "They look so much better this way than wearing the same on both feet. That would be *boring*. It's way cooler this way."

"You still have to choose," Tessa insisted. "And I'd suggest the dark blue pair on both feet."

"But why?" Kayden wailed. "Why do I have to choose? I like them both."

Eventually Kayden ended up throwing a tantrum in the middle of the store, and they didn't buy either pair of shoes. However, his words echoed in Tessa's ears for the next several weeks. She instinctively kept these incidents a secret from Sean. As he was hardly home and rarely spent a lot of involved time with the kids, he seldom noticed these issues, but when he did, his reaction convinced Tessa further to not divulge these pieces of information to him.

After the purple princess shirt episode, Sean's negative reaction, and Kayden's obvious despair, Tessa decided that it was time to ask Kayden some questions. She had dreaded this talk, but she felt that she couldn't postpone it any longer. Once Kayden calmed down, she carefully began, "Baby, I know you like that shirt. Can you explain to me why?"

"Because it's pretty," Kayden claimed.

"Yes, it is," Tessa hesitated. "But… you know that it's a shirt for girls, right?"

"Yeah," Kayden agreed. "But I don't like that. I think it's a shirt for anyone."

"If you could… would you rather wear that shirt and clothes like Kammie's all the time if you could?" Tessa asked cautiously.

"No," Kayden protested. "That would be boring. I'd still want to wear my clothes. I'd just wear Kammie's clothes when I feel like it."

"So…," Tessa paused. "So, if you could choose, would you choose to be Kammie rather than you? Do you like being a little boy, or would you rather be a girl like Kammie?"

"I wouldn't want to be a girl," Kayden announced with a contemplative look.

Tessa felt a sense of relief, at least until Kayden continued, "I wouldn't want to be a girl, especially not all the time, but I'm not sure I like being a boy only. I don't understand why you have to choose. I'm a boy, sure, I know, but I'm not just a boy, and I don't like to be called just a boy. I'm so many things. I'm me. I'm Kayden. Sometimes Kaydie. I can be something today and something else tomorrow. I don't get it why some things are for boys and others for girls. I think everything is for everyone."

Tessa was confused, but also amazed by the profoundness of her young son's words. She realized that she, and even more so, Sean, and the rest of society had been pushing something on Kayden from the time he had been born. In fact, it had started before he was born. Tessa hadn't really had a preference for a boy or a girl before she had children. She had wanted two or three children, but she had truly not cared about what sex they were. She had always believed in destiny and that she would ultimately be given the children she needed to have, regardless of their sex. However, Sean had had a different mindset. As soon as they learned that she was pregnant, he expressed his preference for a boy. When she turned out to carry twins, he was hoping for two boys and was slightly disappointed to find out that one of them was a girl. Having at least one boy, though, consoled him. Ironically, these days he seemed to be more drawn to his daughter than his son, probably because his son sometimes didn't behave in gender-conforming ways, whereas Kamryn did. Kayden's occasional unconventional demeanor puzzled and frustrated Sean.

While Tessa hadn't had a sex preference for her children, as soon as she learned that she was carrying a boy and a girl, she found herself engaging in some gender stereotyping as well. She was drawn to pink, frills, and dresses for Kamryn and darker colors, pants, and collared shirts for Kayden. She automatically went to the girls' department to shop for Kamryn and the boys' for Kayden. Even before they were born, she had bought gender-specific clothing for both. Furthermore, color-coding had influenced her decisions on how to decorate the nursery as well. She had chosen a dark crib for Kayden and a white one for Kamryn. She had painted the wall next to Kamryn's crib lavender, complete with flowers, butterflies, and clouds. She had painted the other wall next to Kayden's crib light blue with some baby animals in the background. Even their bibs, car seats, high chairs, and later, potties were color-coded, and no matter how tired she was, Tessa never mixed them up. Kayden did, of course, or tried to, from the time he was around 2 years of age.

Tessa had never consciously thought about her choices of clothing, toys, and other items for her children based on their sex, but subconsciously internalized beliefs and norms guided her selections. Logically, as they were the same age, Kayden and Kamryn could have shared some of their objects, and they didn't need separate, color-coded versions, but Tessa didn't follow this kind of logic. She was easily influenced by commercials and separate, almost segregated, departments for boys and girls in stores. Commercials also had a great impact on Kamryn, but not so much on Kayden, except when he expressed occasional enthusiasm about a toy that was advertised for girls. Other times he criticized why some toys meant for boys weren't available in a wider variety of colors.

People around Tessa had reinforced her ingrained ideas on gender-specific items as well. For instance, no one had purchased any gender-neutral clothing or baby toys for her baby shower. Kayden's and Kamryn's grandparents kept giving them color-coded gifts as well. The children's great-grandmother on Tessa's mother's side was the only one who had expressed at the

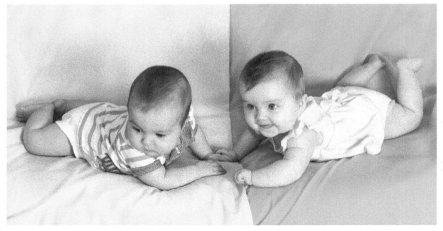

baby shower that it wasn't frugal to buy all these separate items for the kids. She mentioned that in her childhood, and even more so when her parents had been growing up, all children in her family wore white or yellow baby clothes, regardless of their sex, passing the clothes down from one baby to the next. It made sense, but Tessa still ended up spending a lot of money on gender-specific objects.

When the children were 3, Tessa took Kamryn to ballet and Kayden to karate. Kayden loved karate some days, but on other days he whined to attend ballet instead. Sean had been convinced that Kayden would love football and baseball like he did and was bewildered when he did not. Kayden was more or less neutral about baseball; he was enthralled by the outfits, but disinterested in the game. As far as football was concerned, Kayden detested it. He wasn't fond of the strict rules in sports, just as he couldn't fathom rigid rules in everyday life.

Preschool turned out to be a challenge for Kayden, too. He could scarcely tolerate the regulations there, and he often got in trouble when he questioned authority or norms. His karate instructor and most of his preschool teachers noticed and tended to curb and correct his gender non-conforming behaviors. He had one preschool teacher who turned out to be more flexible and told Tessa that he should be left alone and allowed to experiment and be himself. A part of Tessa agreed instinctively, but she was still apprehensive of the potential consequences and people's disapproval. She was most afraid of Sean's reproach, who would view any examples of Kayden's sometimes unconventional gender expression as a reflection on his own masculinity, or lack thereof.

As Kayden was thoughtful, bright, funny, and entertaining, he had some close friends in preschool and in karate, but some kids judged his unorthodox behaviors somewhat harshly and made fun of him. Tessa was concerned that older children might be even more rigid, and if Kayden remained the way he was, he could encounter more trouble or even bullying in late elementary, middle, and high school. She was worried that he might lose the spark that made him unique. She was anxious that he might lose some friends, or even his father's support and love, and she might come to a point where she might have to choose between her son and husband. She had no doubt that she would choose Kayden, but the consequences could be challenging. As Kamryn was the apple of her father's eye and highly adored by him, if Sean ended up rejecting Kayden, it could drive a wedge between the twins.

Tessa mused back to her childhood and realized that her gender nonconformity hadn't been met with as much animosity as Kayden's. She had been labeled a tomboy, but the term was harmless, almost endearing. For example, her father had said it with apparent pride. Tessa was born as the third child after two older brothers. Her father had expected another son and didn't know what to do with a girl. Her mother had been used to boys by that point as well and didn't force girly outfits, toys, or pursuits on her. Tessa had played rough with her brothers, and they had almost considered her one of the boys as well. She had loved to play outside, climb trees, and even have some innocent physical fights with her brothers. She had played baseball with them and her father and learned to fix cars and things around the house relatively young. She could get more excited about a toolbox and trucks than dolls. She played with dolls with her brothers, but those dolls were more likely to engage in warfare than tea parties. Tessa was the only child in her family who showed interest in her father's favorite hobbies, fishing and hunting, which filled him with incredible pride.

When Tessa was 9 and her brothers 10 and 12, their sister, Jenna, was born. Jenna was petite and feminine from the very beginning. She turned out to be the most girly girl Tessa had ever known. Their parents treated them somewhat differently because by that point they were ready for a girl, and because they were slightly older themselves by then. Their parents pampered Jenna and sometimes her older siblings did, too, but other times they just avoided her or picked on her because they didn't quite know what to do with her, as she didn't fit into their tight-knit trio.

The contrast between Tessa and Jenna had always been stark, and in her sister's presence Tessa felt even more of a tomboy. She didn't mind it, though, because she still felt like a girl but could enter and enjoy the world of boys with all of its fun and freedom. Wearing a dress, uncomfortable shoes, and headbands had always seemed restricting to Tessa, and she was happy she wasn't forced to do it. Being a grown woman, she enjoyed dressing up and wearing makeup sometimes, but mostly only when she felt like it, and it was her choice. Given her relatively gender-neutral upbringing she slightly surprised herself with buying all the pink and frills for Kamryn, but she was caught up in the frenzy that the world around her seemed to project, and Kamryn appeared to enjoy girly things much more than Tessa ever had.

When Tessa had entered adolescence, she started to feel her parents treating her somewhat differently from her brothers. Her brothers had a later curfew and were allowed to do some things that she wasn't. Her dates were screened with much more scrutiny than her brothers' as well. Her father started to worry about where she was going and whom she was seeing. It was frustrating and limiting, especially after a freer childhood. Tessa suddenly experienced stricter gender rules, and she wasn't thrilled about them. It wasn't only her family, the boys she had used to play with, including her brothers' classmates, began to see her and treat her differently, and the gap between them seemed to have widened.

Despite some negative experience in her middle and late teens, Tessa felt that she had been offered more flexibility than Kayden in her gender expression as a child. She wondered why that was and if this was true for their case only, or for boys and girls in general. Tomboy was an innocuous label in her case, and it didn't harm her being accepted among her peers. In fact, it elevated her respectability among some of them, especially the boys. However, with Kayden the opposite seemed to be a more prevalent reaction. In many ways, Tessa had been much more gender nonconforming than Kayden because she had nearly constantly violated gender norms, whereas Kayden only occasionally did, but he still seemed to be more firmly punished for it than she had ever been.

Tessa was perplexed about that contrast as she recognized that boys sometimes had it more difficult than girls. Yes, girls were undoubtedly restricted in some ways, but boys arguably were even more so. If boys showed the slightest deviation from gender norms, they tended to be called very offensive names and ran the risk of becoming outcasts. Their emotions tended to be more strictly regulated than those of girls as well. Girls could become upset, cry, or even throw tantrums, but boys were usually discouraged from these behaviors—that is, they were inhibited from expressing or even feeling the emotions that generated these behaviors. Sometimes Tessa told Kayden not to cry as well, but she never particularly enjoyed doing that because she was perturbed that she might be teaching him to suppress his emotions, or that his emotions didn't count.

Tessa wondered what was considered normal in terms of gender expression. The term "normal" made her slightly uncomfortable because it implied that everything (or worse, everyone) outside of the realm of normal was *not* normal or was abnormal. Not normal could involve some horrible labels. It could also entail that something or someone needs to be *fixed* to become normal, and that approach seemed troublesome as well. She would have been the last to judge her son, but she was aware that he might become the subject of other people's judgment, so she still found it important to figure out what they were dealing with.

The term that had been flashing in her mind for a while was *transgender.* She didn't know what that meant exactly, so she decided to look it up. After the kids and Sean had gone to bed, she settled down in front of the computer to conduct some searches. When she typed in transgender, she got over 60 million hits. It seemed overwhelming at first, but she managed to develop a better idea of what transgender stood for by

kaetana / Shutterstock.com

scanning through some articles and definitions. Her understanding was that transgender individuals had a gender identity that didn't match the biological sex they were assigned at birth. They felt as if they were born in the wrong body. Some, usually referred to as transsexuals, had a strong desire to change their bodies to fit the gender they identified with. The change could involve hormone therapy and/or sex reassignment surgery. If the perceived mismatch between body and mind persisted for a while and caused significant distress, affected individuals could be diagnosed with gender dysphoria (formerly gender identity disorder).

Tessa also learned that some cultures recognized a third gender and/or trans individuals. Examples of this included the *hijra* in India, the *muxe* in southern Mexico, and two-spirits (formerly *berdache*) in some Native American cultures. The Bugis in Indonesia had as many as five genders. To understand all of this, Tessa also had to clarify the difference between *sex* and *gender* and realize that sex was biological and physical, whereas gender was psychological, cultural, and social.

Tessa continued by watching some videos online on transgender children. Some stories tugged at her heart and filled her eyes with tears. It seemed that transgender individuals tended to show signs from early childhood. Some met an inordinate amount of resistance from their families and other people around them, and, as a result, they went through considerable struggles in trying to be true to themselves. Tessa watched with horror how some trans children were bullied, and how some ended up hurting themselves, or even committing suicide. It was all extremely disheartening.

Prejudice, discrimination, and violence toward the transgender community also appeared to be rampant. Bathroom use troubles were exceedingly common. Trans children and adults frequently had to fight to be able to use the restroom that fit their gender identity. Most of them reported fear and harassment as they entered a specific restroom. Many addressed lack of knowledge and prejudice in the medical community as well. Tessa felt the most disturbed when she heard about assaults and murders of trans individuals.

Tessa moved on to more cheerful and inspiring videos. If families accepted and supported trans children, allowing or even encouraging them to live as the gender they identified with, they seemed to thrive and radiate confidence and peace. They might have encountered some prejudice from others, but it was easier to overcome if they had their families' full support.

What struck Tessa the most was that the majority of trans children had a strong, persistent, and consistent identification with the gender that didn't match their biological sex. For example, most trans children who were born as boys insisted from early on that they were girls. This unshakable resolution was especially prevalent among transsexuals, predominantly those who were eventually diagnosed with gender dysphoria. After her thorough exploration of trans children, she concluded that Kayden didn't seem to fit this category because he didn't entirely reject being a boy, sometimes he was even happy with it, and he didn't express a compelling desire to be a girl or identify as one.

In her search of gender nonconformity, Tessa came across another term that she didn't understand. It was *intersex*. She looked it up for clarification. She learned that intersex meant being born with a sexual or reproductive anatomy that didn't fit the typical definitions of female or male. She was amazed to find out that chromosomally, there were five sexes among humans, so the picture was much more complex than the XY and XX she used to hear about in school. Tessa was exasperated when she realized that doctors still often suggested early surgery on infants in these cases to "fix" or "correct" atypical genitalia.

Tessa also read that intersex anatomy didn't necessarily show up at birth, especially if the condition didn't affect the genitalia. Some intersex conditions could become apparent during puberty or not even then. It was common for intersex children to demonstrate some gender nonconforming

behaviors. In their case, when they had a mix of male and female reproductive and/or sexual anatomy, it was more ambiguous what constituted gender nonconforming behavior at all. The main difference between transgender and intersex seemed to be whether sex or gender was involved. Trans children tended to be born with an unambiguous sex, but identified as the other gender, whereas intersex children had a more obscure sex, which could impact their gender expressions.

At first, Tessa thought that Kayden couldn't be intersex, as he was explicitly pronounced a boy at birth. Further research raised some questions in her, though, because some intersex conditions weren't obvious at birth. She wondered if Kayden might be affected. They might not know before puberty or never find out without an array of medical tests. She wasn't sure if embarking on that journey of exploration might be worth it, especially at this point, when he was only 4 years old. She could see how Sean could excuse Kayden's occasionally unorthodox gender expressions more if there was an undeniable biological explanation for it. However, she was also petrified that if the doctors found something, and surgery was a possibility, or even a recommendation, Sean would opt to do it.

She didn't want to get stuck on intersex because she had no way of knowing if that might impact Kayden. She chose to delve into other possibilities as well. She discovered a sea of terms and definitions to describe gender non-conforming children. One of them was *gender variant* (or *gender diverse*). This meant exhibiting gender behaviors or expressions that didn't fit conventional gender norms of masculinity and femininity. *Genderqueer* (or *nonbinary*) was an umbrella term that stood for gender identities that didn't fit into the gender binary, indicating identities that were not exclusively masculine or feminine. Genderqueer individuals could identify as neither genders, both genders, or a combination of two or more genders. *Genderfluid* (with different spellings, one word, two words, hyphenated, and so on) described a gender identity that varied over time. They could identify as male, female, neither, both, or a combination of any genders, and it could vary depending on the situation and over time. It was mostly associated with identity shifts and fluctuations.

Tessa was getting somewhat confused, even dizzy reading through all the different terms and their definitions. There were so many more, but she didn't have the energy and perseverance to explore all of them tonight. As far as she could judge, Kayden seemed to fit the gender variant label for sure, and possibly the genderfluid and genderqueer concepts as well. Some appeared to overlap, and Tessa was finding it difficult to distinguish between them.

She was wavering whether finding a label for Kayden might be more helpful or harmful. It could be beneficial because she could potentially gain a more profound understanding of him, and he could have a community with whom he would have many things in common. At the same time, labels were labels, and Tessa was hesitant whether a label could ultimately lead to a greater level of prejudice and discrimination. Also, Kayden was so young; he might be in a passing phase, he might simply be imitating his sister sometimes, and even if not, what was the use of identifying what might fit him? Even more so, most of these terms referred to gender identity, and Kayden was the only one who could decide about his own gender identity, and he might be too young for that at this point. Kayden's words from today echoed in Tessa's ears: "I'm me. I'm Kayden. Sometimes Kaydie." Maybe this was the bottom line in all of this. He expressed a desire not to be defined as anything other than himself. Could Tessa ask for a more evident answer to all of her questions?

Discussion Questions

1. How do you envision Kayden's and his family's life in the near future? What about 20 years from now?

2. When do you think gender socialization starts in families? Also, list a few examples of gender socialization in families.

3. There are many agents of socialization; families are one of them. Besides families, where do we learn about gender socialization? Also, list some of the messages about gender that we learn outside of families.

4. Do you think it is possible to raise a genderless/genderfree/completely gender-neutral child in today's society? Why/why not? Would it be *advisable* to do so? Why/why not?

5. West and Zimmerman (1987) explained that gender was a routine, everyday accomplishment. It is something that we do in interaction with others, as opposed to something that we are. Discuss a few examples of how characters in the story *do gender* (or fail to do gender in conventional ways).

6. Lumping is emphasizing similarities between certain groups and discarding their potential differences, whereas splitting is concentrating on, or even exaggerating, differences between certain groups (Zerubavel, 1991, 1996). Do most people tend to do more lumping or splitting in terms of gender socialization? Draw parallels with the story as well.

7. In his labeling theory Becker (1997) explained that an individual became a deviant only when the label was successfully applied to him/her. (A deviant is someone who diverges from social norms in some way.) First, the individual's behavior is labeled deviant, but then the label extends to the person. The individual often internalizes the label and starts acting accordingly, so it may become a self-fulfilling prophecy. (This last step is not unavoidable, but it is a common result of labeling.) Discuss the role of labeling in Kayden's life and in the lives of other gender nonconforming children.

8. Hegemonic masculinity is the most accepted, dominant, and normative way of masculinity in a particular society at a given time (Connell, 1987). Usually it operates by subordinating femininity and alternative forms of masculinity, which are considered effeminate, thus, inferior. Discuss hegemonic masculinity in the story and how it affects Kayden's life.

9. Lorber (1994) argued that gender was a social construction, a product of socialization and human creation. It is something that varies across cultures and over time, but many still view it as universal and essential, forgetting our role in constructing and perpetuating it. Apply this theory to the story and to gender nonconformity in general.

10. Boys are frequently restricted more in terms of gender expression and behaviors than girls—for example, pink clothes, frills, nail polish, and Barbie dolls tend to be discouraged among boys, especially by heterosexual fathers (Kane, 2006). Why do you think this is? Why are girls often given more gender leeway than boys?

Find the Answers

Go to http://www.transequality.org/sites/default/files/docs/usts/USTSBlackRespondentsReport-Nov17.pdf to find answers to the following questions.

1. List two key findings (p. 3).

2. Discuss the most common reactions from families (p. 6-7).

3. Discuss unemployment and poverty rates among the respondents (p. 8).

4. Mention two statistics regarding health (p. 18-19).

Mini Research Assignments

1. Survey at least seven individuals, asking them to rate their agreement with the following statements on a scale of 1–10 (1 meaning complete disagreement and 10 indicating full agreement): 1. "I wouldn't mind it at all if my son (or a boy in my immediate family) played with Barbie dolls and wore pink clothes and nail polish sometimes." 2. "Girls are allowed more freedom in gender expression than boys." 3. "Gender socialization usually starts before birth, once parents know the sex of a baby." Summarize the results. Discuss the role of gender, age, and other factors in the responses. Draw parallels with the story as well.

2. Visit the baby aisle and the children's department in at least two department stores of your choice, paying close attention to clothes and toys. Can you easily tell which clothes/toys are for boys and which ones are for girls? How? Can you find any gender-neutral clothes and toys? If yes, how easy are they to locate? What do your observations tell you about gender socialization in early childhood? Did you notice any difference between the two stores? Draw parallels with the story as well.

3. Watch parents interact with their children at a public place (e.g., mall, playground, restaurant). Discuss how the observed children are socialized in terms of gender based on their appearance, clothing, behavior, names (if you can tell), the instructions parents give them (or don't give them), and so on. Do mothers and fathers seem to treat children differently? If yes, how so? Summarize your observations. Draw parallels with the story as well.

4. Watch a movie, documentary, or an episode of a TV show on either transgender or intersex children. How are they depicted? How are they treated and socialized by their families? How are they treated and socialized by others (e.g., other relatives, school, media, church)? How do they identify? How do they seem to see themselves? Summarize your observations and draw parallels with the story as well.

References

Becker, H. S. (1997). *Outsiders: In the sociology of deviance* (new edition). New York, NY: Free Press. (Originally published 1963)

Connell, R. W. (1987). *Gender and power: Society, the person, and sexual politics*. Stanford, CA: Stanford University Press.

James, S. E., Brown C., & Wilson I. (2017). 2015 U.S. transgender survey: report on the experiences of black respondents. Washington, DC: National Center for Transgender Equality. Retrieved from http://www.transequality.org/sites/default/files/docs/usts/USTSBlackRespondentsReport-Nov17.pdf

Kane, E. W. (2006). 'No way my boys are going to be like that!': Parents' responses to children's gender nonconformity. *Gender & Society, 20,* 149–176.

Lorber, J. (1994). *Paradoxes of gender*. New Haven, CT: Yale University Press.

West, C., & Zimmerman, D. H. (1987). Doing gender. *Gender & Society, 1,* 125–151.

Zerubavel, E. (1991). *The fine line: Making distinctions in everyday life*. New York, NY: Free Press.

_____. (1996). Lumping and splitting: Notes on social classification. *Sociological forum, 11,* 421–433.

CHAPTER 10

"But we only did it once."
TEENAGE PREGNANCY

Vicente Barcelo Varona/ Shutterstock.com

Sierra Lewis hit the snooze button on her phone alarm for the third time. She simply couldn't find the energy to get up. She had felt immensely exhausted lately, no matter how much she slept. She chalked it up to loads of schoolwork and frequent tests as the school year was coming to an end. She sat up in bed and was immediately hit by a wave of dizziness. These episodes of dizziness were a novel experience as well. She had never felt dizzy before, except on some tough amusement park rides. She sat in bed for a few more minutes, avoiding to get up too quickly. She heard voices from the kitchen, as her mother and her sister, Sage, were talking. A faint smell of cooking bacon oozed into her nostrils, and she almost gagged. That was very surprising, as bacon was one of her favorite breakfast meals. Battling a sudden wave of nausea, she sank back onto her bed.

"Sierra, come on, you're going to be late," she heard her mother calling.

Sierra took a couple of deep breaths, sat up cautiously, got dressed slowly, and eventually walked into the kitchen. She fought another bout of nausea as the smell of bacon hit her with full force.

"Finally," her mother sighed. "Come, eat breakfast quickly before it gets cold and before the school bus gets here."

"No, thanks," Sierra gulped. "I don't have time. I'll just grab some crackers and eat them later."

"Are you sure?" her mother asked with a hint of concern in her voice. "Breakfast is very important. It's hard to concentrate in school without it."

"It's fine, mom," Sierra assured her, thinking that what would make it hard to concentrate in school were the dizziness and nausea. She didn't want her mother to worry, so she didn't mention that she wasn't feeling well. Probably it was just a passing bug anyway. She had experienced about the same the day before, and after about noon she suddenly felt much better. She hurried to the school bus, munching on a few crackers on the way.

When she got to school, after some more waves of dizziness and nausea and sizable fatigue, Sierra decided to see the school nurse. After the nurse examined her and asked several questions about what she had eaten lately and whether she had encountered any significant physical and/or mental strain, she posed a question that stupefied Sierra for a second.

"When did you have your last menstrual period?" the nurse repeated, as Sierra failed to respond the first time.

"Umm," Sierra hesitated. "Just now. I mean, not too long ago."

"Do you remember the date?" the nurse inquired.

"Umm, about a week ago," Sierra answered slowly. It wasn't true, but suddenly she couldn't figure out what to tell the nurse. She needed to gain time, but as she needed to react fast, she panicked and continued lying, "You know, what? I just remembered that I ate a sandwich from the fridge the other day. It tasted kind of funny, but I was very hungry, so I ate it anyway. I don't know how long it might have been there. I'm sure that's what made me sick."

As the nurse gave her some medicine to soothe her stomach and offered some additional instructions, Sierra was unable to pay attention and blocked her words out. She was still trying to calculate when she had had her last period, but she couldn't remember. She needed to get rid of the nurse so she could have some peace and quiet and look at the calendar on her phone.

Finally she could leave and rushed to a relatively private corner of the school to check the calendar on her phone. Her mother had been instructing her to keep track of her periods, but she usually forgot. Occasionally, she put the dates in her smartphone, but as she didn't do it regularly, it didn't help. The last date that she found was from 2 months ago, but that didn't mean she hadn't had her period since then. Maybe she did and forgot to make a note. She wracked her mind trying to remember, but she couldn't. It seemed that it had been a while since she had had her last period, but she had been so busy, so maybe time just *appeared* to pass more slowly than usual. She suddenly recalled having some light bleeding about 2 to 3 weeks ago. Yes, it was very light and didn't last long, but that must have been her period. It was difficult to tell because her period was mostly irregular, sometimes it even skipped a month, and its heaviness tended to vary as well.

Sierra was truly relieved to have figured out that she did have a period rather recently. The nurse's question had terrified her, and she was befuddled as to why. She understood that the nurse attempted to find out whether a potential pregnancy might be causing her symptoms. But why did she panic at that suggestion? It would be impossible for her to be pregnant; she was a virgin. At least she was pretty sure she was still a virgin. Or could she *not* be a virgin? Could she actually be *pregnant*?

At barely 16, Sierra felt somewhat underinformed about sex and pregnancy sometimes. Her parents had shied away from discussing these topics with her, and sex education in school was kind of vague and focused mostly on abstinence. Sierra had intended to abstain, even if not until marriage, but at least until she had a serious boyfriend. She was well aware that many of her classmates were having sex, she had heard the rumors, but as her closest friends were still virgins, she hadn't been able to discuss sex and birth control with her peers either. She had googled a few things, but was too shy to read what came up, and when pictures or videos emerged as well, she was almost horrified and closed her search immediately. She was careful to clean the search history and make sure that her parents didn't find out how she circumvented some of the parental controls they had set on the computers at home. Too bad that she had a younger sister, not an older one because she would have felt comfortable enough to ask an older sister, especially someone as cool as Sage.

Sierra was familiar with the basics, she knew about condoms and birth control pills. She just thought that she didn't need to think about protection until she had a boyfriend and was ready to have sex. Even then, she assumed that her boyfriend would have condoms and know how to use them.

About 1.5 months ago Sierra attended a birthday party that one of her friends threw. Sierra's parents believed that Becca's parents would be at home and that the party was a sleepover for girls only. However, Becca's parents were actually out of town and thought that Becca arranged a sleepover for a couple of her best friends only. They had no idea that boys would be invited as well, and how huge the party would eventually get. They were also unaware that there would be alcohol.

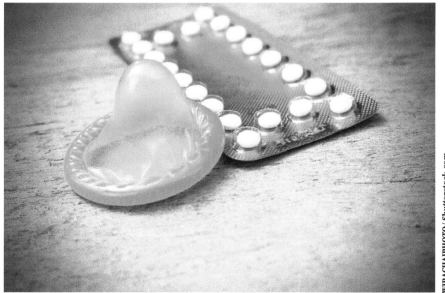

Sierra arrived in a casual, conservative outfit and was slightly embarrassed to discover that most of the other girls had dressed up. Becca quickly came to the rescue and offered some clothes from her closet. She also applied some makeup on Sierra. Sierra wasn't sure whether she was fully comfortable with either the somewhat tight outfit or the makeup, but finally Becca's compliments and encouragement convinced her that she looked great.

As Sierra entered the party, she immediately got some stares from a few boys. She smiled modestly and secretly enjoyed the attention. She didn't care too much about the boys; she was having way too much fun with her girlfriends. However, when Tanner Dunn started to chat with her, Sierra couldn't turn her back. She had had a small crush on Tanner for a while. He was very good-looking and popular. She could hardly believe that he knew her name and was paying attention to her now. Her heart swelled with pride as she noticed some jealous glances from several girls around them.

Tanner turned out to be very funny, which was a side of him that she hadn't been familiar with before. He seemed to be a good listener and very attentive, which surprised Sierra even more, as Tanner had the reputation of sometimes being a jerk. He was standing very close to Sierra and whispered some jokes into her ear. He was drinking, which Sierra found bold and appealing, even if slightly dangerous at the same time. He was doing his best to convince her to drink, too.

"Hey, come on, just one drink," he hummed.

"No, that's okay," Sierra refused.

"What's the matter? You've never drunk before?" Tanner laughed.

"Of course I have," Sierra lied. It wasn't entirely a lie; she had taken a few sips of alcohol before, but never a full glass.

"Then why not now?" Tanner asked teasingly. "You don't want to drink with me? Just a sip? Here, take a sip from my drink."

Sierra was too embarrassed to blatantly reject it, and it excited her that he offered his own drink. It was as if they shared something very intimate. She glanced around and took a small sip. She started coughing a bit. She didn't know what it was, but it seemed to be very strong.

"Atta girl," Tanner smirked. "I bet this was your first drink, wasn't it?"

"No," Sierra protested. "It was a little strong, I'll admit, so it took me by surprise for a moment."

"You're a good girl, aren't you?" Tanner asked jokingly, looking into her eyes. Sierra blushed, as both his look and tone embarrassed her. She had an inkling that he wasn't just talking about alcohol anymore. Tanner inched even closer to her, and his closeness was so exhilarating and his cologne so intoxicating that Sierra didn't feel like moving away. They continued talking, and every 5 minutes or so, Tanner offered another sip of his drink. Sierra refused about half of the time, but couldn't the rest of the time, and she took an increasingly bigger sip each time. In the meantime, Tanner refilled his glass and about 50 minutes and eight sips later, he leaned

Yellowj / Shutterstock.com

even closer to kiss her. Sierra was slightly surprised by the kiss, but not too much. In a way, it was obvious that this was where the flirting would lead. Sierra was pleased and proud that Tanner turned out to like her. He might have even had a secret crush on her, as she had had on him.

As the kiss deepened, Tanner opened one eye, glanced toward the room they were standing next to and started to pull Sierra toward the door. Sierra pulled back and tried to cement her feet to remain standing in the hallway. It seemed a little bit more difficult than expected, as she wasn't very steady on her feet. Tanner continued to guide her toward the room, and she was stepping back, as if they were engaged in an odd dance.

Tanner eventually stopped kissing her and looked at her questioningly, "What's going on? Something wrong? Don't you want a little more privacy? It'd be more comfy in there, too."

"Yeah, maybe," Sierra whispered, flushing. "It's just… I don't want you to get the wrong idea. I… I just want to kiss. I don't want anything else to happen."

"Sure thing," Tanner beamed. "Don't worry. We're just going to make out."

He pulled Sierra into the room and closed the door. She didn't resist it anymore. They continued kissing for several minutes, then Tanner's hand inched down from her shoulder, beginning to explore her body.

"Hey," Sierra protested. "Just making out, remember?"

"Can't we have a little more fun while making out?" Tanner asked, his voice hoarse. "Don't you like this? I bet you do."

Sierra was hesitant because Tanner's caresses did feel thrilling. Her body would have wanted more of them if she had had a guarantee that they would absolutely not go further than this. At the same time, she was worried that things might get out of hand, especially because she was buzzed, and her body felt funny.

"I like it, I guess," Sierra murmured. "But… I don't want… And I feel kind of funny."

"You're supposed to feel kind of funny; that's the point," Tanner laughed. "Funny in a good way."

"Wait," Sierra exclaimed. "I do feel funny. It's the booze, I think. I might get sick."

"Oh, come on, don't ruin the party," Tanner whined. "We were having so much fun."

"I think I need to lay down for a minute," Sierra muttered.

"Yeah, baby, lay down for a minute," Tanner said. "I'm happy to lay down with you."

"Stop joking around please," Sierra begged. "I don't feel good. I think I might pass out."

When Sierra woke up, she had no idea where she was and what had happened. She struggled to get up, trying to fight off dizziness and a splitting headache. It was dark and quiet. She eventually remembered Becca's party and Tanner. She looked around in a frenzy, suddenly terrified to find Tanner next to her. She was relieved to discover that she had all her clothes on, and Tanner was nowhere to be seen. Not that she would have ever presumed that Tanner might do something while she was out, but it was still reassuring to find that he was gone, and she was safe and alone in bed.

She realized that she should have never come to this room with him; he might have taken it as encouragement. Even more so, she shouldn't have drunk and let herself lose control. Maybe she shouldn't even have allowed Becca to push these clothes and makeup on her. They might have been the only reason why Tanner had noticed her in the first place. Why hadn't he approached her in school before? Although her head was still throbbing, Sierra suddenly saw things clearly. Probably Tanner didn't truly like her; he was just having some fun with her. She realized that he wasn't who she had hoped he was, and she felt her crush on him dissipating. Yes, making out with him was exciting, but it might not have happened without the alcohol, and she knew that he wasn't boyfriend material. At least not the kind of boyfriend she had been dreaming about. She was relieved that things didn't get out of hand.

For the next few days, Sierra couldn't shake off a sense of unease. What if something did happen while she was out? When she passed Tanner in the hallway in school, he turned his head, or he simply might not have seen her. Or he might not have recognized her without the makeup. Sierra felt even more embarrassed to approach him now, but she finally gathered the courage to do so when he was alone for a moment.

"Tanner, can I speak to you for a minute?" she asked, her voice quivering.

"Sierra, hey," he responded with a forced smile. "What's up? I'm in a hurry actually."

"I just…," Sierra began slowly. "I was just wondering what happened at the party. I passed out."

"You don't remember?" Tanner looked at her quizzically.

"Not really," Sierra admitted.

"Nothing happened," Tanner asserted. "We made out for a while, then you passed out, so I left."

"So… you left right away?" Sierra asked.

"Sure, why would I have stayed?" Tanner confirmed. "Are you accusing me of something?"

"No, of course, not," Sierra protested. "Just wanted to ask because I didn't remember."

"You have your answer now," Tanner declared. "Look, I gotta go now. See you around."

One and a half months after this conversation, having just left the school nurse's office, Sierra was overcome by a sense of disquiet. Was it possible that Tanner lied, and he did do something at the party, which she didn't remember? Also, how come she couldn't recall what had happened? How come she had passed out so quickly? Yes, it was a strong drink, and she wasn't used to alcohol, but was it possible that the drink had something else in addition to alcohol? Sierra wracked her brain to remember the drink. She wasn't sure, but she had a vague recollection that Tanner didn't drink after he had refilled the glass. Sierra was hit by a sudden wave of anxiety and a horrible suspicion. What if Tanner did have sex with her while she was out? What if he had even spiked the drink he offered her? What if he *did* have sex with her and didn't use protection? What if she was pregnant?

Sierra felt panic rising in her chest at an alarming rate. She had to take several deep breaths to calm herself down. The nurse had given her a note that would excuse her absence for the rest of the school day. She decided to take a pregnancy test, as she knew that she couldn't get this dreadful suspicion out of her mind otherwise. She wanted to avoid going to the pharmacy that her family regularly used, so she walked nearly 5 miles to a pharmacy that they never went to. She was truly embarrassed to buy a pregnancy test, but she couldn't think of anyone who she could ask to purchase it for her. She circled around in the pharmacy, waiting for customers to disperse. Finally she grabbed a pregnancy test, chewing gums, nail polish, and a small bag of diapers from the shelves and approached a cashier to check out.

"Hi, how are you?" the cashier asked automatically.

"Hi," Sierra forced a smile while the cashier scanned her items. "You know, parents are so embarrassing. My parents had a baby a year ago, and my mom might be pregnant again. Kind of tacky at their age and in mine to have baby siblings," she blurted out, pointing at the diapers and pregnancy test.

The cashier looked at Sierra quizzically, but didn't utter a word.

Sierra was relieved to leave the store and released the deep breath she had been holding. She discarded the diapers and receipt a block later and sank the pregnancy test into her pocket. It had been kind of visible through the thin plastic bag. She quickly calculated that neither her parents nor Sage would be home at this time, so she hurried home to have some privacy to do the test.

As she unwrapped the pregnancy test at home and read the instructions, she was thinking that she would not have assumed to ever do a pregnancy test at 16. She had been planning on having children eventually, probably two or three, but she imagined going to college and establishing a career first and not start having children until she was at least 28, or even 30 years old. Of course, it would also depend on when she would meet the One, settle down, and get married. Becca had sometimes teased Sierra for her firm belief in the One, but Sierra was unshaken in that belief and looked forward to the day when she would meet him.

While Sierra was waiting for the test results, she was dreaming about her future life: a wonderful guy and a nice family when the time was right. When she glanced at the test and saw two lines, she couldn't fathom what her eyes communicated to her. She checked the instructions, read and re-read them several times. According to the test, two lines meant that she was pregnant, but that wasn't possible, was it?

As she bought a double pack, she wanted to do the second test immediately, but she didn't have to pee. She walked to the kitchen mechanically and drank a huge glass of water. She waited about half an hour, staring into space and intentionally not thinking about the two lines. She did the second test, moving like a robot. When the two lines emerged on the second test, too, Sierra threw it away, ran into her room and started to sob uncontrollably. It was as if a floodgate had broken, and all the panic and numbness of the last hour had tried to escape, all at once. She felt a sense of such deep despair that she had never known before. Ironically, although she had just learned that there was a child growing inside of her, she felt as if she had lost a child: herself. She had grown up in the last few minutes. She felt as if her life was suddenly over, or, if not her entire life, but as if a period of her life, childhood, had just ended.

Dread had also grabbed her throat and heart. She had never felt so scared before. What would happen now? What would happen to her? How would she tell her parents? What would happen to this baby? She couldn't quite think of it as a baby, but ultimately, that's what it was, or, at least, that's what it would or could end up being. She suddenly thought of how afraid she had used to be of the dark as a child. That fear appeared to be so trivial and so childish now. What she felt at this moment surpassed every fear that she had ever experienced. This type of darkness that now enfolded her with all its lurking shadows and unfamiliarity was much darker and much more dreadful than the literal darkness she had used to fear as a child. This was another reminder that she had abruptly left childhood behind and entered adulthood. She couldn't afford the luxury of childish fright anymore; even her fears had had to grow up and expand.

She wanted to run to her mother and cry on her shoulder, but she realized that this wasn't so simple anymore either. She would have to strategize and plan how to tell her parents. She yearned for their help, sympathy, and support, but she had no idea how they would react, and if she could actually count on them to provide what she desperately needed. She felt utterly alone and didn't know who she could turn to.

When it dawned on her what the pregnancy meant as far as Tanner was concerned, she gagged. She ran to the bathroom because she felt she would get sick. Eventually she just ended up gagging and sank down to the bathroom floor as the tide of nausea had passed. She felt extremely vulnerable and violated. Did this mean that Tanner took advantage of her? Did this mean that Tanner *raped* her? Could it even be called rape? She flirted with him, she drank, and went to the room with him. Was she just as responsible as he was then? Did she encourage him? Did she give him the green light? Was it her *fault*, at least partly? As these angst-ridden thoughts plagued her, Sierra was overwhelmed by a sense of guilt and self-blame. How could she put herself in that situation and make herself so vulnerable? She should have known better. She should have never trusted him.

For the next few hours, Sierra was overcome by a myriad of different emotions: fear, anxiety, despair, helplessness, disbelief, denial, guilt, and shame. She forced some calmness on herself before Sage and her parents came home, which took an enormous effort. She cleaned up the traces of the pregnancy tests and hid them in her backpack, wrapped in several tissues and a plastic bag. She washed her face to conceal any sign of crying. When her parents came home, she told them that she didn't feel good and was fighting a bug, and she went to bed early. She was awake for most of the night, tossing and turning and stayed home from school the next day as well.

She went to school 2 days later, determined to confront Tanner. It was extremely difficult to catch him alone, especially because he seemed to be avoiding her. She finally cornered him, and while he tried to escape, announcing that he was late for practice, she didn't let him go.

"Then you might just have to be late or miss practice," Sierra asserted. "You need to listen to me. You lied to me. You said nothing had happened at the party. That's a lie."

"No, it's not," Tanner countered. "You said you didn't remember anyway. So what's going on? Did you suddenly remember something? If you think you did, you were probably dreaming, and now you're trying to pin it on me."

"Really?" Sierra exclaimed, her voice trembling. "If you did nothing to me, how do you explain I'm pregnant?"

"You're *pregnant*?" Tanner blurted out, his eyes suddenly filled with disbelief and fear. A moment later his expression changed, and he smirked, "Do you want me to explain how you got pregnant? You really didn't get much out of sex ed, did you? You had sex, and you got pregnant. But don't blame me. I told you we didn't have sex."

"I didn't have sex with anyone," Sierra cried. "I *thought* I didn't have sex with you either. I *believed* you. How could you lie to me like that? How could you take advantage of me like that?"

"Whoa, what are you saying?" Tanner protested. "I never took advantage of you."

"Well, you must have; I wouldn't be pregnant otherwise," Sierra insisted.

"Look, I left you right there in that room," Tanner argued. "I have no idea how long you were in there. Maybe someone went in there and did something to you. But it wasn't me. There were at least 20 guys there. You can go around and start asking *them*. Good luck on that, though."

Sierra was horrified by his suggestion. Was that possible? Maybe it wasn't even Tanner? Maybe it wasn't even one guy, but who knows how many? She had to fight a strong wave of nausea and panic, and this might be a possibility she might have to consider, but she had to stick to this conversation for now and not let Tanner get off so easily.

"I guess it's very easy to tell by a paternity test," Sierra said, her voice shaking. "If you know it absolutely can't be you, you don't need to worry about a paternity test. And there *will* be a paternity test, I guarantee you. On you first, but then on all the other guys, if necessary. I didn't sleep with anyone. At least not out of my free will. If I'm pregnant, someone made me have sex, and it'll turn out who."

Tanner's face turned white. "You know, that's a pretty serious accusation. Look, you don't want to keep the baby anyway, do you? You should just have an abortion and forget about this."

"I have no idea what I'll do," Sierra declared. "But no matter what I end up doing, I can't just forget about this. I won't, either. Whatever happens, I'll figure out who the father is, and he won't get away with this. I don't expect responsibility for the baby, but there has to be responsibility for making me have sex against my will."

CHAPTER 10: "But we only did it once." Teenage Pregnancy

219

Tanner cursed for a minute, then stared at Sierra venomously, "Against your will? If that's your story and want to stick to it, I have a story and will stick to it, too. How about you forced sex on *me*? You seduced me and didn't take no for an answer. You climbed on me and didn't even let me put a condom on first. People saw us kissing and you coming in the room with me. You were asking for it. Do you think anyone would believe that you changed your mind later and didn't want it? Why else would you have come in the room with me?"

"I told you I just wanted to kiss," Sierra cried. "And I wasn't even conscious."

"Why did you drink then? And, by the way, you said you wanted to hook up, and based on the signals you were giving, you didn't mean just the kissing kind."

"I did not say that," Sierra protested.

"Well, you said you didn't remember anyway," Tanner said sarcastically. "*I do*. And how do you know I don't have video proof of what happened later? Would you like to show the whole world what a bad girl you are?"

Sierra felt exasperated and helpless. She did *not* remember what had happened. What if she *did* go along with Tanner's advances or even initiated more? She was suddenly ashamed, and while she was still very angry at Tanner, her anger shifted to herself as well. She turned her back to Tanner and walked away. She recalled how she couldn't turn her back to him at the party when he started flirting with her. That's where she should have done so. She felt desperate and confused.

She decided to turn to the school counselor. She had seen her a couple of times before when she had been battling test anxiety in school. That seemed so long ago now, and she wished for a more innocent time when test anxiety used to be her greatest concern. The counselor was a woman of incredible empathy and skill. She would know what to do. She could confirm whether what Tanner did (if it was even him) was wrong, whether it actually might have constituted rape, and if so, what course of action could be taken then. She could help her tell her parents. She could guide her through this process emotionally and logistically. Of course, the biggest issue was what to do about the baby. Sierra couldn't imagine aborting it, but she couldn't fathom keeping it and raising it either. And adoption? That seemed to be such a foreign concept as well. Either way, she was cognizant that this would be the most difficult decision she had ever had to make, and it would change her life forever.

*

Maria Symchych/Shutterstock.com

Adriana Salgado leafed through a bridal magazine, her eyes shining and her smile widening. She had been dreaming about her wedding all her life. She had been to several weddings and had served as a flower girl at a few of them. She loved weddings so much that she could even imagine becoming a wedding consultant one day. Of course, her own wedding and family would come first, but maybe one day she could help others prepare for their big day.

As she was barely 15, it hadn't been long ago that she had played bride with her siblings and cousins, putting on her First Communion dress and attaching a small lace tablecloth to her hair, pretending that it was a bridal veil. Soon, she might get married for real and become Ignacio's wife.

She had known Ignacio Cuevas practically all her life. He was best friends with one of Adriana's cousins. Although Ignacio was nearly 4 years older, they used to play together as small children. Adriana's play grooms rotated, but when she played wedding, Ignacio was one of her favorite grooms. Ignacio seemed to be into those pretend weddings as well, which he would have never admitted to Adriana's cousin and the other boys. He said he was just being nice playing with Adriana as a little girl.

About a year ago, when Adriana had turned 14, and Ignacio hadn't yet reached 18, they started dating. Their relationship began to blossom very slowly. Most of the time Adriana's parents didn't let them go on a date on their own. Either Ignacio could come to their house and hang out, while Adriana's parents and siblings were also home, or they could go on a group or double date with one of Adriana's older siblings or cousins and their significant others. So, they were seldom alone, except for a few minutes here and there. They stole some kisses, but their rare private moments were usually interrupted. They held hands and could hug without anyone raising any objections.

For a while, they didn't mind the close supervision, and Ignacio was very respectful of Adriana and her parents' rules. In a way, they didn't mind the limitations because this way they could just get to know each other even better without any potential temptations arising. They might have been young, but after about 6 months of dating both of them were sure that they wanted to get married someday.

Ignacio had dropped out of high school in the eleventh grade and started working. His family needed his income, and he could neither afford college nor did he have any ambition of obtaining a college degree, so he didn't see the point of finishing high school. He probably couldn't have acquired a better paying job even if he did. So, he had the income to potentially support a family. Yes, it was a meager income, and it couldn't provide a luxurious, or even very comfortable, lifestyle, but it could be sufficient to get by. Adriana's parents wanted her to finish high school. She preferred to do that as well, but she didn't think she could wait over 3 more years to marry Ignacio. He proposed to her on their 7-month anniversary. This was a "someday" proposal, with an unspoken agreement that it would be repeated for real when the time came, most likely in a few years. Still, he wanted to express his love and commitment, and it meant a lot to both of them that they were more or less engaged.

After about 8 months of dating Adriana started to sense a heightened level of restlessness in Ignacio. He began to work longer hours and also to work out more often. Sometimes he seemed to be avoiding Adriana, especially being alone with her. Some days he sabotaged even those few minutes that they could have had alone. After some prodding, he admitted to Adriana that he was finding it difficult to restrain himself and not initiate sex. He was 18, and hormones were raging through his body. Being so much in love didn't make it any easier for him to avoid thinking about sex. He respected Adriana, and he wanted to wait as well, obeying the teachings of their church and the morals of their families. They wanted to be married the first time they had sex. However, waiting a couple more years to tie the knot was beginning to appear more and more challenging.

Ten months after they had become a couple, Adriana and Ignacio were hanging out at one of Adriana's grown cousin's place. Adriana's cousin, Valeria, was cooking dinner and ended up accidentally cutting her finger. It was a pretty deep cut, and it seemed obvious that it would need to be stitched. Valeria's husband, Diego, decided to drive her to the emergency room. They asked Adriana and Ignacio to stay and make sure their baby, Gabriel, was okay until they got back. They didn't want to wake the baby and take him to the emergency room with them.

As Valeria and Diego hurried out of the apartment, Adriana checked on Gabriel, who was fast asleep. She had babysat him before, just as she had watched other children in her nuclear and extended family. When she returned, she found that Ignacio had moved away from the sofa, where they had been sitting together.

"What's going on? Do I have the cooties all of a sudden?" Adriana joked.

Ignacio stared at her silently, then shook his head, "No, of course not. I'd like to sit by you more than anything. That's exactly why I shouldn't. Do you realize we're all alone? This is the first time we've been alone like this."

"Oh, I guess that's true," Adriana muttered, suddenly embarrassed. "But that's okay, you can still sit by me."

Ignacio moved back on the sofa, sitting down next to her. He moved somewhat slowly and reluctantly.

"Do you want to watch a movie?" Adriana suggested.

"Sure," Ignacio sighed, relieved.

They began to watch a movie. Ignacio inched slightly closer to Adriana and put his arm on her shoulder. About 15 minutes later Adriana placed her head on his shoulder. She found his closeness intoxicating, and it was incredibly exciting to be alone with him. She planted a light kiss on his cheek. He turned his face away, then stared at her with desperate longing. His expression melted her heart, and she kissed him on the mouth. He moaned and returned the kiss with a passion that he had never allowed himself in the past. Adriana was taken aback, but thrilled at the same time. They started kissing with even more fervor, and Adriana experienced feelings that she had never known before. Ignacio finally pulled himself out of the kiss and stared at Adriana, out of breath.

"Adriana, we can't," he whispered.

"Please, Ignacio, we're not doing anything wrong," Adriana breathed. "We're just kissing. And we've never had the chance to be alone like this, and who knows when we will again. Let's just enjoy it a little bit. We'll be careful."

Ignacio gave in, and they continued where they left off. Things started to heat up with neck-breaking speed. They lost track of time and suddenly shed all reservations and teachings. One thing led to another, and before they had time to catch on and realize what was happening, everything had

CHAPTER 10: "But we only did it once." Teenage Pregnancy

223

happened. Everything that they had been discouraged from, everything that they had tried to avoid.

Afterwards they looked at each other in disbelief. It was astonishing how easy it was to be tempted and to be unable to resist. They were happy and sad at the same time. They were ecstatic to have become even closer to each other and express their love for one another in novel ways. They were also disappointed in themselves for giving in to temptation the first time they had the chance to do so. Being a few years older, Ignacio felt that he had more responsibility than Adriana.

After that day things got back to normal, and they didn't have any opportunities to be alone for more than a couple of minutes. Now that they had crossed a line and released their passion for each other, it turned out to be more difficult to go back to more innocent ways of spending time together. It wasn't just about lust either; they were also yearning for the incredible emotional closeness that they had felt in each other's arms. They both started considering marriage even more seriously than before.

About six weeks later, Adriana began to suspect that she was pregnant. She had been around so many expecting mothers before that it was easy to recognize the signs. When they were swept away by desire, they didn't think about using protection. They had been planning on abstaining, so they weren't prepared for other possibilities. Using birth control was contrary to what they had been taught anyway, and they didn't intend to use birth control once they were married.

Although Adriana was slightly scared of how their parents might react to learning that they had had premarital sex, she was so delighted about the baby that this joy surpassed any fear. She didn't mind becoming pregnant at all; she even had an inkling that subconsciously she might have wanted to get pregnant because it could help speed things up. They could soon get married and become a family instead of having to wait a few more years. It was never a question whether she would keep the baby. Abortion was unheard of in her family, and it was against her own beliefs as well.

Adriana assumed that she most likely wouldn't finish high school once the baby was born. She was slightly disappointed, but, in a way, she was looking forward to motherhood, which she considered her main desire and obligation in life. She was aware that her parents had imagined her life in a different way; that was one of the reasons for immigrating to the United States, but she simply couldn't view education as more important than family. She also knew that life wouldn't be easy; Ignacio barely made enough to support a family, but they were used to poverty anyway. Even like this, their standard of living was so much higher than it used to be.

Poverty in Guatemala versus poverty in the United States were widely different. Adriana didn't remember it because she had been under 5 years of age when they had left Guatemala, but she heard the stories from her relatives and from Ignacio as well, who had turned 9 just before his family emigrated, old enough to have memories of his own.

Ignacio was taken aback at first when he learned about the baby, "But we only did it once," he kept repeating. When he finally fathomed the news, he was ecstatic. He felt some shame, especially when he thought about telling their parents, but the dominant emotion was happiness. Beyond his love for Adriana, his sense of responsibility kicked in, and he modified his "someday proposal" right away, suggesting that they tie the knot as soon as possible. They didn't have any illusions that life would be easy, but they were convinced that all potential struggles would be mitigated by their love for each other and determination to make it work.

When they finally told Adriana's parents, her father was angry and her mother wept.

"You knew the rules," Mr. Salgado said with pursed lips, shaking his head. "You should have known better, especially you, Ignacio, you should have known better. You were supposed to respect my little girl."

"Yes, I know, sir," Ignacio responded, bowing his head in shame. "We made a mistake, and I'm sorry, but we can turn it for the better. For the best, actually. We're getting married and will have a nice family."

"We were hoping for a better life for you," Mrs. Salgado cried. "Do you know how hard this life is? You could have had so much more. You still could have had children, of course, just not so young."

"But, mami," Adriana quietly interjected. "You two got married younger. You had Felipe when you were 14. And it worked out so beautifully for you. Did you ever regret it?"

"No, not for a minute," Mrs. Salgado declared. "But it was a different time. A different country. In my village everybody got married and had children at 14 or 15. It was normal. It's different here. People will frown, people will talk; they won't like it."

"That's okay," Adriana smiled. "I don't care. I'd rather follow Guatemalan traditions than American anyway. More importantly, I'd rather follow my heart. We will be so happy, mami, you'll see."

Adriana beamed at Ignacio, who smiled back at her. She could feel love radiating from him toward her and their unborn child. In her mind she was already planning their wedding and dreaming about the incredible life they would have together. No matter what anyone might think, she was convinced that it would indeed be a beautiful life.

Discussion Questions

1. How do you think Sierra's story will end?

2. How do you envision the life of Adriana and Ignacio?

3. Discuss the role of age in the stories and teenage pregnancy in general. Do you see a difference between teenage pregnancy at the age of 12, 14, 16, and 18? Why/why not?

4. Discuss the role of culture, ethnicity, and nationality in views on teenage pregnancy, referring back to the stories as well.

5. Discuss the role of social class, socioeconomic background in teenage pregnancy.

6. What do you see as the main potential challenges and consequences of teenage pregnancy?

CHAPTER 10: "But we only did it once." Teenage Pregnancy

229

7. Do you think that there is any stigma regarding teenage pregnancy? Remember, stigma is a salient, usually enduring, negative label that is applied to individuals who do not follow social norms (Goffman, 1986). If yes, does the stigma vary by different factors (e.g., age, religion, culture) and circumstance? How so?

8. Brekhus (1996) argued that marked categories tend to be perceived as less natural or potentially more problematic than unmarked categories. Do you think that marking teenage pregnancies by placing the term "teenage" in front of them suggests that they are different from and maybe more problematic than other pregnancies? Why/why not?

9. Blumer (1969) identified three premises of symbolic interactionism. The first is that humans act toward things based on the meanings those things have for them. The second is that meanings are created through social interaction. The third is that meanings are understood and potentially transformed through an interpretative process. Apply this theory to definitions of teenage pregnancy and different approaches to it in the two stories.

10. West and Zimmerman (1987) highlighted that gender was a routine, everyday accomplishment, something that we do in interaction with others, as opposed to something that we are. Discuss a few examples of how characters in the two stories do gender.

Find the Answers

Go to http://www.cdc.gov/teenpregnancy/about/ to find answers to the following questions.

1. Have birth rates declined or increased among women aged 15–19 in the last few decades?

2. How do teenage birth rates vary by race and ethnicity?

3. What are some social and economic costs of teenage motherhood?

4. Go to the following article: http://www.who.int/maternal_child_adolescent/topics/maternal/adolescent_pregnancy/en/ How do teenage birth rates in low-income and middle-income nations compare to teen birth rates in high-income countries?

Mini Research Assignments

1. Survey at least seven individuals, asking them to rate their agreement with the following statements on a scale of 1–10 (1 meaning complete disagreement and 10 indicating full agreement): 1. "Sex between teens aged 14–16 is always wrong." 2. "Sex between teens aged 12–14 is always wrong." 3. "Teenage pregnancy has severe social, emotional, and economic costs." 4. "Teen pregnancy could easily be prevented." Summarize the results and analyze the potential role of gender, age, ethnicity, and other similar factors in the responses. Also, draw parallels with the stories.

2. Conduct a search on teenage pregnancy in other high-income countries (e.g., European countries, especially in Northern and Western Europe, Canada, countries in East Asia, such as Japan, Singapore, South Korea). Either find at least two articles on this topic or at least two brief documentaries. Another option is to work with one article and one video. Compare and contrast the two articles/videos. How are they similar and different? How does teenage pregnancy in the selected country (countries) compare to teen pregnancy in the United States? How do you explain the differences? If you find any pertinent parallels with the stories as well, discuss those, too.

3. Watch a movie and/or TV show or documentary that depicts at least one incident of teen pregnancy. How is teen pregnancy depicted? Discuss the gender, race/ethnicity, age, education, and socioeconomic background of the characters and how the story might be different if they were from a different background. Do you detect any stigma toward teenage pregnancy in the movie/TV show/documentary? Draw parallels with the two stories as well.

References

Blumer, H. (1969). *Symbolic interactionism: Perspective and method.* Englewood Cliffs, NJ: Prentice-Hall.

Brekhus, W. (1996). Social marking and the mental coloring of identity: Sexual identity construction and maintenance in the United States." *Sociological Forum, 11,* 497–522.

Goffman, E. (1986). *Stigma: Notes on the management of spoiled identity.* New York, NY: Touchstone. (Originally published 1963)

West, C., & Zimmerman, D. H. (1987). Doing gender. *Gender & Society, 1,* 125–151.

CHAPTER 11

SINGLE-PARENT FAMILIES

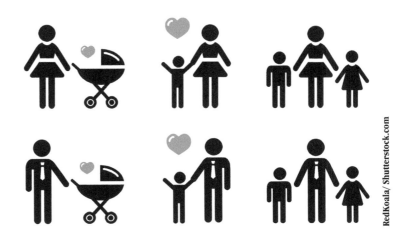

RedKoala/ Shutterstock.com

Lauren Thornton despondently stared at her divorce decree. She still couldn't fully comprehend that Daniel had really gone through with the divorce. She was hoping until the last minute that he would eventually change his mind. Sometimes he could be easily influenced, and maybe he still was in this case as well, just not by Lauren anymore.

When they had met and fallen in love, Lauren had truly believed that this marriage would last a lifetime. Her parents had divorced when she was 7 years old, and Daniel's parents had separated when he turned 18. Lauren was aware of statistics and probabilities; she knew that individuals whose parents had divorced were more likely to obtain a divorce themselves, and she was also cognizant that close to half of all marriages ended in divorce. Nevertheless, she had cherished the fervent hope that they would be the exception, that they would make it.

She and Daniel had met 8 years ago, at a party. She had been immediately drawn to him; he seemed like a very strong, capable, and intelligent man. He was also accomplished by that point. He had passed the bar and started working as a lawyer, showing incredible promise. She had just finished college, majoring in philosophy and having no idea what to do with her life, so his determination and success had really attracted her. They engaged in a deep conversation at the party, and she was delighted when he asked for her number. She didn't hesitate to give it to him and was looking forward to continuing what they had started at the party.

The next day someone told Lauren that Daniel had a girlfriend. She was considerably disappointed, but firm in her decision not to get involved with him then. She even told him that much when he called her 2 days later. He explained that he and his girlfriend had been going through a rough time and were on the brink of a breakup. Lauren asserted that she wasn't willing to see him until he was completely free and available. She didn't hear from him for 3 weeks after this phone call, and she was about to give up on him and move on. Then, one day he called and informed her that he had ended his relationship and wanted to see her. She was slightly hesitant at first, but was finally convinced that he was telling the truth. She felt somewhat guilty and sorry for his girlfriend, but was hoping that they had really not been doing well, and she had been just as ready to move on as he.

Lauren's excitement soon surpassed any other feelings she might have been harboring, and she enthusiastically jumped into a relationship with Daniel. She fell in love with him almost instantly and realized that she had never been so much in love before. She was soon convinced that they were meant for each other. He asked her to move into his condo 5 months later and proposed to her on their 2-year anniversary. Their wedding day was the happiest day of her life, and she could hardly believe that a person's heart could contain so much love and bliss.

Noah was born 3 days after their first wedding anniversary, and Lauren's happiness reached even more unexpected heights as they became a family. Noah wasn't an easy baby; he often had trouble sleeping, and he was also frequently sick in the first year of his life. Daniel was working a lot, but he was usually home for a late dinner and to put Noah to bed together. Some days he managed to make it home by Noah's evening bath, and he gave him his bath those days. They could spend more time together on the weekends and did their best to do something memorable every weekend, such as going to the zoo, to a park, or to the playground.

Lauren was always exhausted, and taking care of Noah tended to absorb all her energy. She didn't pay too much attention to her appearance, and she seemed to have given up any ambition to find a career that suited her. She felt that she had found her calling by motherhood. She thought that she might work once Noah was in school, but probably not before that. They didn't particularly need the money; Daniel could support them and provide a very comfortable lifestyle.

Lauren had been dreaming about another baby since Noah had turned 3, but Daniel argued at the time that they should wait. She wasn't very keen on waiting, but respected his wishes. In the 2 years that had passed since then, she had brought up the idea a couple more times, but she didn't want

to push Daniel. By the time Noah had turned 5, Lauren felt she couldn't wait any longer, and the day after Noah's fifth birthday she communicated to Daniel that she really wanted a baby, and they should get started on it. Daniel stared at her for a few minutes, and he seemed immensely sad. She began to prepare herself for him admitting that he didn't want a second child, but she wasn't prepared for what he ended up saying next. He told her that he had been having an affair for about a year, that he was in love with the woman and wanted a divorce.

This had happened 5 months ago, and even with the divorce being final, Lauren still couldn't believe that it was happening. She was partly in denial. Other times she blamed herself; she had to admit that she had been very preoccupied with Noah and let herself go. There were also days, though, when she blamed Daniel and was extremely angry at him. Then, she was suddenly dejected and simply very sad. The lowest blow was when she learned that Daniel's girlfriend was pregnant, and they were getting married soon after the divorce was final. She felt as if the woman had taken her place and were living her life. She should have been the one expecting a child with Daniel.

As the emotional part of the divorce had struck her really hard, she didn't deal with other implications of their separation for a while. Then, one night she woke up covered in sweat, panicking about the future. She didn't have a job; she didn't have a career or even good prospects for a job. How would she support Noah? Would they need to sell the house? Would

CHAPTER 11: "We all need two parents. Or don't we?" Single-Parent Families

237

they need to move? Would she have to start working right away? What could she even do with her degree in philosophy? How much could she even earn? Who would take care of Noah while she worked? How would Noah endure his father's absence? And would his life change in other ways as well? And if yes, how would he deal with that?

Lauren called Daniel the next day, who reassured her that he would continue taking care of them. He offered that he wouldn't sell the house; Lauren and Noah could stay and live there for 3 years so that Noah didn't have to lose his home in addition to his father. After that, he would sell it, but give 60% of the money to Lauren and Noah, which could be sufficient to buy a small, but comfortable place in a good neighborhood. He would even pay 70% of the bills and utilities for 3 years. Lauren could also keep her minivan that she used to drive Noah to preschool and for other purposes. Daniel agreed to pay not only a generous child support, but also alimony for 3 years. This way, Lauren would have 3 years to figure out what she wanted to do for a career. She could even go back to school and obtain another degree, at least an associate's level or some kind of certificate. Daniel would continue to pay for Noah's private preschool so that he didn't have to change schools.

Lauren was relieved that at least she didn't have to worry about their home, finances, and Noah's future. She couldn't have imagined having to deal with all of that in addition to everything else. It was already difficult enough. She was almost grateful to Daniel for his generosity, but then she reminded herself that he had still cheated on her and had left her and Noah.

Noah had some trouble with the transition. He missed his father and yearned to spend more time with him. He was angry at Daniel's girlfriend, subconsciously sensing that she had something to do with his parents separating. Sometimes he was also mad at Daniel, and even more so Lauren, blaming her that she had driven Daniel away. Noah had overheard Lauren screaming and yelling at Daniel to go away after Daniel had admitted the affair. Noah didn't understand the context, of course, but when he heard his mom being so upset, he thought that Lauren was the one to have sent Daniel away.

Noah had been a poor sleeper as a baby, but for years he had been sleeping relatively well. However, his sleep troubles returned now. He was also often short with Lauren and threw some tantrums. A few of his preschool teachers also complained that he acted up in school. Lauren struggled with him and was helpless in terms of what to do and how to help him. As Daniel only spent Sundays with Noah, and he was more or less calm then, although sometimes mean with his girlfriend, he didn't notice Noah's problems so much and accused Lauren of exaggerating them.

Lauren once thought she had been primarily the one raising Noah. She just realized how wrong she had been and how big of a role Daniel had actually had in Noah's upbringing. He often used to give him his bath, play with him, read to him, and drive him to some extracurricular activities. Also, he had handled the bills, taken out the trash, mowed the lawn, grilled meat for dinner on occasion, and vacuumed the rugs. Lauren was surprised to find how incredibly difficult it was to do everything on her own. And she wasn't working outside of the home. She could hardly imagine how hard it would get when she would begin to work, too. Sometimes she almost hated Daniel not only for leaving them, but leaving her *alone* with Noah and everything.

Lauren still had no idea what to do with her life, but she knew she had to figure it out soon. Yes, she had 3 years, but even that could pass relatively fast, so she needed to act. At least she needed to think about what steps she would take, or even where to begin. While she was still grieving losing Daniel and couldn't imagine being with someone else, she was also aware that she was young and the type who didn't like being single and alone. She would eventually start dating and want to find someone, maybe even remarry. Of course, it might not be easy, especially because she would have to look not only for a husband for herself, but a good stepfather for Noah. These prospects scared her at the moment, but she suspected that they would eventually come. She viewed being a single parent as a temporary state, not a permanent condition.

Lydia Burns couldn't stifle a yawn. She had been used to feeling exhausted and sleeping no more than 4 or 5 hours a day, but today she found it especially arduous to stay awake and be productive. She had an hour until her children would come home from school, and she still had a lot to do around the house. She ran another load of laundry and washed the dishes. There was no dishwasher in the apartment, and hand-washing dishes seemed to take forever sometimes. Both laundry and dishwashing were never-ending tasks at their household of four.

She heard a sound, which sounded like a faint shot. She ran to the window, but couldn't see anything unusual. As the noise appeared to have come from far away, she wouldn't be able to identify the source anyway. Nevertheless, the constant worry that she felt about her kids grabbed her throat. She was aware that their neighborhood wasn't very safe, at least it was relatively close to an infamously unsafe area. This particular neighborhood wasn't immensely crime-ridden, but its proximity to the one that was tended to scare her. She was somewhat used to it by now, and as she didn't have a choice because she couldn't afford another place, she had to make peace with their surroundings, and the only thing she could do was pray for the safety of her children. The area could be especially dangerous for her sons, Anthony and Brandon, but she reassured herself that they would be fine.

Brandon was still young enough at 10, but at 13, Lydia knew that Anthony could be exposed to numerous potential dangers, including violence, guns, gangs, and drugs. She tried to involve them in church activities to provide positive role models and productive activities. Anthony had become less interested in church lately and more restless and impatient. Lydia hoped it was due to adolescence and hormonal changes, but her ex-husband, Rick, set a bad example that haunted her sometimes. She wanted her sons to avoid his fate.

Rick got involved with drugs relatively young, but when they got together and decided to create a family, he swore to have given them up. It lasted for a while, but eventually he reconnected with his old buddies and was tempted by drugs again. He could resist at first, but not very long. Besides using, he started dealing as well. He kept it a secret, but Lydia began to suspect it when they suddenly had more money than before. Not that it lasted long because Rick usually ended up squandering it on drugs. Lydia considered leaving him, but was scared and didn't know where else they could go. She worked part-time then, and wouldn't have been able to support their three kids on her own.

Rick was finally caught, arrested, and sentenced to prison. That was the last straw, and Lydia was determined to divorce him. The cost of the divorce seemed almost insurmountable to her at the time, but she was firm to separate from him and try to provide a better life and example for her children. She would have preferred to move as well, but while she could move to a different apartment, she couldn't afford to relocate to another neighborhood.

She turned her part-time job to a full-time one. She worked as a janitor, cleaning office buildings at night. The job didn't pay very well, but she wasn't qualified and didn't have the experience for a different type of job. The hours also worked for her because this way she didn't have to pay for a babysitter while she worked as the children were sleeping. At first, she was concerned to leave them home alone, but she didn't have a choice. Paying for a babysitter would have cost more or just as much as she was making at this job. At the time, Anthony was 11, Brandon 8, and Jade 7. They all slept very soundly and hardly noticed that she wasn't there at night. Still, she incessantly felt guilty for leaving them alone.

The apartment itself was relatively safe; being out in the streets in the afternoon or at night was more unsafe. Working at night she could be there when her children woke up and went to school and also when they got back from school in the afternoon. She could watch them more closely and ensure that they weren't wandering around the streets, potentially mixing with bad company. This meant that she could only sleep while they were at school, and not the whole time either because that was the only time to do household chores or run errands.

This way, she was at home and available to help with schoolwork as well. Not that she could be of great assistance; her relatively limited schooling prevented her from always being able to help with homework. She wished her children could attend a better school, because the public schools in the neighborhood were underperforming, but she could never afford a private school. She heard that the high school had especially poor performance, and less than half of the students graduated. She knew that education could be the key to a promising future for her children and was worried that these neighborhood schools wouldn't be able to do the job. She would never even dream of a college education for them, but at least a high school diploma could provide a more or less secure future.

Lydia earned a few cents more than minimum wage, and with full-time work and three dependents that put her under the poverty line. She was eligible for some government assistance. At first, she was ashamed to use it, but she soon changed her mind, as there was absolutely no way they could have survived otherwise. Her pride could never overshadow her concern and love for her children.

Even with her wages and the benefits that she received, their family was struggling. Although Rick had been making only slightly more than the minimum wage—before dealing—and she had been working part time, the two incomes made a huge difference. One minimum-wage income was not sufficient to support a family of four with three children, no matter how much she tried to stretch the budget.

Lydia became extremely efficient in finding and using coupons, discounts, and sales. Unfortunately, she couldn't go to the grocery stores that offered even more discounts and a wider variety of products because it was impossible without a car. She usually purchased the cheapest groceries, and even then, sometimes she, herself, had to run on one or two meals per day to ensure that the kids were fed three times a day. They ate fruit or vegetables maybe once a week, as they were the most expensive types of food.

Malnutrition, exhaustion, and stress put an incredible strain on Lydia's body, and her health was beginning to deteriorate. She became pre-diabetic, and if it turned into full-blown diabetes, she would be in trouble. She had no idea how she could take care of herself then and afford medication. They didn't have health insurance, and a medical bill, even a relatively small one, could potentially bankrupt them. When Brandon had broken his arm a year ago, the cost had nearly ruined them. Lydia constantly prayed that nothing happened to either her or the children. A tooth had been giving her some pain in the last few months, but a dentist was absolutely out of the question. If the pain persisted, she might have to figure out how to pull the tooth herself. Maybe a neighbor could assist.

To save water, the four of them generally used the same bathwater to take a bath. She needed to do laundry, especially because they hardly had any clothes, and the boys' clothes got dirty so rapidly. They did not have a computer, only a small, old TV with a few channels, and they saved on the lights, but because the apartment was so energy inefficient the power bill tended to be costly.

Brandon and Jade were so sweet and rarely complained, but Anthony had started to rumble more about their situation in the last 6 months or so. This was the main reason why Lydia was concerned that he might eventually turn to a more profitable, albeit illicit, source of income. He was doing poorly in school as well, not because he was unable to excel, but because he seemed to have lost motivation.

Lydia wished to be able to offer a respectable male role model for her children, especially Anthony, who seemed to be needing it the most. Brandon would also soon reach the age when he might miss a male role model. Church members appeared to help somewhat, but a male in the house would be even more beneficial. However, what mattered the most was what kind of role model that male could provide. Lydia had lost trust in men after the disappointment she had experienced with Rick. Most of the men that she encountered were similar to Rick. Finding someone at church could be a feasible option, but it was a small church, and all the men around her age were married. She knew that a man could be helpful not only for her children, but her as well. It would be immensely relieving to be able to share the emotional, physical, and financial burdens of child-rearing.

Lydia's father had been a great man whom she admired, but he died when she was 9 years old. Her mother raised Lydia and her three siblings on her own, with some help from her own mother. Lydia witnessed the struggles of her mother as a single parent and vowed at the time to try to avoid a similar situation. Life got in the way, and this didn't work out for her. She found herself as a single parent, and in some ways, her circumstances were even more arduous than her mother's had been. Her mother at least had her own mother, who could help some financially and by babysitting Lydia and her siblings. Lydia wished her mother were still alive, as she knew she would be more than happy to help her with the children. Unfortunately, she had passed away a year after Anthony had been born.

Lydia's siblings had their own struggles; they were plagued by divorces, illness, disability, financial and mental troubles, so she couldn't count on them. In fact, sometimes she was the one who needed to help them. She didn't have time to maintain friendships, even though she was aware that friends could offer some emotional, and maybe even physical, assistance.

She didn't trust most of the neighbors, but there was one elderly woman, Mrs. Washington, who could occasionally babysit the kids and provide Lydia with some beneficial advice. Unfortunately, she had been battling some health issues lately, so she was rarely available to help out. Lydia got her some groceries sometimes when she had the time. Mrs. Washington used to be able to even lend Lydia some money when she really needed it, but she wasn't able to do that anymore. In fact, she tended to need loans. Lydia felt guilty, but she couldn't help her with money, as she was struggling, too.

Coming home from school, Jade complained of a sore throat and ran a very high fever. Lydia tried everything to bring the fever down, but nothing helped. She eventually realized that Jade needed a doctor. Her stomach churned at the thought of the cost, but she couldn't risk her daughter getting worse. She hoped that she might be able to obtain a discount once she got the bill, considering her vulnerable financial state.

She was reluctant to call in sick at work for fear of putting her job in jeopardy. She already missed a few days from work in the last couple of months when the kids were sick, and her boss had told her that she couldn't miss any more this year. She was hoping that he would understand the situation and give her a pass. That didn't happen; her boss was furious and ended up firing her. Lydia briefly considered begging him to take her back and going to work after all. Maybe Jade could wait to be seen by a doctor until the morning. However, glancing at her face and feeling her extreme fever convinced Lydia that it wasn't the case. She couldn't go to work, even if that meant losing her job.

She was extremely worried about Jade. She was also plagued by anxiety about how they would get by if she was unemployed, even just for a few weeks. She trusted to find a similar job, but even then, the same situation could occur. Her children had to come first, and if anything happened to them, she would have to miss work. She wished that she could acquire a certificate or training for a better, more flexible, and higher paying job. However, how would she ever have the money for education? How could she even attend school? She felt trapped because the only experience she had was as a janitor; she most likely couldn't get another type of job, especially when she didn't have the resources to train herself in another area. She still had some hope for the future, especially for her kids' future, but she was aware that even if there was a road leading to better prospects, it wouldn't be devoid of hardship.

*

Grant Brewster sat down at his kitchen table, slowly gulping coffee. It was his fourth cup today, but he was used to drinking large quantities of coffee. As a single father, working full time, he didn't get a lot of sleep. His daughter, Abbie, ran into the kitchen and popped herself on one of the bar stools. He preferred her to sit on one of the chairs at the kitchen table, but she just loved the bar stools. It used to be more of a problem in the past; she was old enough now not to fall. Abbie could be stubborn sometimes, and Grant learned to choose his battles. The bar stool might have been a priority when Abbie was under 5 years of age, but at 8 it wasn't anymore.

"Hey, daddy," Abbie exclaimed. She tended to speak loud, full of enthusiasm or outrage, depending on the situation. "Guess, what? Ms. Jablonsky assigned us an essay today. We have to write about why our mom is the best mom. How do I do that? It's so annoying. Why do people think that everyone has a mom? And that everyone has a great mom, one who's the best? I think I'll just change the title and write about you."

Grant sighed. He understood Abbie's dilemma, and his heart ached for her. She didn't have the best mom; that was undeniable. He had met Abbie's mom, Kelly, 10 years ago. They had fallen in love almost instantly and decided to get married and start a family soon after. Kelly had had some doubts, as she had been young and had cherished dreams to become a dancer. She was worried that pregnancy could ruin her figure, and a child could destroy her career, but she was so much in love that she went along with the plan. Grant realized now that he might have pushed her. He was over 30 and ready, and while he suspected that Kelly wasn't, he chose to not see it.

When Kelly got pregnant, Grant was over the moon. She was fine with it at first, too, but began to panic when her belly started to grow and she had to stop dancing. She dieted in secret, not admitting to Grant that she was terrified of gaining too much weight and not being able to lose it after the pregnancy. Grant became suspicious when she stopped gaining weight and even lost some, but Kelly denied dieting. She ended up giving birth at 7 months, and the baby was premature and underweight. The doctors told Grant that Kelly's dieting might have played a role in it. It soon turned out that Abbie had a mild case of cerebral palsy, too, a condition affecting muscle tone, movement, and motor skills.

When Kelly learned about cerebral palsy, her face froze with utter terror. She was a perfectionist, and as a dancer, perfect movement was especially crucial for her. She soon told Grant that she couldn't deal with a child who wasn't perfect. She already had doubts about having a child, but if she wasn't perfectly healthy, she couldn't handle it. Grant couldn't believe his ears, and it was the moment when he had forever fallen out of love with Kelly. For him, Abbie was perfect, no matter what.

Before Abbie turned 1 month old, Kelly had moved out. She regained her figure and stamina very quickly and could continue dancing. Grant found himself alone with Abbie. He had never planned on becoming a single father, and the task suddenly seemed daunting. His mother lived about 3 hours away, so she couldn't come and help all the time. She did her best, but Grant still needed to handle everyday tasks on his own. In the first few weeks he hired a baby nurse to show him the ins and outs of infant care. He quickly learned everything that needed to be done around a baby, and he managed acceptably. He wished he could afford the baby nurse for a longer period of time, but even those few weeks put a strain on his budget.

Grant was making a living as a musician, and sometimes he had acquired moderate success, other times he was struggling. When Kelly left them, he was torn because he needed to be with Abbie, but, at the same time, they would have needed the money that he could earn pursuing his career. He ended up turning down some gigs, and his career started to suffer. He didn't care about fame anymore, but he cared about being able to support his daughter. He began to work as a bartender, which he had had some experience in before his career in the music industry. He still took some gigs when he had the time and a babysitter. He didn't entirely give up his dreams of becoming a successful musician, but those dreams had to wait now.

A secure job and health insurance became extremely important, especially because Abbie needed regular medical care. She had to go to frequent

Maria Symchych/ Shutterstock.com

physical therapy for the first few years of her life. As her cerebral palsy was relatively mild, and physical therapy really helped, there were hardly any noticeable signs of her condition now. All the time and money they had invested into physical therapy truly paid off.

Grant was very proud of Abbie and the beautiful girl she had become, not only on the outside, but on the inside as well. Luckily, she had a bigger heart than her mother. In fact, she instinctively stood up for anything or anyone who appeared to need help. She was gentle with animals and a great proponent of animal rights. She had many friends, and she would have given anything for them. She showed incredible empathy anytime someone she loved, or even somebody she didn't even know, was hurt or suffering. As far as Grant knew, Kelly was a relatively successful dancer by now, and he found it sad that she had no idea that her biggest contribution to the world wasn't her career, but Abbie, who would leave an indelible mark in this world, he had no doubt of that.

After Abbie didn't require care practically every moment of the day, and Grant had some time to notice the world beyond the two of them, he realized how much recognition and attention he got as a single father. Abbie's physical therapists, teachers, mothers of kids in her kindergarten, preschool, and school, and even strangers expressed their admiration for Grant. He was delighted to hear their compliments, but knew that he didn't do more than what millions of single mothers around the world did every day. Yes, the responsibility and time investment were huge when only one parent was present, but it wasn't any less in the case of single mothers. He found it unfair that he got more recognition than single mothers for doing the same. He suspected that actually he might have been offered more assistance than single mothers. Sometimes he got home-cooked meals from random acquaintances, as well as offers to babysit.

It surprised him how often he got longing stares and date invites from women. Abbie turned out to be a magnet to attract women, or the attraction might have stemmed from his status as a single father. He rejected most offers for a long time, except for a few brief affairs when he was very lonely. He didn't even introduce those women to Abbie. He wanted to provide stability for her and make her his priority, so finding and maintaining a serious relationship would have been a challenge. His short marriage with Kelly didn't leave him unscathed either. The only female he was interested in was his daughter.

In the last few years his friends and their wives had become more aggressive sending blind dates his way. They thought that it was time that he started dating more seriously. He rejected most offers, but there were a couple that he couldn't turn down. He noticed that he began to scrutinize women based on their mother potential. A beautiful face or figure couldn't excite him for more than a few seconds or minutes; he really paid attention when a woman turned out to be very nurturing, motherly, especially if she had a child or children of her own. He almost started dating a woman that he wasn't attracted to, just because of her motherly potential. Then he realized that it wouldn't be fair to the woman, or even himself if he built a relationship on those grounds.

Abbie seemed to be perfectly satisfied with not having a mother in her life, but Grant knew better what she was missing. He hoped to be able to provide a mother for her eventually. When Abbie was done with her essay, and Grant read it, he was immensely moved by the love and profoundness of her work. His heart burst with pride, and he was relieved to conclude that he might really do a good job with Abbie, and she wasn't suffering due to the lack of a mother. He used to think that we all needed two parents. Or didn't we? Her essay read like this:

"Why my dad is the best dad and mom,

I decided to change the title because I don't officially have a mom. I don't know her, and she's not the best mom. Not every mom is the best mom, but that's okay. That's why we have dads, too. Let's not forget about the dads. They do a great job, at least some of them do, like my dad.

My dad does all the things dads do in my friends' families. He's strong, and he can chase away anything or anyone scary. I feel safe with him. He works, earns money, and takes care of us. He pays the bills and can fix our car or anything around the house. He likes football and baseball. He kind of likes all sports. He watches many games on TV, and I usually watch them with him.

My dad is also the best mom I could wish for. I don't think someone has to be a woman to be a mom. My dad is a good mom as a guy. He is there and calms me when I'm sad or cry. He cooks yummy food. He does my hair. He plays with Barbies with me. He shops for clothes with me. He takes care of me when I'm sick. He takes care of me all the time. I couldn't wish for a better dad. And mom. I'm glad to have him."

Discussion Questions

1. What do you think comes next in each story? How do you envision the future for each of the three families?

2. Discuss the role of gender in single parenthood. Do you see any difference between single mothers and single fathers? Why/why not?

3. Discuss the role of social class/socioeconomic background in single parenthood. What is the impact of social class? Compare and contrast the stories.

4. What is the relationship between poverty, gender, and single parenthood?

5. Many people in the United States struggle with numerous aspects of poverty, even if they work full time, earning minimum wage (Ehrenreich, 2011; Shipler, 2005). Illustrate this through Lydia's story.

6. A sizable portion of low-income women in urban neighborhoods place children before marriage. They might have a high respect for marriage, but they might not see it feasible to find an eligible, honorable man in their neighborhood. As having children is an absolute priority, many of these women bear and/or raise children on their own. Children bring a sense of accomplishment and social status for them (Edin & Kefalas, 2011). Draw parallels with Lydia's story.

7. Lumping is focusing on similarities between certain groups and discarding their potential differences, whereas splitting is concentrating on, or even exaggerating, differences between certain groups (Zerubavel, 1991, 1996). Do most people tend to do more lumping or splitting in terms of single parenting? For instance, are single mothers and single fathers generally lumped together, or are there mechanisms of splitting between them? Are single parents usually lumped together or split from two-parent households? Draw parallels with the stories as well.

8. West and Zimmerman (1987) argued that gender was a routine, everyday accomplishment. It is something that we do in interaction with others, as opposed to something that we are. Discuss a few examples of how characters in the stories *do gender,* and how doing gender can be independent of biological sex (e.g., how a male can do femininity in terms of parenting, or vice versa).Brekhus (1996) contended that marked categories tend to be perceived as less natural or potentially more problematic than unmarked categories. Do you think that marking single parenthood by placing the term "single" in front of it suggests that single parenting is different from and maybe more problematic than other forms of parenting? Why/why not?

9. Brekhus (1996) contended that marked categories tend to be perceived as less natural or potentially more problematic than unmarked categories. Do you think that marking single parenthood by placing the term "single" in front of it suggests that single parenting is different from and maybe more problematic than other forms of parenting? Why/why not?

Find the Answers

Go to http://www.childtrends.org/?indicators=family-structure to find answers to the following questions.

1. How have the living arrangements of children under 18 changed since the 1970s?

2. How common are mother-only families compared to father-only families?

3. How do living arrangements for children under age 18 vary by race and Hispanic origin?

4. What are some of the characteristics of children in cohabiting (unmarried) families?

★ Mini Research Assignments ★

1. Survey at least seven individuals, asking them to rate their agreement with the following statements on a scale of 1–10 (1 meaning complete disagreement and 10 indicating full agreement): 1. "Single-parent families tend to have more struggles than two-parent families." 2. "There are significant differences between single-mother families and single-father families." 3. "Single parenthood is only problematic if it's combined with poverty." Summarize the results and analyze the potential role of gender, age, marital status, and other similar factors in the responses. Also, draw parallels with the stories.

2. Go to the following site: http://playspent.org/
   Play the game until the end. Discuss the outcome and the most difficult decisions you had to face during the game. What made them so difficult? What have you learned from the game? Also, analyze the combined impact of poverty and single parenthood. Draw parallels with the stories as well.

3. Watch a movie and/or TV show or documentary that depicts at least one incident of single parenthood. How is single parenthood depicted? Discuss the gender, race/ethnicity, age, education, and socioeconomic background of the characters and how the story might be different if they were from a different background. Do you detect any stigma toward single parenthood in the movie/TV show/documentary? Draw parallels with the three stories as well.

4. Run a search online on stepfamilies/blended families. Read at least three articles or thoroughly study at least two pertinent websites. Summarize the statistics, trends, and issues related to stepfamilies/blended families and compare them with single-parent families. Draw parallels with the stories as well, speculating what could happen if either family became a stepfamily/blended family.

References

Brekhus, W. (1996). Social marking and the mental coloring of identity: Sexual identity construction and maintenance in the United States." *Sociological Forum, 11,* 497–522.

Edin, K., & Kefalas, M. J. (2011). *Promises I can keep: Why poor women put motherhood before marriage.* Oakland, CA: University of California Press.

Ehrenreich, B. (2012). *Nickel and dimed: On (not) getting by in America.* New York, NY: Picador.

Shipler, D. K. (2012). *The working poor: Invisible in America.* New York, NY: Vintage.

West, C., & Zimmerman, D. H. (1987). Doing gender. *Gender & Society, 1,* 125–151.

Zerubavel, E. (1991). *The fine line: Making distinctions in everyday life.* New York, NY: Free Press.

_____. (1996). Lumping and splitting: Notes on social classification. *Sociological Forum, 11,* 421–433.

CHAPTER

"Second shift, third shift, and more? Yes, I can do it all."
WORKING WOMEN WITH CHILDREN

Macrovector/ Shutterstock.com

Sidney Fuller was driving home from work, glancing at her watch nervously and pushing the gas even more. If she hurried, she would be home before 6 p.m. and be able to make dinner before her family got too ravenous. She suddenly realized that they were out of milk, bread, and juice, so she had to stop at a grocery store to grab those items. She was practically running through the store, checking her watch a few more times. She thought that this rush could also be counted as exercise, especially because this was the only exercise she would get today.

She was out of the store in under 10 minutes and back on the road, accelerating toward home. She really had to pee, but she didn't want to waste time in the store, although she knew that it would still have to wait when she got home. As she walked through the door, her 5-year-old, Finn, and her 13-month-old, Freya, ran to her and hugged her legs. Finn started to talk about his day in preschool with full volume and abundant detail. Freya began to cry and lifted her tiny arms to signal that she wanted to be picked up. Sidney kicked off her shoes, stroked Finn's head, scooped Freya up, and paid Anna, the babysitter, with her one free hand. Sidney

Renaud Thomas/Shutterstock.com

was informed that Finn ate a little bit too much sugar, so he might be slightly hyper, and Freya was somewhat fussy all afternoon. Sidney was extremely grateful to Anna for all her work, but still gulped as she paid her approximately 25% of what she made that day. Yes, 75% was still left, and Sidney was aware that other working mothers spent even greater portions of their salary on childcare, but it was still a sizable sum.

With Finn and Freya in tow, Sidney walked into the master bedroom and changed to more comfortable clothes, which reminded her that she had to do laundry. She threw some clothes into the washer, cradling Freya in one arm, who asked to be picked up again. Sidney started dinner, but the process was interrupted by Freya's cries and signals that she wanted to be in Sidney's arms. Sidney tried to put her down several times to wash and cut some chicken meat for dinner, but as Freya loudly protested, she had to wash her hands after handling raw meat and pick her daughter up again and again. She asked Finn to entertain Freya for a while, but it didn't work for longer than a couple of minutes, especially because Finn was also too active and running around. Finally, the chicken was cooking, and Sidney put together a quick salad. She even had time to go to the bathroom now.

She had been planning on cooking and blending something fresh for Freya, but she realized there was no time for that, especially with her being so fussy. Sidney took a jar of baby food from the pantry, deciding that this would be Freya's dinner. Her stomach was squeezed by a wave of familiar guilt. She had been determined to give Freya fresh, homemade food at least 6 days a week, but she had to settle for a jar of baby food the second day in a row. She silently vowed to cook and blend her something for tomorrow after both of the kids were in bed. She inadvertently glanced at the ingredient list on the jar, and she was almost overwhelmed by another wave of guilt. Although this was a relatively healthy and expensive brand of baby food, it still contained some questionable ingredients. This was one of the main reasons why Sidney had intended to give Freya home-cooked meals in the first place, but she didn't have a choice now.

Sidney fed Freya the baby food, while she was singing some educational songs with Finn. Although he attended a relatively respectable preschool, Sidney noticed some gaps in his education, which she tried to fill. The only problem was that she rarely had time to focus on his educational activities only; usually they had to be done while she was paying attention to something else as well. Multitasking had become her forte, and she smiled as she recalled having included on her resume when she had been looking for her first job how skilled she had been in multitasking. She had had no idea then how much more gifted she would become in it after years of work and having children.

By the time Freya had been fed and several songs had been sung with Finn, dinner was ready, although slightly overcooked, and Sidney's husband, Tom, arrived as well. He worked even longer hours than her, and today was actually a day when he came home relatively early at 6:45 p.m. They ate dinner together, while Finn was talking incessantly about his day in preschool. Halfway through dinner Freya needed to be picked up again, so Sidney ate the rest of her dinner with Freya in her lap. At least she was more or less calm when being held.

After dinner Tom gave both kids a bath at the same time, and Sidney cleaned up leftovers and the dishes. She was seriously tempted to sit down as she caught a glimpse of the super-comfortable couch in the living room, but she was afraid she wouldn't be able to get up then, and she would have to clean up even later in the evening. When they had purchased the couch with Tom, they had dreamed about spending long lazy hours lounging there. However, with life running at full speed, they rarely had even some lazy minutes, let alone hours.

Finn begged after his bath to watch an episode of his favorite TV show online. Sidney didn't like him to watch TV every day, but she was too tired to protest. One episode wouldn't hurt him, and at least he would be quiet for half an hour. She took Freya to her room and read her a story. Freya loved to look at the pictures and play with the foldouts in the book. After the story Sidney breastfed her. She still breastfed her twice a day, in the evening and at night when she woke up. She had read so much about the benefits of breastfeeding, and it really calmed Freya, too. Sidney noticed that she was starting to have less milk, and it scared her because she didn't think that Freya would be ready to give up breastfeeding soon. Sidney had been able to breastfeed Finn until he was 17 months, so she hoped she would be able to do the same with her daughter.

Freya took a while to fall asleep. When she finally did, Sidney read Finn a story and put him to sleep. She was about to sink down on the couch, next to Tom, when she thought of the laundry. She still had to put the clothes in the drier. She also realized that she had to do some ironing, so she grabbed the clothes, iron, and ironing board, and set it up in the living room. She and Tom discussed their day while she was ironing, and he was watching the news, but not listening to them. Sidney sometimes missed the long hours of talking they had shared before they had children. She wouldn't have exchanged them for the kids, of course, but occasionally she just yearned for Tom, the husband. She saw him mostly as a father, being with the kids, and they didn't have too much time alone, as husband and wife.

When done with the ironing, Sidney curled next to Tom on the couch. They whispered quietly for about 10 minutes, until Sidney fell asleep. Tom gently woke her later, and they went to bed. Sidney had been planning on washing her hair and applying a face mask that evening, but she was too tired and even forgot. She just took a brief shower the next morning. She didn't wash her hair; she put it up in a bun, and it still looked acceptable. She knew that she paid hardly any attention to her looks. She tried to compensate for her hair and chipped nail polish with putting on nice clothes and some quick makeup. She didn't look bad, but she didn't *feel* beautiful. She also realized that she had fallen asleep last night, again, without making love to Tom, or even kissing him goodnight. She swore to wash her hair, throw on a baby-doll, and seduce him tonight. She felt almost ashamed to recognize that she simply put love-making on her mental to-do list, like any other activity or duty. She didn't view it that way; in fact, she often felt a desire for it, but she usually dreamed about it during the day, when she was more active and awake, and exhaustion might have prevented her from realizing those dreams by the time she was actually in the same room with Tom, and the kids were asleep. They still made love about once a week, but it was a little bit less than either of them would have desired.

It also occurred to Sidney that she had been meaning to get up early and exercise before her family was up. She managed to do so about once or twice a week. At least they biked together during the weekends, so that partly met her target dose of exercise, and it was a fun family activity as well. Tom tended to have to go to work earlier than Sidney, so she handled the children partly alone in the morning. Anna came to take care of Freya during the day, and Sidney drove Finn to preschool. Anna did some light cooking and housework, but they would need to pay her more to do more, so Sidney did most of the chores around the house. Tom took out the trash and completed yardwork.

Sidney sometimes felt that her work was never done. She worked at her job during the day, then she came home and continued working. Taking care of the children and the house occupied most of her evenings and part of her weekends. She had already relaxed her standards of cleanliness because she would have to clean all the time otherwise, and she preferred to spend some of that time with her family. She worked so much, but she still tended to feel that she was lacking in every area. She knew she could have a cleaner house.

She could spend more quality time with the children, and she could teach them even more. She could be more patient with them. She could be more consistent with them. She could also be a better wife. Sometimes she hardly listened to Tom, or even fell asleep while he was talking. She used to give him small surprises; now the surprise was if she occasionally still did so.

Guilt had become one of the most familiar and pervasive feelings she experienced. She might have been a perfectionist, but she definitely rarely met her own standards. While she had learned to manage guilt about keeping a messier house and postponing errands indefinitely, she couldn't brush aside guilt when she failed her children or Tom. Hopefully they didn't experience it as a failure, but she did. She also felt that she was in a hurry all the time. She had learned to do things more rapidly, which often made her irritable and impatient because it wasn't her own, comfortable pace. She seemed to rush from someplace to somewhere else all the time, frequently being late. Not too late, just a few minutes, but it still bothered her.

Dealing with the unexpected was also difficult. An illness, whether it was hers or one of the kid's, threw off her schedule. She didn't really have time for illness, but had to accept that it was a part of life. Usually when the children were sick, if it was more than a little cold, she took a day off, which made her feel guilty because she hated to miss work. She was more conscientious than that, and she wanted to avoid becoming the stereotype of working mothers and being less capable of performing or exceling at work as a result of being a mother as well. From the second day when a child of hers was ill, Sidney usually went to work and left them with Anna, which stirred guilt for other reasons. Sometimes she felt that she had let them down. She had a single friend without children who generally told her how much she admired Sidney's efforts and successes at work and at home. Sidney appreciated her praise, but it still didn't always make her feel better.

Parenting advice and critiques could drive her crazy sometimes. Her mother and mother-in-law were especially keen on sharing their opinions and suggestions. They rarely criticized Sidney openly, but even their implied negative views could shake her. Sidney's mother didn't work outside the home when raising children, and her mother-in-law had worked part time, so they didn't seem to comprehend the difference that it made. Sidney simply didn't have time for all the things they suggested, nor did she agree with some of them.

Mothers at Finn's preschool were the worst. Some always seemed to know better and never failed to boast with their children's milestones and accomplishments and inadvertently put Finn and Sidney down once in a while. Tom tended to tell Sidney not to make a big deal out of it, but as she was more sensitive and anxious than him, the advice didn't work as beautifully for her.

After dropping Finn off at preschool and warding off some judgmental stares when it turned out they didn't bring cookies they were supposed to bring that day, Sidney sped up toward work. She mentally switched gears from mom-mode to work-mode. The transition wasn't always easy, even though she had had plenty of experience by now. She mentally worked out some details of the project she was working on before she reached the parking lot of her office building. She worked as an accountant, handling any accounting issues for clients. She didn't have as many clients as before, and she noticed that her childless colleagues got most of the very important clients. Sidney could have made a complaint, but she didn't want to risk her job, and realistically, she wouldn't be able to handle some of those prestigious clients who had more demands and might require more overtime.

Sidney worked diligently for the next 3 hours, not stopping to have coffee or even go to the restroom. She could be very efficient when she completely immersed herself in work. As she answered emails, she read one from a client with the last name, Finn. That made her think of her son, and her mind couldn't help wandering off. There were some complaints of Finn in pre-school that he was too loud, he talked too much, and he was too restless. Sidney hadn't known enough boys of his age to be able to compare his behavior to others. She noticed that he was often hyper and very talkative, but she thought that was the characteristic of most boys his age. Nevertheless, she was worried about him sometimes and wondered if he might be seeking attention because he didn't get enough at home. Sidney was aware that she focused more on Freya than Finn these days, but she was still so small, needing her mom, and she could be fussy. Sidney hoped that Finn understood, but she was sometimes plagued by concerns that she was neglecting him. At the same time, she was worried when Freya was so fussy. Finn hadn't been that way at this age. Sidney believed that she should be able to figure out what was wrong with Freya and be able to comfort her. She suddenly realized that Freya was due for a routine doctor's appointment, so she quickly called the doctor's office and set up an appointment. Then she put it on her mental

to-do list, along with a reminder to shop for clothes for Freya, as she was growing out of most of her clothes. Freya was slightly small for her age, so it hadn't been necessary to use a size for 12-month-olds until now.

Sidney abruptly realized that she hadn't been working for the last 20 minutes or so, and she diverted her attention back to work, feeling slightly ashamed. It frequently happened that she thought about the kids at work, but she also thought of work occasionally when she was with her children. She tried to do her best to be fully present in the moment, but she didn't always manage to do so. Sometimes she felt split and wished that she could clone herself. Actually, she would need several clones: an accountant, a mom, and maybe even one clone for each kid, a wife, a maid, a daughter, a friend, and so on. She had mostly learned to reconcile the several roles and identities that she was expected to fulfill, but when two roles seemed to require completely different behaviors from her, it could be very demanding.

Tom had been trying to persuade Sidney to have a third child, as he had always dreamed about a large family. She had also wanted the same, but she hadn't been aware of everything that it entailed. She used to talk about having three or even four children. Before they had Finn, Sidney planned on having another child within 18 months. However, when Finn was born, and they didn't have a lot of help, she was almost overwhelmed by taking care of him. As a new mother, she wasn't immensely informed about infant care. She hadn't counted on her own recovery time either. She needed to have a caesarian both times, and it wasn't easy to recover physically while struggling with the novel physical and emotional challenges of motherhood. She had been concerned about work as well, and she needed to return to work 8 weeks after giving birth. Sidney was actually lucky, though, because her workplace was one of the more flexible ones. Most workplaces didn't offer more than 6 weeks of leave. Her leave was also unpaid. Fortunately, Tom's salary proved to be sufficient to support their growing family, but unpaid maternity leave could be a nearly insurmountable obstacle for other families, especially those with low incomes, and even more so, families with one modest income instead of two.

Considering the unexpected difficulties, Sidney had reconsidered having a second child so soon and ended up waiting almost 4 years to get pregnant again. The second time around she wasn't so naïve; she was more prepared and knew what to expect. Although she had hard deliveries, at least her pregnancies were relatively uneventful, and she could work until a few days before giving birth. In the beginning of her second pregnancy, however, her joy was somewhat overshadowed by several fears and concerns. She was mostly worried about how she would manage with two children and a full-time job. She was praying for an easy, calm baby and for Finn to adjust to the infant without too much hassle and jealousy. Unfortunately, Sidney's prayers weren't answered, so she was struggling on both accounts ever since. Finn's jealousy had started to subside, so she could get some relief in that area, but Freya was far from being an easy baby or toddler. Sidney loved her to death, but she had to admit that she found it difficult to deal with Freya sometimes. She sensed that her daughter really missed her and would have needed more time with her mother, but there was nothing Sidney could do to help her. At least there was nothing she could do without giving up her job.

After having Freya, when her 8 weeks of maternity leave were completed, Sidney considered not going back to work. She mused about quitting her job, staying at home, having another baby within a few years, and potentially attempting to find another job once the children were older, preferably all of them in school. However, she was cognizant that it would practically mean discarding her career altogether because in her field missing several years of work could be a kiss of death. If she stayed at home for a couple of years, especially several years, she would realistically not be able to return to work, or she would have to start from scratch. She thought about years of studying and her student loans, her dreams and ambitions, which would all be for naught then. Still, she considered this option to be able to be fully present for her children. Finally, it was Tom who had dissuaded her from giving up her job. He knew how much it meant for her, and he feared that she would lose a crucial part of herself by leaving it behind.

However, now it was Tom who wanted to have a third child. Sidney believed that it wasn't feasible without her becoming a stay-at-home mom. Sometimes when Sidney was exhausted and felt that she might not be able to go on any longer, she kept repeating a mantra: "Second shift, third shift, and more? Yes, I can do it all." This mantra empowered her and kept her going. Once in a while, she almost felt like a superhero by being able to juggle so many roles and responsibilities. However, she frequently sensed that she was very close to dropping at least one of the balls that she was juggling. In fact, she nearly dropped a ball almost every day. She was aware of her limits and was terrified that adding one more ball to her act could lead to her dropping balls all the time, or maybe her act collapsing entirely.

Sometimes Sidney mused whether having a different system in terms of parental leave could make things easier. Sidney's sister, Casey, lived in Finland with her family. Her husband was from there; they had met when he had come to the United States as an exchange student. They decided to move to Finland soon after they had both graduated. At first, Sidney had been worried about Casey, fearing that she wouldn't be able to adjust to living in a foreign country.

However, the opposite turned out to be true: Casey had fallen in love with Finland. She had grown fond of the language, the culture, their coffee and cuisine, their saunas, and last, but not least, their family leave policies. Casey had found a job teaching English, and when she decided to have children, she was pleasantly surprised to discover how family leave policies made her decision to have a family and to work relatively easy. She could have a maternity leave of 26 weeks, which was paid at nearly 90% of her original salary. In addition, as there was a paternal leave of several weeks in Finland, Casey's husband could also stay at home with the children for a while. Casey's children were very smart, well adjusted, well behaved, and relaxed, and Sidney suspected that their parents having been able to stay at home with them for so long probably played a significant role in how they turned out.

Sidney wished that she could do the same with her children. She also knew that Tom would have been very happy if he had been given an option to stay at home with them, too. Sidney joked sometimes that maybe they should move to Finland or another European country with more generous family leave policies than the United States. An English-speaking country with similar policies, such as Canada, New Zealand, or Australia could also work. This was mostly a joke, of course, as they both had their jobs and lives here, in the United States, but Sidney couldn't believe that their country didn't provide them and other working parents with more options.

It wasn't only Tom who wanted a third child; if the circumstances were right, Sidney would have wanted it, too. Maybe not now, while Freya was still young and needed her so much, but in a few more years. However, Sidney knew that realistically it wouldn't fit into their lives. With a third child she might have to give up her career or neglect her children. It wouldn't be real neglect, of course, but according to her own standards, it might as well be. Sidney hoped that it wouldn't come to a point when she would have to literally choose between her career and her children, or at least having a third child. In small ways, she was choosing between her children and job more than once every day. She had grown up in an era when women had made enormous strides, and she had been told that she could have it all: a career and a family. She was sort of having it all, but the price was already significant sometimes, and it might get to a point when it could become too high to pay.

*

Sarah Whitney tried to shake off the exhaustion that clouded her head. She needed to work. She had been staring at the screen, wishing, hoping, and praying for inspiration, but it wouldn't materialize. She had been working on a book, a collection of poems and philosophical essays. This type of writing was virtually impossible to complete without inspiration.

She structured her days by following a rigid schedule. The only time she had to write was about 1.5 hours midmorning, 1.5 hours midafternoon, and at night. Her writing schedule had to revolve around the needs of her 8-month-old, Forrest. She could only write when he was asleep. The problem was that inspiration didn't always cooperate with his schedule, and sometimes Sarah stared at the screen, not being able to write anything during his entire morning or afternoon nap. Other times a wave of inspiration flooded her during his nap, and she was extremely productive, but it was very difficult to have to stop and stifle her creative drive when he woke up and demanded her attention.

Sarah usually needed about an hour to mentally prepare for writing, so during the day she often had to stop before she even had time to delve into it. As a result, she did most of her writing at night while Forrest was sleeping more soundly and a longer stretch of several hours at a time. Sarah had more time then, but exhaustion frequently got the best of her. Luckily, she was very disciplined, so she made herself stay awake and write. However, the quality of her writing suffered sometimes. Once in a while she ended up deleting a whole poem or essay that she had spent an entire night working on because she considered it substandard.

This was the first book contract that she had been offered, and she was very excited. Before this she had been working as a freelance journalist, but it wasn't her true calling. She took a big risk by devoting her time to writing a book full time, but it was her dream, and finally it was being realized. The timing wasn't perfect; Forrest was 3 months old when she got the book contract. She had completed several poems and essays that she had submitted for the book proposal, but there were still many more to write because the publisher wanted to present a thick volume. She also had to write some freelance articles and use her savings to live on while working on her book. In addition, there was no guarantee that the book would become a success, and it wasn't the type of writing anyway that would yield a substantial income. Financially, she would be better off writing a popular literature bestselling novel, but, again, that wouldn't satisfy her true talent and literary thirst.

With a baby and a book Sarah's two biggest dreams were coming true. She had wanted a baby for a long time, but she had been putting it off, placing her education and career first. Also, she had been waiting for the right man to come along. She had waited too long for him. She had had several relatively brief relationships in her twenties, and a 7-year relationship in her thirties. She had truly loved the man whom she had been involved with for 7 years and hoped that they could build a life together. They sort of did, but things were progressing slowly, as he was postponing commitment. They finally moved in together after 4 years of dating, and Sarah was hopeful that a proposal, marriage, and a baby could soon follow. He talked about marriage and children once in a while, which was enough for her to continue believing that they were in their future. However, after 7 years of dating, he eventually blurted out that he realized he didn't want to get married, nor did he desire to have children.

Sarah could have continued the relationship without getting married. As long as some form of commitment was at least present, she didn't necessarily need a piece of paper to legalize and solidify the relationship. However, she wasn't ready to give up ever having children just to stay with him. So, she decided to go for the baby project on her own. She would soon turn 40, and she felt that she couldn't afford to wait around for a man any longer. She considered many options and ended up choosing a sperm donor.

Selecting a sperm donor was an interesting experience. Sarah had tried online dating before, and scanning through profiles of sperm donors reminded her of that, minus the profile pictures. However, it required a much greater level of responsibility to choose a sperm donor than to select an online dating partner. First off, she had to let go of her dream to have and raise a child in a two-parent household, and for a child to be conceived in a loving relationship. It felt odd to create a baby with a stranger, but, at the same time, she could choose a man much more wisely this way, with no emotional involvement, which used to cloud her judgment. She knew now, for instance, that her ex would not have been a great father, and potentially even his genetic makeup wasn't ideal. By choosing a sperm donor, she could screen the future father in many ways, especially medically, instead of being emotionally and sexually involved with him.

Sarah decided to purchase sperm online. She looked through the profiles of at least a hundred donors until she settled on one. The profiles included several pieces of information about the donor, such as his race, ethnicity, weight, height, eye color, hair color, blood type, psychological and physical health, education, and occupation. Sarah chose someone of her own race and ethnicity, average height and weight, good health, high educational level, and a blood type, hair and eye color different from her own. She ended up paying $400 for the sperm and close to $200 for shipping. She scheduled for the shipment to arrive during her ovulation. It was her birthday, and she found it especially significant and symbolic to potentially create a new life on the day when she had been born 40 years ago.

She followed the instructions, inseminated herself with the syringe that was provided in the package, and waited for the results. She hoped that she would get pregnant the first time, especially because she focused so much on the timing, but she was aware that it might take more than one attempt. Three weeks later she did a home pregnancy test and was ecstatic to learn that she was pregnant. She knew that she was very lucky, and she felt grateful for that.

She didn't tell anyone about the sperm donor and even the pregnancy until she was 12 weeks along. Even then, she only informed the people closest to her about the sperm donor and let others assume whatever they wanted to believe about the father. She faced various reactions when people around her heard about her decision. Her parents were sad, and her mother even called it a desperate move. Her father was more supportive eventually, being happy that at least she would have a child, and they would get a grandchild. Some of her friends praised her for being brave and going for it, others were slightly worried about her becoming a single mother without even knowing the father. Sarah thought that it might actually be better to have a child with an anonymous stranger than with an unsuitable man, who might be in the child's life but present a bad example.

Sarah was happy with her decision and firmly believed that it was much better to have the child of a stranger as a single mother than not to have a child at all. She didn't regret her choice and was convinced that she never would. There was no question either about being a *working mother*. Even if she had a partner, she would want to keep working, but as a single mother, she even had to. She could opt for a more reliable and stable income, but she would have to sacrifice her dreams then.

Also, there were advantages of being able to work from home. In fact, in the beginning, she found it ideal to be able to stay at home with Forrest, taking care of him and working at the same time. Those of her friends who were also mothers, working outside of the home, kept repeating how lucky she was that she could work from home. She didn't have to worry about childcare or pay for a babysitter, and she had the opportunity to spend more time with Forrest. At the same time, she discovered the challenges of working from home with a baby as well. She had to write and complete chores around the house while Forrest was asleep, and she never seemed to have sufficient time for anything. She hardly slept at all to make the best of Forrest's naps and be able to spend time with him when he was awake. Working from home could offer a relatively good balance between work and motherhood, but it undeniably took some sacrifice, too.

Sarah knew a few other mothers who worked from home, and they usually reported the same upsides and challenges that she experienced. There were also some differences, depending on what kind of job they did at home. One of her friends did a phone customer service job, serving customers who called mostly from Europe, usually at night for Sarah's friend, which was morning in Europe. Another friend of hers gave up her job as a fashion designer after her second child was born and created her own small business, designing and selling maternity clothes. She didn't earn as much as a fashion designer, but her business was relatively successful, and it worked beautifully around her children's schedule. She predominantly worked at night as well. Both of these friends slept even less than Sarah, but it worked out for them, and they said it was worth it.

adriaticfoto/ Shutterstock.com

One of Sarah's cousins who got married and had children young, dropping out of college, operated a small daycare in her own home. Besides her own two children, she had four or five other children in her home every day. Even after her divorce she could support herself and her kids, living on the income her daycare generated. She enjoyed her daycare as well, although she sometimes complained that while she spent all day with her children, she didn't have so much individual time for them because she had several other children there to focus on.

Virtually all of Sarah's friends and female relatives who were mothers also worked. Except for a few, the majority of them worked outside of the home. They complained about being away from their children, the difficulty of finding reliable and affordable childcare, and feeling torn between work and the home. At the same time, they also mentioned that sometimes it felt refreshing to be able to leave from home, have to dress up, and converse with adults, not only their own children. For those working from home there was no separation between work and home, and sometimes they felt that hardly ever leaving home was driving them mad. Sarah knew the feeling; occasionally she wished she could go to work, too. Nevertheless, she was happy to be able to spend Forrest's infanthood with him and that she never had to miss any important moments. Women working outside of the home often complained to her that they missed so many milestones, such as first steps, first words, school events, and so on.

Taking everything into account, Sarah was satisfied with her life. She finally had a baby, and motherhood truly suited her. She was finding her calling, too, and writing her book fulfilled her. She couldn't imagine not working. She also found working from home ultimately beneficial both for her and for Forrest. While some people felt sorry for her or criticized her for some of the decisions she had made, as far as she was concerned, she thought that her life was very fulfilling.

Discussion Questions

1. Continue the two stories. How do you envision Sidney's and Sarah's lives in a couple of years?

2. Compare and contrast mothers working from home and outside of the home.

3. A role conflict is encountering different expectations and having to fulfill potentially conflicting roles when occupying two different statuses, such as a mother and a working individual (e.g., employee, employer, entrepreneur). Mention examples of role conflict from the stories.

4. Multiphrenia is defined as splitting into multiple self-investments (Gergen, 2000). Discuss examples of multiphrenia from the stories.

5. Hochschild and Machung (2012) explained that working women often faced a second shift, returning from work and having to work a second shift at home, taking care of the household and children. Illustrate the second shift based on the stories.

6. Discuss the role of gender among working parents. Do you see any difference between working mothers and fathers, and if yes, what kind of difference?

7. How does social class make a difference among working parents, if at all?

8. Do you think that there is any stigma regarding working mothers? Remember, stigma is a salient, usually stubborn, negative label that is applied to individuals who do not follow social norms (Goffman, 1986). If yes, does the stigma vary by different factors and circumstance? For instance, are there any jobs that would be stigmatized for mothers? Any jobs that would stigmatize motherhood?

9. West and Zimmerman (1987) underlined that gender was a routine, everyday accomplishment, something that we do in interaction with others, as opposed to something that we are. Discuss a few examples of how characters in the two stories do gender.

Find the Answers

Go to https://www.dol.gov/wb/stats/NEWSTATS/latest/laborforce.htm#eight to find answers to the following questions.

1. Compare and contrast the labor force participation rates of men versus women.

2. Which racial/ethnic group has the highest and lowest labor force participation rate among men and women?

3. What difference does education make in labor force participation?

4. What are the key differences between the labor force participation of mothers and fathers?

Mini Research Assignments

1. Survey at least seven individuals, asking them to rate their agreement with the following statements on a scale of 1–10 (1 meaning complete disagreement and 10 indicating full agreement): 1. "Children benefit more from having working mothers than having mothers who stay at home." 2. "It is better for mothers to work from home than outside of the home." 3. "Working mothers usually face more challenges than working fathers." Summarize the results. Discuss the potential role of age, gender, marital status, education, and other factors in the answers. Draw parallels with the stories as well.
2. Interview at least two working mothers. Ask them about the joys and challenges of being mothers and working at the same time. Inquire about the different roles they fulfill and the identities that they endorse as a mother, employee, and so on. Compare and contrast their answers. Draw parallels with the stories as well.
3. Conduct a search online on parental leave policies in other countries. You may use articles or videos/documentaries in your discussion. Compare and contrast the policies of at least three other countries with those in the United States. Discuss the potential benefits and disadvantages of each policy for families and for society as a whole. Draw parallels with the stories as well.

References

Gergen, K. J. (2000). *The saturated self: Dilemmas of identity in contemporary life* (reprint ed.). New York, NY: Basic Books.

Goffman, E. (1986). *Stigma: Notes on the management of spoiled identity.* New York, NY: Touchstone. (Originally published 1963)

Hochschild, A., & Machung, A. (2012). *The second shift: Working families and the revolution at home* (rev. ed.). New York, NY: Penguin.

West, C., & Zimmerman, D. H. (1987). Doing gender. *Gender & Society, 1,* 125–151.

Part 3

Families around the World

CHAPTER

13

"Parenting from a world apart."
TRANSNATIONAL FAMILIES

Annasunny24/ Shutterstock.com

Rocio Hernandez wiped her hands. She had been doing dishes and cleaning the countertops in the kitchen. The grey granite was shining, reflecting glittering rays of the sun that found their way into the kitchen. It was a beautiful kitchen, complete with dark grey granite countertops, white cabinets, a huge island, and the most up-to-date and costly stainless steel appliances. The kitchen was simply one of the many rooms of the house. Although it was midsummer in southern Florida, the house was nice and cool, due to the wonders of air conditioning.

The first time Rocio had seen the house, 3 years ago, she was breathless. It was grand and impressive, and by far the largest residential building she had ever laid eyes on. She had never known that houses like this even existed. She could have seen one on TV, but she didn't use to own a TV. She envisioned her tiny house back in Chiapas, a southwestern state in Mexico, which was one of the poorest, if not the poorest, region in Mexico. In fact, the house wasn't hers; it was owned by her in-laws. The house had been shared by her in-laws, Rocio and her husband, Alvaro, their children, Estela and Fernando, as well as one of Alvaro's brothers, his wife, and their three children. So, the house used to accommodate 11 people at a time, although a few of the family members almost always seemed to be away. It had two rooms, a small kitchen in the corner of one of the rooms, and an outhouse.

They had electricity, but air conditioning was unheard of, which is why Rocio was so taken aback by the coolness of the huge Florida home in all seasons. The double-oven and all the other appliances were a great surprise, too. The number of TVs and other electronic devices astonished Rocio as well. She didn't know how to use most of them, but she didn't have access to the majority of them anyway and learned what she needed to use. The house had four bathrooms, which amazed Rocio, especially as the house she used to live in didn't have any. She had her own room in Florida, which she had never had before either. She used to share a room with her siblings, then her in-laws, husband, and children. At a minimum, she had always shared a room with at least three or four other people, sometimes more. Her own bathroom in Florida also seemed like a miracle. In a way, it was all too much, and she missed living with others.

Several years ago, unable to find a lucrative job and chasing dreams to provide better lives for their families, Alvaro and his brother, Manuel, left for the United States to work and send money home. They tried to get papers to work legally, but they didn't succeed, so they decided to go a different route. They put together all their saved money, borrowed some more, and hired a coyote to take them across the border. It was a dangerous trip; they had heard of others who hadn't made it, but they signed up for it because they couldn't let their families starve. They got across the border

Frontpage/ Shutterstock.com

and found a job, working at construction sites. The money they earned was insignificant according to U.S. standards, but they could send more than half of it home, which turned out to be a relatively significant amount for their families back in Mexico. Rocio and her sister-in-law, Mariana, put most of the money aside, saving it to buy their own homes eventually.

Alvaro and Manuel were away for about 3 years. They weren't able to return at all during that time because they would have risked not being able to go back to the United States. It took an immense sacrifice to give up seeing their wives, children, and parents. Estela had been 18 months and Fernando 6 months old when Alvaro had left, and they were 4 and 3 years old when he finally returned. Although Rocio had sent him some pictures, Alvaro hardly recognized the children, and they didn't recognize him. It took them almost 6 months to get used to him again. One of Manuel's children had been born while he was away, so the first time he saw him face-to-face, he was already 2 years old. The little boy cried when Manuel hugged him, as he was scared and clueless about who he was.

Although the 3 years away seemed like an eternity, Alvaro and Manuel would have stayed longer if they had had the chance. However, the economic crisis slowed down new constructions, and Alvaro and Manuel eventually didn't have enough work. They hadn't been able to earn sufficient money to build their own homes in Mexico. They found menial jobs in their hometown, but they didn't pay much and were mostly seasonal, not yielding stable, permanent incomes.

About a year later, Mariana started to talk about the nanny positions her sister and one of her cousins found in Florida, and she considered seeking one herself. She shared the stories with Rocio about the relatively good pay and comfortable living standards. The more they talked about it, the more excited they became. Maybe they could earn the money their families desperately needed. They felt heartbroken to leave their children behind, but they could take care of them much more effectively by sending them money than by starving together with them. This could provide not only their own homes in the long run, but nutritious food and good schooling in the short run. Rocio's late parents and her in-laws were illiterate, like many in their region. Rocio and Alvaro had 8 years of schooling, whereas Mariana and Manuel had even less. They wanted to provide a better future for their children, and education was an avenue for that.

When Alvaro and Manuel heard about Rocio and Mariana's plan, they tried to dissuade them fiercely. Their pride was hurt; they felt that they were the men, the heads of their households, so they should be able to support their families. They offered to go to the United States themselves, but

CHAPTER 13: "Parenting from a world apart." Transnational Families

283

the opportunities in construction were still scarce. It took nearly 6 months to convince them, but eventually they gave in, especially when Mariana's sister found a nanny job for both Mariana and Rocio, which paid even more than construction would have.

Rocio felt extremely hesitant to leave her children behind, not having any idea when she would see them next. It was very difficult to say good-bye to her husband as well. She was aware that her parents, if they had still lived, would have convinced her not to go, and she might have listened. It was an odd concept to help her children from so far away, but it made logical sense, so she had to stifle the emotional battles that it involved. Estela had turned 6 by then, and Fernando had been 5. They were still young, but not babies anymore when they used to need their mother even more. Also, they had started school at the time, at least Estela had, and Fernando soon did, too, so the timing was advantageous because with Rocio's income they would have access to better schools.

When they said goodbye, Estela was crying inconsolably, as she sort of understood what was going on. Fernando didn't, but his sister's grief made him scared and upset, too. Rocio strengthened herself and didn't shed a tear, at least not until her children were out of sight. The trip across the border was long and dangerous. Rocio and Mariana didn't leave each other's side, and fortunately a male cousin of Mariana was going to work to the United States as well, accompanying them on the trip. This way they were less fearful of potential dangers, such as rape, that could affect solo women on the trip. They had heard other women whisper about how they had been raped on their way to America.

They had to walk for most of the trip, and it was extremely hot and dry in the desert. Although the coyote asked for a lot of money, it was worth the investment because without him they could have lost the way, wandered around in the desert, and died. They knew a few people who had met this fate. They were also familiar with stories of people getting killed crossing the border. This was one of the reasons for not bringing their children with them. Also, they were aware of how hard they would have to work in the United States. They wouldn't have time to take care of their children or be able to pay for childcare. Living as undocumented immigrants could result in other complications or even dangers for their children. They were safer back in Mexico, and their money would go farther there.

Before Rocio had left Mexico, Alvaro had taught her basic English. He didn't know much of the language either, but at least he shared what he knew. It turned out to be very limited right away. Rocio had a hard time understanding even the basic instructions of her employers. It took her nearly a year until she felt more comfortable with the language. Until then she often felt lost. She hardly spoke with anyone else but the family that employed her. Mr. and Mrs. Lennox had high expectations from her from the very start. They had just had twins, identical boys, Eli and Abel, which is why they needed a live-in nanny.

Rocio had had her own babies by then, and they were only a year apart, but taking care of the twins on her own still proved to be very challenging. Fortunately, the Lennox family had a live-in baby nurse for the first few weeks, who showed Rocio how she needed to take care of the babies, who were premature and needed extra care, things that Rocio had never had to do with her own children. It was lucky that the nurse could demonstrate what to do instead of explaining it because in the beginning the language barrier had been especially salient. Rocio learned to feed the babies at the same time, as well as everything else that was involved in taking care of them. Once the nurse left, Rocio found herself solely responsible for the twins. She was expected to do all the feedings, including the ones at night, so she was working around the clock. She realized that she spent almost more time

Dave Clark Digital Photo/ Shutterstock.com

with Eli and Abel than with her own children when they had been babies because there had been so many other family members around and involved then.

Rocio was also assigned some household chores, such as cooking, washing dishes, doing laundry, and ironing. There was a maid service handling heavier cleaning around the house once a week, so at least that wasn't Rocio's responsibility. For the first 1.5 years she didn't have any full days off. She had one afternoon off, approximately 4 hours, every Sunday. From the time the twins turned 18 months, Rocio was given all day Sunday off. Her hours or days off were the only time she could leave the house, except when she was instructed to take the children somewhere. She had never spent so much time inside a house, and sometimes she felt the beginnings of depression, yearning to have more freedom. At the same time, she was cognizant of practically selling herself, at least her labor, to the Lennox family, and she had to do it for the money and for her children.

There were other rules, too. For instance, she had to cook separately for herself, and she couldn't eat with the family. She wasn't allowed to have a cell phone, but she might not have been able to afford it anyway, as she was sending almost her entire salary home. The Lennox family allowed her to use their landline to call her family once a week. They told her that the call was very expensive, so in the beginning she had to limit each call to 15 minutes. A year later, they allowed her to extend the call to 30 minutes. This limited time was extremely brief. Rocio waited all week for it, and when it finally came, it flew. She used most of it to talk to Estela and Fernando, so she could only speak with Alvaro for a couple of minutes every week.

She felt that she and Alvaro had begun to grow apart. It hadn't been easy when he had worked in the United States either, but it was even more difficult now, especially because Rocio could sense that his male ego was hurt, and, in a way, he was upset with her for leaving and being able to provide a better income than he had been capable of doing. After a couple of years, based on some of the things her children told her, she began to suspect that he might have a girlfriend. She was heartbroken, but couldn't blame him. She was hoping that it wasn't serious, and it would end once she returned. Fernando also hinted that Alvaro worked less than he used to, and he drank more.

Alvaro didn't spend a lot of time with the children, either. The children viewed him almost as a stranger, and he couldn't take the effort to try to get closer to them. The children were raised mostly by Rocio's in-laws, especially her mother-in-law. She had suspected that this would be the case, but she truly trusted her mother-in-law, and she knew the children were in good hands. Alvaro couldn't do many of the things that his mother could.

Fortunately, Estela and Fernando got along really well with their grandparents, as well as their cousins, with whom they shared a home. In fact, the cousins really understood each other because they were all in the same situation—that is, first with their fathers, then their mothers being away. In the last few months, Estela had started to become a little bit short with Rocio on the phone. She was fed up with not having her mom, and she felt sort of betrayed. Rocio began to notice that she didn't only miss most of her children's milestones and lives in general, but Estela began to talk to her less about those events as well. She wrote less frequently, too, and she didn't go into too many details either. Rocio still wrote letters to them at least twice a week. Just last week, Estela had an outburst and yelled to Rocio across the phone line, "You can't be parenting from a world apart." Rocio was stunned and begged to differ for a moment, but then she realized that Estela was sort of right. She couldn't be parenting from so far away, at least not in the traditional way. Maybe it was also more difficult for Estela; as a girl, she might have missed her mother even more than Fernando.

Her in-laws sent photos of the kids about twice a year, and Rocio always cried when she saw how much they had grown. In fact, she cried almost daily anyway, at least in the first year. Then, she began to strengthen herself deliberately, but she still shed tears thinking of her children at least once or twice a week. Sometimes their absence physically hurt, other times the pain was more dull, or she almost felt numb, like a robot fulfilling her duties and discarding her emotions. She often wondered if it was worth it, but she was convinced that it was when she heard how well they were doing in school, or how much they enjoyed their nice meals or clothes. If they could all be united at the end in their own little house, that would be heaven. Once in a while, Rocio had some doubts if there was still a family to be united, if Alvaro would want to remain her husband, or if she and the kids, especially Estela, would become too estranged. She usually stifled her fears because she wouldn't have been able to justify staying and go on otherwise.

Eli and Abel were adorable babies, and they offered some solace. Although Rocio worked nearly 24/7 taking care of them, their very presence and smiles were so refreshing that sometimes she hardly felt tired at all. Being there for all their important milestones, such as first smiles, first words, and first steps almost compensated her for missing key events in her own children's lives. Almost, not entirely, of course. She had fallen in love with the boys and loved them nearly as much as her own children. She knew that the twins loved her, too, which felt wonderful, as they were the only people in the entire town who loved her. Mariana worked in another city, being just as busy as Rocio, so they couldn't really be there for each other either.

Sometimes Rocio felt guilty for growing so close to the twins, showering them with all the attention her own children should have received from her. She was even worried that she might miss these children, too, when she returned to Mexico. It was likely that Eli and Abel would forget her, and she would never hear about them and from them again. Once in a while she almost felt like their mother, but she soon realized that she wasn't. Although the children might have viewed her that way, especially when they were very young, her employers didn't let her forget where her place was, at least according to them. Rocio recalled one occasion when the twins were about 15 months, and Eli called out to Rocio, "Mama." It was one of his first words, and it wasn't addressed to his own mother. Unfortunately, Mrs. Lennox overheard it, and she didn't fail to correct Eli, her voice ice-cold, "No, honey. *I'm mama*. This is Rocio. She is your nanny. *She's the help*." Of course, Eli was too young to understand and made the same mistake a few more times, and so did Abel. When Mrs. Lennox was present, she didn't let it slide, and one time she specifically asked Rocio to correct the boys, too, if she noticed them doing the same.

These were the harshest reminders for Rocio about what her place was in the family. Although she lived with the Lennox family, she wasn't a family member; she wasn't viewed or treated as one. She had heard of some rare examples when American families truly considered their live-in nannies family members, but she found her case to be more typical. She talked to other nannies on the playground once in a while. In this neighborhood, it was much more common for children to be at the playground with their nannies than with their parents. There were some other Hispanic women, as well as girls from less privileged parts of Europe, such as Ukraine. Although the girls from Europe were still underpaid and overworked, when they compared their wages, Rocio found that they were often still paid more than their Hispanic or black counterparts. The women with visas and work permits were paid much more than those who were undocumented, which made sense, but still seemed unfair.

Soon, Rocio's workload would increase to a great extent. Last night Mr. and Mrs. Lennox called her to the living room after the boys were asleep and shared some news with her, "Rocio, we have something to tell you. We're expecting a baby. It's one baby this time, not twins. Eli and Abel are getting a little brother or sister."

"So nice, congratulations," Rocio smiled.

"This means that you'll become pretty busy again," Mrs. Lennox highlighted. "We're not hiring a baby nurse this time. Hopefully this baby won't be premature. We're expecting you to take care of him or her, handling everything that needs to be handled. I might need to go back to work even sooner than last time, so it'll all be on you. Do you understand?"

"Yes, ma'am," Rocio nodded.

"Look, we know it'll be a little more work," Mr. Lennox added. "But we can't give you a raise. We can't give you more money. In fact, probably we'll have to reduce your Sunday off to only Sunday afternoon off again. Understood?"

"Yes, sir," Rocio replied. She knew that she wasn't in a position to negotiate a raise. If she tried, she would probably be advised to leave, and her employers would find someone else, who would do it for less money. Rocio couldn't afford to jeopardize her job; she needed the money. She calculated that she needed to stay at least 3 more years in the United States to be able to send enough money home for a modest house back there. In the meantime, she would raise another baby for the Lennox couple. At least raise him or her from a baby to a toddler. It was inconceivable that she wouldn't see her own children for 3 more years. Alvaro might divorce her in the next 3 years, or he might get bored with his girlfriend and welcome Rocio home when she returned. Her children, especially Estela, might grow further from her, or she might come around and understand why she had signed up for this. A home and a family—hopefully ultimately they would be worth all the sacrifice.

*

Attila Lendvai was thrilled to be able to visit home. He had just finished a 4-week work shift in Germany, and finally he would return to Transylvania and see his family again. His shifts usually lasted for 4 weeks, then he got 2 or 3 weeks off. Transylvania was a region in Romania that once belonged to Hungary prior to World War I. Therefore, many of its inhabitants were still of Hungarian ethnicity, although their nationality might have been Romanian. Attila spoke both Hungarian and Romanian fluently. His German wasn't flawless, but it was sufficient to get by.

The trip from Germany to Attila's hometown in Transylvania was about 11 hours by train, across Eastern Germany, Austria, Hungary, and Western Romania. He had to take four trains to get there. He was sitting on one of the trains, which was speeding through Eastern Hungary. The trains themselves were fitting representations of the economic situations of the countries he was crossing. As he was heading East, the quality and comfort of the trains was declining. The

ekler / Shutterstock.com

CHAPTER 13: "Parenting from a world apart." Transnational Families

289

one in Hungary was still fine, but not as much as the ones in Germany and Austria.

It would have been faster to fly, but Attila couldn't afford to spend his hard-earned income on a plane ticket. As he lived in a village in Transylvania, he would have had to complete the last stretch of the journey by train or a local bus anyway. He didn't mind taking a train for the entire trip; it was his favorite mode of transportation anyway.

An elderly lady boarded the train at the next stop. She struggled with her luggage, and Attila jumped up to help her and place it in the overhead compartment.

"Let me help you, ma'am," Attila said, eager to assist her, grabbing the luggage.

"Thank you, young man," the lady exclaimed, and her face shone with gratefulness. "It's so rare these days to meet such a gentleman."

"Don't mention it," Attila smiled. "It was my pleasure."

"Whew, long day," the woman sighed, fanning herself. "And it's so hot outside. But at least there's air conditioning on the train. I remember the days, not even that long ago, when there was no air conditioning on trains either. Some trains still don't have it, actually."

"Yes, it's very useful on hot summer days," Attila agreed.

"Are you traveling all the way to the final stop?" the lady asked.

"Yes," Attila nodded. "Actually, even longer. I'm going to Transylvania."

"Oh, wow," the woman cried out. "Where are you traveling from?"

"Germany," Attila responded.

"Oh, really?" the lady shot back with growing surprise and curiosity. "If you don't mind me asking, do you work there? Or were you on vacation?"

"I work there," Attila confirmed.

"How wonderful," the woman asserted. "At least I hope it's wonderful. Do you like it?"

"Yes," Attila replied. "It's a lot of work, but I don't mind hard work. I work in a restaurant in 4-week shifts. During those few weeks I have to work 15 hours per day, including the weekends. But it's worth it because I get a couple of weeks off afterwards. This schedule works."

"Must be exhausting, though," the woman said with sympathy.

"It is, for sure," Attila agreed. "But I'm used to working hard."

"Great job, you should be proud of yourself," the woman complimented him. "I'm Margit, by the way."

"Attila."

"I suppose you're paid much better, too, than you would be at home," Margit commented. This remark could have seemed too forward, or even impolite at some places, but it was not out of the ordinary in Hungary.

"Yes, I am," Attila confirmed. "They pay me well. I wouldn't do it otherwise. I'm doing it for the money. My family and I need it badly. It's not only the pay, though; there are hardly any jobs where I'm from. I didn't use to have a regular job. Some days I had trouble being able to feed my family."

"Do you have a big family?" Margit queried.

"Not that big," Attila smiled. "I have a wife and three children. That doesn't count as very big there."

"How old are your children? Boys, girls?"

"Two boys and a girl. They're 8, 5, and 1."

"How nice," Margit stated jovially. "I bet they miss you when you're away."

"Yes, they do," Attila sighed. "I miss them, too. But when I'm back and have a few weeks off, I can spend quite a lot of time with them. It's not very balanced; not seeing them at all for a month, then seeing them a lot, but it kind of works. My weeks off make it all worthwhile."

"And how's your wife handling it?"

"She's great," Attila stressed. "It's not easy for her when I'm not there. She's practically a single mother then. She takes care of everything beautifully, though. I respect her for it."

"I'm glad to hear that," Margit beamed. "So many young people get a divorce these days. It's always wonderful to hear about a couple that is doing so well."

"We have our little disagreements, too, sometimes," Attila admitted. "But we're a team. We're working for the same goal, which is preserving the unity of our family and providing the best for our children."

CHAPTER 13: "Parenting from a world apart." Transnational Families

291

"Have you considered moving your family to Germany?"

"Yes, I've thought about it," Attila affirmed. "But we like our home-town. That's our home, and our families are there. My wife and I have parents who are getting older, and they might need some assistance soon. And at this point my wife still needs some help with the kids, and it's nice to have relatives and friends nearby. We don't want to leave for good. We just want to provide better opportunities for our children so that they can do whatever they want to."

"I understand," Margit nodded. "When I was young, times were different. You couldn't leave for a while and then return. Under communism there were severe restrictions on even travel, and if somebody left the country without a permit, they would have been arrested and imprisoned when they returned. My uncle left and immigrated to Canada in 1957. He was sentenced to prison in his absence, so he couldn't come back. His father, my grandfather got very sick about 5 years later, but my uncle still couldn't risk returning. He got the news about his father's death in Canada. He couldn't even come to the funeral. I know that some people in the family were mad at him, but others understood. He had a good life in Canada, and what would he have had here? Imprisonment?"

"Yes, those were rough times," Attila said slowly. "I had a distant relative who emigrated, too. He went to Germany. No one in the family saw him again; he probably died there. Or started a completely new life. Who knows? I wouldn't want to leave like that. If I could never return, I couldn't leave. I'm glad I don't have to make that choice."

"No, fortunately you don't," Margit agreed. "The European Union makes it easier, too. There are practically no borders these days. People from member countries can work and live in the other countries. This is a great opportunity, and so many young people make the best of it. Do you know any other people from Transylvania where you work in Germany?"

"Yes, there are a few others," Attila confirmed. "There are workers from other European countries as well."

"Do they usually have their families there?"

"Some do, but most of them don't," Attila explained. "Many work in shifts like mine, so they leave their families in their homeland and go visit instead."

"I think it's great when you can make it work without moving there. It's probably better for your family, especially your aging parents. I have two grandchildren who work abroad. One works in Switzerland in a similar arrangement to yours. She spends about a month there, taking care of elderly people, then she comes home, and another young woman takes her place for a few weeks. It's kind of ironic that she's over there taking care of elderly people when she has a grandmother here. Of course, I couldn't pay her for it, especially as much as she's paid there. And, fortunately, I don't need to be taken care of; I manage on my own. For how much longer, I don't know. I'm 78, and I'm not getting any younger. I don't feel sorry for myself, don't misunderstand me. Yes, it'd be nice to have my grandchildren nearby, but it's their lives, they have to follow their heart and the opportunities they are offered. I just miss my grandchildren sometimes. The other one is even worse; I get to see her even less. She not only works in Spain, she also lives there. She's married to a Spanish man. I can't talk to that guy at all. I don't speak Spanish; he doesn't speak Hungarian. He looks nice enough, but I have only met him a couple of times. They're so far away. And my granddaughter is expecting a baby, which thrills me, but I worry that I will hardly ever see the baby. I'm not very young, but I still have enough stamina that I could even help my granddaughter with the baby if she needed it. But not if they're in Spain. I'm so concerned that she'll be all alone with no family to rely on. At least not her own family, as her husband's family is there, of course. And the baby might be a little Spaniard, with no ties to Hungary. He might not even end up speaking any Hungarian. What if I couldn't talk to my own great-grandchild? That would be so sad! Of course, my granddaughter says that he'll be bilingual, and he'll speak Hungarian fluently. I

CHAPTER 13: "Parenting from a world apart." Transnational Families

293

hope so, but who knows? So, I really miss this granddaughter, Erika, and I'm a little worried about her, but at least she's found her place. She has a great job in Spain and a nice husband, even if he's a foreigner. But I'm even more concerned about my other granddaughter, Evelin, the one who works in Switzerland. I get to see her a little bit more, but I don't know if she's on the right track. She graduated from college here, but she couldn't find a job in her field. So, she just up and left, finding this job in Switzerland, taking care of elderly people. She doesn't need her degree for that, so all those years of school might go to waste. It's a good way to earn money, maybe, and she says she only wants to do this temporarily until she becomes more financially established, and then she'll come home and seek a job in her own field. But she won't have any pertinent work experience, so I think it'll be hard. Also, she used to say she'd only do this job for a couple of years, but it's been 4 years. I worry that she might get stuck. And she doesn't have a family of her own. Yes, she's still pretty young, but it's so sad that she's all alone. She needs a nice young man. At the same time, I worry that she'll find one in Switzerland and stay there like Erika did in Spain. Even if she got married to a nice Hungarian man, she couldn't have a baby if she continued this lifestyle and work schedule. How could anyone do that with a baby? She couldn't leave her baby for a month and go to work in Switzerland. She couldn't take the baby either because she works really hard and extremely long hours there. But if she came home for good and didn't find a suitable job, she might not be able to have a baby for financial reasons."

"I think they'll be fine," Attila declared. "Don't worry about them. It sounds like they're making a good future for themselves."

"I hope you're right," Margit said wistfully. "This new globalized world and the European Union provide great opportunities for young people, but they also intervene with families. When I was young my husband and I used to live with my parents, and it was so natural. Many people lived that way, especially if they couldn't afford their own place. But it was also beneficial because parents could help with the grandchildren, and grown children could assist with aging parents or grandparents. Families had stronger bonds, and they could rely on each other. Who can you rely on when your family members live so far away?"

"That's true," Attila mused. "Don't you have some family members nearby?"

"Oh, I do," Margit said. "Not that close, but nearby. My son, Erika and Evelin's father, lives about 2 hours away. It's not ideal, but at least it's within the same country. He's really busy, though, so I rarely see him. But I've just visited him now, that's where I'm coming from. He has a son who still lives at home; he's in high school. So, I still have a grandchild relatively close. You know, when my son moved 2 hours away, I used to say it was really far. But now that my granddaughters are in different countries, I've reevaluated what I consider far. Two hours in the same country is not that bad."

"No, it's not," Attila echoed.

"I wonder what families will be like in 20 or 30 years?" Margit mused. "Families have changed so much in my 78 years. I wonder how much more they can shift in another few decades, or in another 78 years."

"That'll be interesting to see," Attila replied. "Maybe we'll meet on the train again in another 20 or 30 years and have a chat about it?"

"Oh, that's nice of you to say that, but I might not be around for that chat," Margit responded.

"Who knows? Why not?" Attila countered. "Yes, families have changed a lot, but medicine and standards of living have, too. For example, you're about to become a great-grandmother. Many people in the past didn't live long enough to experience that. Yes, people are having babies later, on average, but people live longer, too. So, maybe this might be one of the changes in families in the future that more of us might get to have great-grandparents, or great-great-grandparents."

"I like that idea," Margit smiled. "We'll see, I guess. In any case, I look forward to having a great-grandchild and seeing where this world goes, and where families are moving with it. The world has been changing so fast that I'm sure I'll witness more changes in my lifetime."

Discussion Questions

1. What do you think will happen to the families in the two stories?

2. How do you define transnational families? Discuss a few variations of transnational families based on the two stories.

3. Discuss the role of gender in transnational families.

4. Discuss the role of education, social class, and socioeconomic background in transnational families.

5. Machismo and marianismo are seen as traditional, somewhat stereotypical gender roles in Hispanic cultures. Machismo represents a strong masculine pride, the ability to protect and provide for one's family. Marianismo is an embodiment of nurturing, self-sacrificing femininity (Dreby, 2006). Discuss examples (and/or counterexamples) of machismo and marianismo in the stories.

6. Due to changes in the labor market and a greater demand for female workers, the structure of transnational families has shifted as well, with women being just as likely, or in some cases even more likely, than men to have to leave their families behind and move to another country for a job (Aranda, 2003; Dreby, 2006, 2010; Hirsch, 2000, 2003; Hondagneu-Sotelo & Avila, 1997; Parrenas, 2005). What can this lead to in families? Draw parallels with the stories, too.

7. Blumer (1969) identified three premises of symbolic interactionism. The first is that humans act toward things based on the meanings those things have for them. The second is that meanings are created through social interaction. The third is that meanings are understood and potentially transformed through an interpretative process. Apply this theory to definitions of families, and how those definitions might shift in transnational arrangements.

8. West and Zimmerman (1987) explained that gender was a routine, everyday accomplishment, something that we do in interaction with others, as opposed to something that we are. Discuss a few examples of how characters in the two stories do gender.

9. Emotion work (or emotional labor) is what we do to suppress or evoke emotions we are "supposed to" or not supposed to feel in certain situations (Hochschild, 2012). Discuss examples of emotion work from the two stories, and how they might be impacted by gender.

10. Discuss the impact of globalization on transnational families. Also, mention how you envision families in the future. Do you expect more transnational families? Why/why not?

Find the Answers

Go to http://www.pewhispanic.org/2018/09/14/facts-on-u-s-immigrants/ to find answers to the following.

1. Discuss changes in the foreign-born population since the 1850s.

2. Discuss changes in the origins of the foreign-born population since the 1960s.

3. Compare the numbers of Asian and Hispanic immigrants among new arrivals.

4. Compare numbers and percentages for authorized and unauthorized immigrants in the United States.

Mini Research Assignments

1. Survey at least seven individuals, asking them to rate their agreement with the following statements on a scale of 1–10 (1 meaning complete disagreement and 10 indicating full agreement): 1. "Families cannot preserve strong ties if their members live in different countries." 2. "Mothers have to live with their children; they cannot be really good mothers if they live and work in another country." 3. "Sometimes family members might have to live apart so that they can find a good job and provide for their children." Summarize the results and discuss the potential role of gender, age, education, and other similar factors in the answers. Draw parallels with the stories as well.
2. Research and summarize immigration policies in the United States and within Europe. Discuss how those policies can affect families. Also, explain how you see the future of transnational families and families in general. Draw parallels with the stories, too.
3. Watch a documentary and/or movie on immigration (documented or undocumented). Summarize in what light immigration is discussed, and how immigrants are portrayed, especially immigrant families. Discuss the impacts of gender and social class on immigration as well. Draw pertinent parallels with the stories.

References

Aranda, E. M. (2003). Global care work and gendered constraints: The case of Puerto Rican trans-migrants. *Gender & Society, 17,* 609–626.

Blumer, H. (1969). *Symbolic interactionism: Perspective and method.* Englewood Cliffs, NJ: Prentice-Hall.

Dreby, J. (2006). Honor and virtue: Mexican parenting in the transnational context. *Gender & Society, 20,* 32–59.

_____. (2010). *Divided by borders: Mexican migrants and their children.* Berkeley, CA: University of California Press.

Hirsch, J. S. (2000). En el norte la mujer manda: Gender, generation, and geography in a Mexican transnational community. In N. Foner, R. Rumbaut, & S. Gold (Eds.), *Immigration research for a new century* (pp. 369–389). New York, NY: Russell Sage.

_____. (2003). *A courtship after marriage: Sexuality and love in Mexican transnational families.* Berkeley, CA: University of California Press.

Hochschild, A. (2012). *The managed heart: Commercialization of human feeling.* Berkeley, CA: University of California Press.

Hondagneu-Sotelo, P., & Avila, E. (1997). 'I'm here, but I'm there': The meanings of Latina transnational motherhood. *Gender & Society, 11,* 548–571.

Parrenas, R. S. (2005). *Children of global migration: Transnational families and gendered woes.* Stanford, CA: Stanford University Press.

Radford, J. & Budiman A. (2018). Facts on U.S. immigrants, 2016. Washington, DC: Pew Research Center. Retrieved from http://www.pewhispanic.org/2018/09/14/facts-on-u-s-immigrants/

West, C., & Zimmerman, D. H. (1987). Doing gender. *Gender & Society, 1,* 125–151.

CHAPTER

14

"But I just want to play."
CHILD MARRIAGES

Xubayr Mayo/ Shutterstock.com

Faridah was walking home from school, still thrilled by everything that she had learned that day. She loved school and had a sizable thirst for knowledge. She almost wished schooldays to be longer so that she could absorb even more information. She had only been going to school for 3 years, but she had already felt as if it had always been an integral part of her life.

The school was located about 5 kilometers (i.e., 3 miles) from her home. She had to walk there every day because there was no school bus or any other form of transportation in her hometown. Her family didn't own a car; in fact, she didn't know any families that did. The reason was not only that they couldn't afford a car, but that there were hardly any paved roads in rural Afghanistan where they lived. They usually walked on dirt roads or the family shared the one donkey that they owned. However, it was mostly Faridah's father who used the donkey; the children normally didn't have access to it.

The road to school was relatively long, and they had to cross one hill to get there, too, so sometimes it could be an arduous journey. Faridah still didn't mind it because the road led to school. She walked to school with two siblings: an older brother and a younger sister. They had two other siblings at home who were too young to attend school. In fact, one of them had just been born a month ago. It was another girl; the fourth girl in the family. When she was born, Faridah noticed that her father was very unhappy and claimed that it was just another mouth to feed, and completely useless as a girl. Faridah wasn't surprised because she knew that girls were less valuable than boys. For example, when they didn't have enough food, her father made sure that the boys ate first, and sometimes there wasn't enough left for the girls. Also, boys were often allowed to go to school longer than girls.

Faridah was aware that their family was poor, and they frequently didn't have sufficient food, but she found it normal because that was the only life she had ever known. Eight of them shared a one-room house with no running water, electricity, or sanitation, but she didn't miss any of those things because she didn't know that they existed. Every family around them had about as much, or as little, as they did, at least in terms of material possessions. They all had a lot in another sense: they all had at least five children. One neighbor had as many as eleven children.

When Faridah and her siblings got home, their father and mother were sitting there, waiting for them, with a stern face. At least, her father's face was stern; her mother looked more dejected. Her father sent all the other children outside; only the baby could stay.

"Daughter, we have something to tell you," her father began solemnly. "As you know, we have a baby in the family now. We do not have enough to take care of all of you. The only solution is if someone else takes care of one of you children."

Faridah didn't comprehend what he was saying, so she simply looked at him expectantly. She also tried to glance at her mother, but she turned her face away, staring at the ground.

Tracing Tea/ Shutterstock.com

Gender, Marriage, and Families: From the Individual to the Social

"You are the oldest daughter, so you're the one to help us in this situation," her father explained. "I've decided that the only solution is for you to get married."

"Married?" Faridah exclaimed, taken aback. "But I'm only 9. Aren't I young to get married?"

"Maybe a little young, but not that much," her father claimed. "Many girls get married at your age, or just a little older. And you are a beautiful, serious girl, pretty mature for your age. For you it's not too early. Maybe we'd wait longer if we could afford it, but we can't. You have to get married."

"But to whom, father?"

"I know a respectable, responsible man who would take you. I trust him. And he's better off than we are; he will take good care of you."

"But who is he; do I know him?" Faridah asked with some trepidation in her voice.

"You don't, but you don't have to. I know him; that should be enough."

"You said he is a man. Isn't he a boy; isn't he my age then?"

"He's not your age. Don't speak silly things. How could he be your age? He couldn't support you then. He's a 38-year-old widow. He's doing quite well for himself. He is giving us five goats after the wedding, which is more than I have ever seen. He also promised to give us a goat or another animal every year while you are married. This will secure your future, as well as your siblings' future. None of you will ever have to starve again."

"Do I have to marry him, father?" Faridah asked shyly. "Isn't there another way?"

"No, there isn't another way," her father asserted. "You have to be obedient and do this. Don't question my decision."

"Do I have to live with him after the marriage?"

"Of course," her father confirmed. "He'll be your husband, so you have to live with him."

"So it's all settled now?" Faridah asked dejectedly. She knew that if it was, she couldn't argue with her father. He expected obedience, and she couldn't talk back, especially as a girl.

"Yes, it's all settled," her father sighed. For a moment, a shadow of concern and sorrow clouded his face, but it passed very quickly.

"When is the wedding?"

"In about 2 weeks," her father responded.

Faridah was stunned by how soon it was, but she knew better than to express her surprise and disappointment.

"Can I still see you after the wedding?"

"Of course," her father replied. "You'll probably see us about once a week."

CHAPTER 14: "But I just want to play." Child Marriages

307

"Can I still go to school when I'm married?"

"You'll have to ask your husband about that. It'll be his decision from then on. Maybe you can still go to school for a while, but most likely, he'll expect you to take care of the household and have children eventually. Not yet, but eventually. I suspect you will have a lot of responsibilities. You will have to grow up soon."

Faridah didn't dare to say anything, but she was screaming on the inside, "But I don't want to grow up. But I just want to play. I just want to go to school." She had been hoping that she wouldn't meet her mother's fate who had attended school only for a couple of years, then dropped out to help take care of her siblings, eventually getting married at 13. She was still only 25, but she had had six children since then, and she started to look like an old woman. Faridah's father was 36; in fact, he was younger than the man he wanted Faridah to marry.

Faridah had no idea how babies came into this world, but she knew that it had something to do with marriage, which her father had just now confirmed, stressing that she would eventually have children when she got married. Faridah was frightened to think about this, as she couldn't imagine to have children yet. She had seen her mother pregnant multiple times, and she had heard her horrible screams, giving birth. She was cognizant that her mother had actually almost died a couple of times during delivery, and one of her babies did die. Faridah wished that she could postpone pregnancy and childbirth, but she was clueless whether that was possible. It seemed not because her mother and all the other married women she knew seemed to be pregnant almost all the time. Marriage appeared to inevitably lead to babies.

Faridah wondered if she would meet her future husband before the wedding. Eventually she didn't; she ended up meeting him about half an hour before they tied the knot. Akbar was tall and lean, and he had a long beard. He seemed very old to Faridah. For a moment, as he was about as old as her father, and he even looked like him a little bit, a glimmer of hope rose in Faridah that maybe he would treat her like her father did, who was usually very stern, and she had to obey him, but he never hurt her physically. She would have to obey Akbar, of course, but hopefully he wouldn't ask anything from her that would be too much to accommodate. Maybe marriage wouldn't be so bad after all. She could still visit her family and maybe even continue to go to school. Plus, she would always have something to eat, which would be a welcome change.

The wedding flew by in a daze, and Faridah couldn't fully grasp that the celebration marked her wedding and her transition from a girl to a married woman. Her mother had made a vague comment about her wedding night, hinting at Akbar possibly doing something that might not be very pleasant. She added that he promised to wait until Faridah was older, but she didn't necessarily believe him. It was all so unclear, and Faridah had no idea what she was referring to. It crossed her mind that it might have something to do with babies, but she pushed the idea out of her mind.

After the wedding, when Faridah and Akbar were finally alone, he started touching her in a way that she didn't like. She asked quietly if he had to do that. He confirmed that he did; it was a part of marriage, and she had to be obedient and cooperate. Faridah knew all about obedience, so she pursed her lips and stifled any sound that she might make. When Akbar did something that hurt more than anything she had ever experienced, she couldn't help crying out in pain. Was this what her mother had referred to? It couldn't be; how could someone be expected to bear this excruciating pain? How often would she have to tolerate this? Would it always hurt so badly?

As Faridah learned later, she was expected to bear it about every second day. It began to hurt less as she got used to it, but it was still very unpleasant. The oddest thing was that Akbar seemed to enjoy it tremendously. Faridah concluded that it probably didn't hurt him then. Faridah suspected that this thing might be the one that led to babies. Maybe it had something to do with the warm liquid that oozed out of Akbar every time. She started to worry that she might become pregnant soon. She finally gathered the courage to ask her mother. She seemed sad and commented that she was disappointed to learn that she was right; Akbar didn't honor his promise to wait until Faridah's puberty. She quickly and sort of vaguely explained to Faridah that she couldn't be pregnant until she was a woman, and she would only become a woman once she would pass blood every month. It all sounded scary and mystical to Faridah. She also asked how could she not be a woman when she was married. It seemed that marriage would transform her to a woman. She undeniably felt much more like a grownup than before her wedding. Her mother couldn't respond; possibly she didn't have the answer either.

Faridah had to get used to all the responsibilities that marriage involved. She suddenly had to take care of a household, cook, and clean. She had helped her mother do all that before, but she had never been solely responsible for those chores. The most unbearable change was not being able to attend school. Faridah timidly asked if she could still go, but Akbar blatantly refused it. He explained that she had been able to walk to school with her siblings before, including a brother, but she couldn't go alone. It would compromise her honor and bring shame on him. Faridah tried to beg her brother to walk to school by her house and accompany her because Akbar might allow her to go then, but her brother wasn't willing to do that, as it would have been too much out of his way. Faridah gathered the courage to plead with her father to talk to Akbar about school, but his father stressed that Faridah had to obey her husband now.

Faridah had never rebelled, but she came very close to it now. She was ready to give up many things, but letting go of school meant discarding her greatest passion in life and her dreams. She had never considered before what if she had been born a boy, but she did now. Her brothers enjoyed much more freedom than she ever did. It was so unfair that her brother, who wasn't as smart as her, got to attend school, and she didn't anymore. It was all because she was born a girl.

Faridah used to be a happy child. She shared numerous moments of play and laughter with her siblings. She had been able to feel incredible joy about small things, such as sunshine or a nice flower. Somehow she had lost her joy; she felt it oozing out of her. It was as if she had had a full cup, which was becoming more and more empty. She didn't know if she might get to a point when her cup might run completely dry.

She couldn't be optimistic about the future anymore, either. What would her future entail? She would forever be married to Akbar, who she couldn't stand. She didn't hate him, but he disgusted her, especially when he forced himself on her. She would never be able to step foot in a school again. She would probably have children in a few years, but she didn't look

forward to that either. It seemed to involve a lot of pain, and she couldn't be too happy about either boys or girls. Girls would eventually meet the same fate that she had to endure, and boys would grow up to be men like her father and Akbar.

Faridah had an inkling that it didn't necessarily have to be this way. It could all be different. There could be a world where girls had other options. At the same time, she was cognizant that it wasn't the world where she lived. After about a year of marriage and darkness, Faridah started to see some hope. She began to cherish dreams that her children could potentially have a different, better life. When she had children, maybe she could raise her sons to be more nurturing and respectful and her daughters to go to school and delay marriage. She knew that it wasn't the standard way of life, and she might not be able to go against tradition, but she could try, and step by step, she could find herself in a world that led to more opportunities, freedom, and happiness.

*

At 13, Nya had been married for a year. Her parents had waited until her puberty, and a month after her first period, they had married her off. They had received seven cows as a bride price. Nya's groom, Mahamat, had been 19 at the time. Nya hadn't been too surprised when her parents had informed her that she was about to be married, as two of her sisters had already been married at the time. One of them had been married at 13, and the other at 11, so the news of her own impending marriage didn't come as a shock to Nya at the age of 12.

Her family had known Mahamat's family for years, and that's why they decided to pair their offspring. Nya had seen Mahamat around, but she hadn't known him very well. He had seemed like a strong, and even somewhat handsome, man, so if she had had to marry someone, she hadn't particularly minded marrying him. Before they had been married, she had even worked up some excitement about their marriage, and she had developed a small crush on him. However, it didn't last long; he had crushed her crush on their wedding night. He had brutally forced himself on her, doing unimaginable things to her. Nya had gathered some information on the wedding night from her married sisters, and she had thought she was prepared. However, she apparently hadn't been prepared for Mahamat's forceful and never-ending desires. When Nya shamefully whispered to her sisters some of the things Mahamat had gleefully done to her, they stared at her with clear surprise, so Nya soon realized that her husband might have a deviant taste in intimacy.

CHAPTER 14: "But I just want to play." Child Marriages

311

Nya had also known that she might get pregnant soon; however, she was still slightly taken aback when it happened within 3 months. By that time, she had begun to consider leaving Mahamat and begging for her family to take her back. Unfortunately, it wasn't customary to do that, and they would have found it difficult to pay back the bride price as well. Also, it would have ruined not only the deal, but the relationship between the two families. When Nya learned that she was pregnant, it was obvious that she couldn't leave.

She was sort of excited about the baby. Maybe someone would love her in her own house because Mahamat clearly didn't. Perhaps Mahamat would become gentler as they became a family as well. The pregnancy wasn't easy in the beginning, but then it became better in the second trimester. In the third trimester it was very difficult again. Nya's small frame turned huge, and she looked almost grotesque with her skinny arms and legs and enormous belly. She started to fear delivery, too. Most of her family members delivered babies easily, but none of them was as young and slender as she was.

When the time came, a village midwife and her mother helped Nya. There was no way she could have gone to a hospital; she was too far in rural Chad, and there were no rapid forms of transportation available either. None of her relatives had ever given birth in a hospital. Nya was puzzled by how strong her pain was; it was nearly unbearable. She was in labor for almost 2 days, and by the end she was nearly delirious and had fainted a few times. Eventually, with some help from the midwife, the baby came. He was huge, at least proportionally, compared to Nya's body, and stillborn. At the time, Nya was in so much physical pain that she didn't even comprehend that her baby didn't survive the long and arduous labor. When she did, she cried for hours, and, 3 months later, the emotional pain remained.

Nya had sustained some physical injuries as well. She had suffered a tear during delivery, which had left her incontinent. Also, she was warned that she might have some injuries, which could make another pregnancy dangerous, if not impossible. This piece of news was especially crushing because having and raising babies was the only thing that gave Nya some hope and perspective for the future.

Mahamat was furious at her when he learned about her condition. He began to view her as damaged goods. He started to talk about taking on a second wife and returning

Anton_Ivanov / Shutterstock.com

Nya to her family. Nya wished that he would do that, but eventually Mahamat reconsidered, taking his family's wishes into account.

Mahamat married a second wife a few months later, and he mostly left Nya alone after that. She was expected to do chores around the house, but having sex with Mahamat was rarely one of them from then on. The second wife was a year older than Nya, and they got along well. She gave birth to a son a year later and two more within 3.5 years. Her fourth child was a girl. Nya loved the children, helped take care of them, and she almost considered them her own. In a way, she felt that she had found a family.

*

Daksha became a widow at 18 after 4 years of marriage. This was potentially the worst tragedy that could have struck her. It was worse than dying. She wished that she had died instead of or along with Zarir. She considered killing herself, but she was afraid of the consequences. She wanted to do her best in this life to ensure the best opportunities for reincarnation in the next life.

Daksha had been a relatively happy child, although she had grown up in extreme poverty. She had been born as the fifth child in a family of nine in rural India. She had often experienced starvation, lack, and illness. Still, she was delighted when she could play with her siblings, and she loved her family. She had always been a dutiful child, and this characteristic was apparent in her adulthood as well.

She considered herself very lucky with her marriage. She was married off slightly later than her older sisters, and she felt she was ready by the time the wedding came. It was an arranged marriage, of course, as was customary, but she didn't mind it, as she had been raised knowing that it would happen one day. She found Zarir a handsome and likable man when she met him. He had been 18 when they got married, 4 years older than her, which was ideal. One of her sisters had married a man who was nearly 30 years her senior, so Daksha was aware that she was very fortunate with Zarir.

When Daksha had married Zarir, love was never a consideration. It was insignificant in an arranged marriage. She had trusted her parents' wise choice. They had undeniably made the best economic decision, but there was an unexpected outcome as well: Daksha had grown to love Zarir. It was a deep, respectful love and attachment. Zarir seemed to feel the same, too. It didn't happen instantly, but they did develop a profound love for each other within a year of marriage. Zarir treated Daksha well, and she thrived in their marriage. They weren't rich; in fact, they did just a little bit better financially than Daksha's family, but it was sufficient for her. She had never dreamed of material comfort; it was not important for her. In addition, she knew that mobility was mostly restricted in Indian society, so she never aspired for much.

After about a year of marriage Daksha started to yearn for a child. Although they were trying, a child never came. Daksha never gave up hope, and Zarir was even more optimistic. He didn't even mind negative comments from his family as years passed by without an offspring. Daksha noticed, however, that her in-laws began to treat her differently. They expected a child from her, preferably a boy, so they were disappointed. Zarir comforted her and encouraged her that she was still very young, and maybe she just needed more time. The more pressure Daksha felt to become pregnant, not from Zarir, but from everyone else, the more anxious she got, and she even suspected that it could have hindered her from becoming pregnant.

A week after Daksha had turned 18, and Zarir had been 22, he had a horrific accident that killed him instantly. Daksha couldn't believe that it had happened, and she was inconsolable. She had never known such vast grief before. It seemed to have swallowed her, to keep her in its grasp, and she couldn't get away. It was always there, and there was no escape from it.

No matter how desperate and grief-stricken Daksha was, she couldn't afford to wallow in grief. Her in-laws didn't give her much time. As a widow, she was considered inauspicious, and especially because she didn't bear an offspring, her in-laws didn't welcome her anymore. They wanted to kick her out right away, but they ended up giving her a week to gather

her belongings and prepare to leave. Daksha didn't blame them; she was cognizant of the customs and also her in-laws' antipathy toward her.

Daksha tried to turn to her family, although she was aware that they couldn't help her in this situation. She was correct; her family turned her away. She didn't want to beg; she was too proud of that, and she was hesitant to bring shame on them anyway. She knew that the best for everyone was for her to go away. She shaved her head and dressed in white, following what was expected of widows. She was aware that she was never allowed to marry again. She had lost all social status by losing her husband.

Daksha had heard rumors about a holy town with many pilgrims, including widows. It was called Vrindavan, but some referred to it as the city of widows because numerous discarded, unwanted, desolate widows visited the city or even settled there. It was mostly lower-class, destitute widows who were treated so badly; sometimes middle- or upper-class ones had more opportunities, and if they could support themselves, they didn't necessarily have to give up their lives. For them, widowhood might have decreased their social status, but membership in a higher class and financial independence could elevate it. However, as Daksha belonged to a lower caste, she didn't have access to these potential advantages.

The trip to Vrindavan was a long and arduous one. Daksha begged for most of the journey, and although it was very hard because most people didn't want to give her any money, she could eventually find her way to the city of widows. As she met a few other widows, she heard about a shelter

CHAPTER 14: "But I just want to play." Child Marriages

315

that took in widows. They didn't have enough space when she arrived, and elderly widows sometimes received preferential treatment, but Daksha hoped that the shelter could eventually provide her with a room and one meal a day. Until then, she continued begging and slept in the street.

She heard about some young widows who turned to prostitution as a last resort and sold their bodies for shelter or food. Daksha wanted to avoid this fate at all cost. She met a young widow one day that was making and selling crafts, acquiring a very modest, but relatively reliable income, making it possible to rent a room with some other widows. Daksha asked if she could join in, as she was somewhat skilled in crafts. The other widow agreed, and Daksha was delighted because it was a source of income and potential friendship as well.

Daksha had always been dependent on others before, and they had always been men, including her father, brothers, and husband. The young widows who sold their bodies still relied on men in a way to support them. Daksha was relieved that she found something that ensured for her to support herself. It was an unfamiliar and an undeniably empowering venture.

While Daksha had made friends with a few widows, she was aware that she would never have male companionship again. She truly missed her husband, but he was never coming back, and she couldn't remarry. No one would marry a widow. This also meant that she would never have a child either. Sometimes she was wondering if she was incapable of bearing children anyway, or if she could have had one eventually if she had had more time with Zarir. She would never know the answer to that question.

One day Daksha met an elderly widow. She was 80, and she had been a widow for 65 years, spending most of them in Vrindavan, begging for money, then living at the shelter. To Daksha, it was almost inconceivable that if she lived a long life, she might live as a widow for most of it as well, maybe as much as 70 years. All those years seemed like a never-ending stretch. She enjoyed making crafts, but it hurt too much to live without Zarir and without children. She spent a considerable amount of her time with religious worship and prayed for a better life after this one. She just hoped that it would come soon, and she wouldn't have to wait several decades for it.

Discussion Questions

1. Continue the three stories. How do you envision the rest of their lives?

2. What do you see as the main causes and potential consequences of child marriage?

3. Discuss the role of gender in child marriages.

4. What does socioeconomic status, social class, and education have to do with child marriages?

5. Discuss the potential impact of globalization on child marriages. Do you think that increasing globalization could decrease child marriage rates? Why/why not?

6. Do you find child marriages deviant (different from social norms in a given society at a particular time)? Why/why not? Do they seem to be deviant in the countries featured in the three stories? Why/why not?

CHAPTER 14: "But I just want to play." Child Marriages

319

7. West and Zimmerman (1987) explained that gender was a routine, everyday accomplishment, something that we performed in interaction with others. Discuss a few examples of how characters in the three stories do gender, and how their gendered behaviors are socially/culturally driven.

8. Do you think that there is any stigma regarding child marriages? Remember, stigma is a salient, generally stubborn, negative label that is applied to individuals who do not follow social norms (Goffman, 1986). If yes, does the stigma vary by different factors and circumstance? Is there more stigma at some places than others? Does there seem to be a stigma regarding widows in India? Why/why not?

9. Do you think that age at the time of marriage makes a significant difference in child marriage? For instance, do you see a difference between girls getting married at 9, 12, 14, or 16? When would you say it is too young to get married? Why? Does the age difference between the partners matter? For example, is it different when both are children, versus only one is a child and the partner is much older? Why/why not?

10. Do you think there is an upper age limit for getting married? Do you think there is an age when one is too old to get married? Why/why not?

Find the Answers

Go to http://www.girlsnotbrides.org/where-does-it-happen/ to find answers to the following questions.

1. List three statistics about child marriage.

2. Which three countries have the highest rates of child marriage?

3. Which world regions have the highest rates of child marriage?

4. Go to http://www.girlsnotbrides.org/what-is-the-impact/ and list at least three common impacts of child marriage.

Mini Research Assignments

1. Study the following website: http://www.girlsnotbrides.org/about-child-marriage/ and click on links to learn about the geography, extent, causes, impacts, and solutions of child marriage. Within the geography section, click on at least five countries to explore their child marriage rates. Summarize the results, including the statistics you find the most surprising and/or significant. Discuss the role of culture, religion, gender, education, and social class, too. Evaluate the proposed solutions and discuss which ones you consider the most effective and suggest any other solutions if you can. Draw parallels with the stories as well.
2. Survey at least seven individuals, asking them to rate their agreement with the following statements on a scale of 1–10 (1 meaning complete disagreement and 10 indicating full agreement): 1. "Child marriage is always wrong." 2. "We have to accept different customs and beliefs in other cultures even if they are widely different from our own." 3. "Child marriage can lead to severe consequences in the lives of affected girls." Summarize the results and discuss the potential role of gender, age, education, and other similar factors in the answers. Draw parallels with the stories as well.
3. Watch a documentary on child marriage. Summarize the main findings of the documentary. Discuss the role of culture, religion, gender, education, and social class, too. Draw parallels with the stories. If there are any proposed solutions to reducing child marriage, mention those as well and evaluate them. You can suggest other solutions, too.

References

Goffman, E. (1986). *Stigma: Notes on the management of spoiled identity*. New York, NY: Touch-stone. (Originally published 1963)

West, C., & Zimmerman, D. H. (1987). Doing gender. *Gender & Society, 1,* 125–151.

CHAPTER 15

"Do I deserve to die for this?"
ADULTERY ACROSS THE GLOBE

Freedom Studio / Shutterstock.com

Nasreen knew that she was in trouble. People would soon figure out her secret. She was pregnant and expected to give birth in about 10 weeks. Her husband had left over 9 months ago. Everybody with just the bare minimum of math skills could calculate that something was off, and it was impossible for her to be pregnant for 12 months. Even if her baby came early, it would still pose problems for her. It would be highly suspicious if she gave birth to a supposedly already overdue baby, who looked premature. If she carried her baby to full term, the baby would arrive almost 3 months after he or she was supposed to. Either way, the time was coming when her secret would be revealed. Nasreen feared for her life, but was even more worried about her child.

Nasreen had been born in Iran 22 years ago. She had always been surrounded by several siblings and numerous other relatives, and was especially close to one of her second cousins, Kasra. They had played together as small children when their families got together. They were almost exactly the same age; Kasra was 10 days older than Nasreen. When they had turned 15, Nasreen noticed that her feelings for Kasra had intensified. She missed him tremendously when he wasn't around, and she could hardly wait for the next time to see him. They could practically never be alone, but Nasreen caught herself yearning for that. She would have given anything for a few private moments with him. She didn't understand how she could feel even more for a second cousin than her brothers, but she still did. She couldn't explain it, but she and Kasra seemed to share something special. She thought that Kasra was aware of it, too, based on how he looked at her sometimes.

A few months before her seventeenth birthday, Nasreen was married off to a wealthy man, Farrokh, who had been 50 at the time, widowed twice. Nasreen had been cognizant that most likely she wouldn't be able to choose her marriage partner when the time came, so the marriage didn't take her by surprise. Nevertheless, she was desperately upset during and after her wedding. Kasra had been there, staring at her, his eyes reflecting the same profound pain she had been plagued by. Nasreen's chest hurt so much that she was afraid she might die. She sank into utter depression in the first few months of her marriage. She cried a lot and thought about Kasra even more than before.

Finally, when one of her sisters noticed her dejection and continued to ask her about it, Nasreen admitted how unhappy she was, and how much her heart ached for Kasra, who she missed much more than any of her other relatives. Her sister looked at her with compassion and a little bit of pity, whispering to her that it sounded like she was in love with Kasra. Nasreen was incredulous at first, but as she thought about it later, she realized that her sister was probably right. Nasreen had tried to chalk up all her feelings to kinship, but they had far surpassed brotherly love.

After this epiphany, Nasreen felt even more upset. She often wept uncontrollably, but made sure to hide it from her husband and everyone

Zurijeta/ Shutterstock.com

else. Her sorrow grew when Kasra got married about a year later. A part of Nasreen wished for a child, although she didn't particularly want Farrokh's child. However, she didn't get pregnant, which was most likely related to some of the issues Farrokh had with his sexual function. She didn't mind it when he stayed away from her for long stretches of time because she detested his touch anyway. He often traveled for business, frequently for months at a time. Nasreen was immensely relieved when he was gone. He wasn't evil, but he could be mean, and when he was in a bad mood, he beat her up.

About 10 months ago Farrokh left for a business trip, which was scheduled to last for 3 to 4 months. Usually Farrokh's elderly mother or another relative moved in with Nasreen for the time when her husband was away, because it wouldn't have been appropriate for her to stay in the house on her own. Her mother-in-law came to stay with her this time as well. Approximately 2.5 months after Farrokh had left, five of Nasreen's relatives, including Kasra with his wife, arrived to visit her. It was still very painful to see Kasra, especially with his wife. It had been several years, but the pain felt just as vivid as it had more than 5 years ago.

The second evening of their visit, after dinner, Kasra whispered to Nasreen to come out to the back of the garden around midnight. Nasreen looked at him incredulously for a moment, then slowly shook her head. She paced in her bedroom for hours, determined to stay in her room. When midnight came, something seemed to take over, and she ran out to the garden, almost on autopilot. She needed to see Kasra and spend just a few moments alone with him.

He was waiting for her in the back corner of the garden, which was also the darkest and completely invisible from the house.

"You came," Kasra smiled, his voice trembling.

"I almost didn't," Nasreen responded, glancing down, avoiding to look at him. "Maybe I shouldn't have."

"I don't know if you should or shouldn't have, but I'm so glad you came," Kasra said, reaching for her hands. Nasreen pulled them away and took one step back.

"I'm sorry, I don't want to scare you," Kasra apologized. "I just… I just couldn't resist. Seeing you after all these years… I thought I'm

over it, that I'm over you, but apparently I'm not. Nasreen, I've never said anything; we've never said anything, but I've always... And I think you, too."

Nasreen jerked away and covered her ears, "Please stop, Kasra. You cannot say that. You shouldn't say that. It's too late. You're a married man, and I'm married, too."

"I know," Kasra sighed. "We were too young. I didn't know what to do. And even if I tried to do anything then, your parents would've never given your hand to me. Farrokh could offer you so much more. I was hoping he would love you, too, and you would be happy. But I'm afraid he doesn't love you, and I'm afraid you aren't happy. I can see it in your eyes."

"You're right on both accounts," Nasreen said quietly. "But it doesn't matter. I'm a woman; maybe I'm not supposed to be happy anyway. I'm supposed to make my family happy."

"It just hurts me so much to see you like this," Kasra exclaimed. "I want you to be happy. I'm not happy either, but I don't care. I don't love my wife, but she's a good woman, and she tries her best. I'm grateful for the two children she has given me. But I don't love her. I've never felt with her what I do with you."

"Kasra, don't do this," Nasreen begged. "Don't be disrespectful to your wife, and don't say things that can't be taken back. Don't torture me and yourself either. You know that we can never be together. Why say all these things then?"

"I just can't help it, Nasreen," Kasra burst out. "I can't help it. Seeing you brings it all back, and I'm not a boy anymore. I'm a man, and it's so much harder to bear it now than years ago."

Kasra reached for her hand, and Nasreen didn't push him away this time. Maybe they could hold hands for a moment; that wouldn't be wrong. Kasra took it as encouragement, and leaned down to kiss Nasreen's lips and neck. Nasreen knew she should really push him away now, but she couldn't work up the strength for it, especially because she didn't want to. She wanted him to be close to her more than anything. Before either of them could stop, they found themselves making love. Nasreen was amazed because she had never realized that such acts could bring so much pleasure. It was the opposite with her husband. They were together until about 4 a.m., then they both sneaked back into the quiet house.

Nasreen felt guilty because this was against everything she was taught and believed in. She was cognizant that adultery was wrong; it was a deadly sin. A small part of her was actually satisfied and happy, which made her feel even guiltier. Kasra couldn't look her in the eye the next morning, and he made up an excuse to leave that afternoon with his wife. As he said good-bye to Nasreen, his suffering glance told her everything she needed to know. He loved her as much as she loved him, but he felt guilty, too, and he knew he needed to be responsible, which he could only do by staying away. They could never be together, and what had happened last night shouldn't be repeated, so the best course of action was to leave, no matter how hard it was.

Nasreen cried a lot after he had left, but she understood, and she was aware that it was the right thing to do. A part of her was delighted that they had been able to have each other at least once in this lifetime, although she realized that it was a sin. She wished the best for Kasra and was hoping that he could forget her and be happy eventually. She doubted that she would be able to do the same.

Around 2 weeks after Kasra's departure and a few days before Farrokh was scheduled to return, Nasreen was notified that her husband had suffered a sudden heart attack and died. She was stunned because the news was so unexpected. She felt sorry for him, but she also felt a wave of relief, which she thought was shameful. She knew she had to go through the motions and mourn for him because it was expected of her. A small part of her began to hope as well that maybe Kasra could divorce her wife, and they could actually be together. She wouldn't expect him to do that, and it would bring shame on them and their families, but it wasn't impossible.

About a month later Nasreen began to suspect that she might be pregnant. In approximately 2 more weeks she was sure. She didn't dare to go to a doctor because the baby's young age would be immediately obvious then. If her husband was the one to have impregnated her, she should have been nearly 5 months pregnant, not 2.5 months. It would be clear that she had committed adultery, which could have severe consequences in Iran.

Adultery was usually difficult to prove because according to Sharia law, the moral and religious code of Islam, there had to be at least four witnesses who could testify to have seen the act of penetration, or the perpetrator had to admit to the sin, or there had to be concrete evidence for adultery. Unfortunately, a baby would be more than sufficient evidence in a case when the husband was first away from home, then dead. Sex for unmarried people could be punishable by 100 lashes, but for married individuals, the punishment for extramarital sex could be as severe as death by stoning. In that case, men were buried up to their waist, and women up to their shoulder, while stones were hurled at them. If they managed to free themselves, they could live, but it was more likely that they died. A confession and repentance could lead to a reduced punishment of 99 lashes instead of death by stoning.

As far as Nasreen knew, there weren't witnesses, especially four witnesses to what had happened between her and Kasra. However, the baby would provide evidence. She might be better off admitting to adultery and pleading for a milder sentence than waiting to be discovered. Although executions by stoning were rare these days, they weren't unheard of, and Nasreen was worried that she might be killed while pregnant, so her baby would die as well. This is why she decided to wait and not give herself up. It was likely that a neighbor or a midwife, or someone else would report her when she gave birth about a year after her husband had been gone, but at least her baby would be born and alive then, although Nasreen had no idea how he or she would be treated as the child of an adulteress.

No matter what would happen, Nasreen swore that she wouldn't give up Kasra; she wouldn't admit that he had committed adultery as well. She couldn't hide her adultery for much longer, but she could try to spare Kasra. In theory, men could receive the same sentence for adultery as women, but, in practice, women tended to get harsher punishments than men. Still, Nasreen didn't want Kasra to get in trouble at all. She prayed for her life, and for her baby's safety, wishing that she could just disappear or move to another country. It wasn't that easy, so if she was discovered, and the punishment came according to the laws of her country and faith, she would have to face whatever came. She was flooded by a wave of rebellion, and a voice yelled in her, "Do I deserve to die for this?" Then, while she was still afraid, she succumbed to her fate, no matter what it would be.

*

Emel had been in hiding for a month. She had no idea how much longer she could get away with not being found, but she had to try her best because her life seemed to depend on it. If her family caught her, she might not be able to survive this time.

Emel had been born and raised in a village in southern Turkey. Her upbringing had been very traditional and conservative. Although most of Turkey was geographically located in Asia, the country had been aspiring to join the European Union. Turkey could boast with several metropolitan areas and highly developed regions; however, parts of the country were lagging behind, and especially the Kurds were following strict religious and moral codes, a subbranch of Islam, which were widely different from mainstream European customs and beliefs. Emel lived in such an area of the country.

Emel had been married off at 16. She had followed her family's wishes and tied the knot with the man her family had selected for her. She never

Yavuz Sariyildiz / Shutterstock.com

questioned their decision and accepted that where she was from women didn't decide about their own marriage; it was a family matter instead. Although her husband was sometimes very rough and aggressive with her, he was no different from Emel's father and brothers and what she had been used to.

Emel was taught to be obedient, and she obeyed the rules. She would have never thought of rebelling against marriage, for instance. She had heard about some girls who did, and some of them ended up being murdered by their own families. By disobeying their families' wishes, they were seen as compromising family honor, which led to so-called honor killings by family members in some cases. Although it was against the law, and it could be seen as a form of vigilante justice, some family members could get away with it, or spend only a few years in prison, which was worth it for them for cleansing family honor. When Emel had been in school, for example, one of her classmates had been killed by her family for regularly talking to a boy in school. Another girl had been raped by three men, and eventually she was also killed by her family for tarnishing their reputation and engaging in premarital sex. Emel had also heard about a boy who had been murdered by his family for kissing another boy, as same-sex relations were also seen as compromising family honor.

Before marriage, Emel had been very careful and avoided boys completely to ensure that she was never viewed as a dishonor to the family. At 16, she got married and became pregnant within a year. She carried the baby to term, but he was stillborn. It had been 2 years ago, and she hadn't got pregnant again since then.

CHAPTER 15: "Do I deserve to die for this?" Adultery across the Globe

331

About 3 months ago a young man, approximately 22, had started to follow Emel around. He had tried to talk to her a couple of times as well, but she rejected him with as few words as she could because she was cognizant that simply talking to him could get her in trouble. He was very handsome, and under other circumstances, at another place or time, she could have imagined talking to him, maybe even liking him. However, here and now, being a married woman in rural Turkey, she couldn't afford that luxury, so she turned him down and attempted to avoid him, no matter how persistent he appeared to be.

In a few weeks, Emel had heard that the man had disappeared. He was reported to have migrated to Europe unexpectedly, but no one heard from him again, including his family. Emel suspected and feared that someone from her family might have seen them together, got the wrong idea, and had something to do with his disappearance. If her family and her husband believed that she was involved with him, she would be considered an adulteress, and her life could be in jeopardy. She felt helpless and didn't know what to do. Before she could come to a decision, she was kidnapped by one of her young cousins in the middle of the night and taken to another family member's remote home. She was informed that the family council, along with her husband, had decided that she had brought dishonor on the family by adultery. She tried to explain that nothing had happened, but they didn't believe her, and her assumed denial actually enraged them more.

A male cousin, who was only 16, was charged with killing her. He was selected because the family thought that his young age could lead to a more lenient, shorter prison sentence for Emel's murder. The young boy was too terrified, and eventually he couldn't work up the courage to use the knife that had been handed to him. The other male relatives were frustrated with him, but they were hesitant to risk the murder and potential consequences themselves. They ended up changing their strategy. They locked Emel up and tried to convince her to commit suicide for the sake of family honor. They handed her a knife and rat poison to choose from. They counted on her obedience and didn't think that she would ever use the knife against them, which Emel eventually did. Her survival instinct kicked in, and she stabbed her younger brother's hand who was standing in guard, and she ran away.

She ran as fast and as far away as she could. For almost a day, she had no idea where she could go. She couldn't go back to her parents' house, for instance, because she knew that her father agreed with the family verdict as well, and so did her brothers. Finally, she decided to go to a widowed aunt's house, who might understand her and take pity on her. She didn't want to get her in trouble either, but she didn't know what else to do.

Her aunt turned out to be compassionate and agreed to hide her for a while. Once, about a week ago, two of her brothers had actually came looking for her, but her aunt had hidden her so well that they didn't find her. Emel was so scared and so relieved when they left. However, she knew that her aunt couldn't hide her forever. The best course of action might be leaving the country and trying to get into the European Union and settle there. However, she didn't have any papers or any money. She didn't know which way to go either. However, this plan started to take root in her mind, and she was gathering up the courage to leave. She was more afraid of her family than any border patrol or government agency. Maybe she could get out of Turkey and start a new life. This seemed to be her only chance.

*

Asta was immensely upset, as she had just learned that her husband, Birger, was cheating on her. Some people might not have considered it cheating, but Asta definitely did. He might not have slept with anyone or had a physical sexual contact with another woman, but to Asta, it was just as painful, or even more so.

Asta and Birger had married 12 years ago, in their native Norway. Their marriage was blissful for years, and they were even happier when their family was complete with two children, a boy and a girl. Then, about a year ago, things had started to change, and Asta could detect some distance between the two of them. At first, she had thought that Birger was exhausted and

stressed by work, but later she began to suspect that he might be involved with someone.

Before they were married, they had many talks on fidelity, and they seemed to agree that cheating couldn't be tolerated. They both wanted total commitment and faithfulness. Of course, maybe it was easy to discuss all of that in theory, and very different years later, in a marriage that was losing its spark. Asta would have never thought to become a woman who would spy on her husband, but her suspicions resulted in so much agony that she couldn't take it any longer. She checked her husband's phone and email when he forgot to sign out once. She was abhorred to find hundreds of texts and emails from someone named Embla. The oldest message had dated back to nearly a year ago.

As Asta read through the texts and emails, crying, she found out that Embla lived in a town that was about 4 hours away. She also realized that her husband had actually never met Embla in person. However, he seemed to have become very close to her and shared many intimate, emotionally, and sometimes even sexually, charged texts. So, it was clear that Birger and Embla hadn't slept together. In fact, they hadn't even met face-to-face, but Asta still felt that her husband had betrayed her and cheated on her.

For a couple of weeks, Asta didn't know what to do. She was upset, frequently crying, and also angry at her husband. Still, she hesitated to ask him directly about the online affair because what if he confessed his love for Embla and left her. Asta used to say that she would leave and divorce her husband right away if he was found cheating. Although Asta considered the online affair cheating, somehow she still hesitated to simply leave.

While Asta was struggling about what to do, one of her colleagues, Geir, approached her and asked her what was wrong. He seemed to have picked up on her anguish. Asta didn't want to divulge her personal issues, but she was so upset, and Geir appeared to be so attentive, that she ended up telling him everything over a drink after work. Geir did his best to console her, but he was even more focused on taking advantage of the situation and getting her to bed. Asta felt so sad, outraged, and ready to punish Birger that she ended up sleeping with Geir. She felt somewhat guilty, but also justified as Birger had cheated on her first.

Her own infidelity had given Asta the strength to address Birger's unfaithfulness with him. Maybe she actually wanted to tell him about her encounter with Geir to hurt him as much as he had offended her. So, one day she sat him down and said slowly, "I know about Embla."

"What?" Birger asked incredulously. "What are you saying?"

"I know about Embla," Asta repeated.

"I… I mean, how?" Birger asked hesitantly.

"That doesn't matter," Asta responded firmly. "I came across a piece of information by accident. What matters is that you've been cheating on me. You've sworn fidelity, and you've cheated on me."

"I haven't cheated on you," Birger sighed. "Yes, I've been corresponding with Embla, and she's become a very dear friend, but I haven't cheated on you. I wouldn't cheat on you."

"Yes, sure," Asta said sarcastically. "There's a woman that you have been talking to all the time. You share so much more with her than with me. You're more confidential with her than with me. And you're saying that you haven't cheated on me?"

"Look, I didn't sleep with her," Birger asserted. "And I'd never do that. I've needed to vent and share some things with an outsider. But I haven't even met the woman in person. How can you say I cheated on you?"

"Because you have," Asta burst out in tears, pushing away Birger's hand, who tried to comfort her. She cried for minutes, while Birger was staring at her helplessly.

"You're so intimate with her," Asta wept. "You're in love with her, aren't you?"

"No," Birger countered. "I'll admit, there have been a few moments when I thought I could fall in love with her, but I held back. I wouldn't do that to you. I *love you*."

"Am I supposed to believe that?"

"Yes, of course," Birger replied. "You've known me for one and a half decades. You know that I love you. We've been going through something; we're not as close as we used to. But I love you."

"And you're saying you never had any sex with this woman?"

"Of course not," Birger protested. "I told you, I've never met her. I've never touched her."

"What about online sex?" Asta asked accusingly.

"What about it?" Birger shot back, looking down.

"Have you had any kind of sex with her, online or otherwise?"

"Look, we've exchanged some racy texts and shared some fantasies," Birger admitted. "But that's nothing. I've never touched her."

"That's *not* nothing," Asta countered vehemently. "You might not have touched her physically because she wasn't here, but it sounds like you wanted to, and you fantasized about it."

"It's only happened a couple of times," Birger contended. "And it was completely harmless, believe me. You know, I don't really get this. You knew that I was watching porn online once in a while. That didn't really bother you. You didn't think *that* was cheating. What's the difference here? Anything that went on with Embla was more innocent than porn."

"It bothers me because she's a real woman," Asta exclaimed. "Porn is like watching a movie, and you don't join in. It's not a substitute for me, but participating in something like this and getting involved with another woman is. I'm not enough anymore? I'm not *good enough* anymore? You know what? *I am.* Other men want me even if you don't."

"What do you mean?" Birger asked suspiciously. "I mean, of course, other men would want you; you're an attractive woman. But what did you mean? The way you said it, and your tone… Are you talking about someone in particular?"

"Yes," Asta burst out. She was still so hurt that she wanted Birger to experience the same kind of pain as well. "I'm talking about a man who's really into me. He wants me. And because I knew you were cheating on me, I didn't turn him down when he hit on me."

"What do you mean you didn't turn him down?" Birger asked, turning pale.

"I mean I slept with him," Asta divulged.

Birger was silent for a few minutes, his face turning even whiter. Finally, he began to talk, "So, let me get this straight. You're accusing me of cheating, which I never did. Yes, maybe I got closer to someone than I should have; I get your point. But I never slept with her and would have never done that. Whatever happened, even the law wouldn't recognize it as infidelity. What you did, however… You're the one who *did cheat* on me. And you're the one who's so upset? How am *I* supposed to feel?"

Asta calmed down for a moment and started to consider the repercussions of her actions. She had felt entirely justified sleeping with Geir, but maybe she was wrong. She had wanted to hurt Birger, but now felt sorry for him and regretted getting involved with Geir. No matter her motives, she did cheat. She felt confused and guilty and had no idea if their marriage could recover from this blow. The consequences of her adultery could be severe because it could lead to losing her husband. She couldn't imagine a more extreme punishment for cheating than this.

Discussion Questions

1. Continue the three stories. What do you think will happen next?

2. Discuss the role of gender in views on adultery and related consequences/punishments.

3. Discuss the potential impact of globalization on opinions and laws regarding adultery. Do you think that increasing globalization could decrease extreme punishments for adultery at some places, as well as honor killings? Why/why not?

4. Do you think that there is any stigma regarding adultery? Remember, stigma is a salient, persistent, negative label that is applied to individuals who disobey social norms (Goffman, 1986). If yes, does the stigma vary by different factors and circumstances? Why do you think the stigma is stronger at some places than others?

5. Blumer (1969) defined three core ideas in symbolic interactionism. The first is that humans act toward things based on the meanings those things have for them. The second is that meanings are created through social interaction. The third is that meanings are understood and potentially transformed through an interpretative process. Apply this theory to definitions of adultery across the globe.

6. Zerubavel (1991) explained that "[t]o define something is to mark its boundaries, to surround it with a mental fence that separates it from everything else" (p. 2). Where are the boundaries of adultery? How do definitions of adultery vary across time and place?

7. Do you see any difference between the following terms: *adultery, cheating, extramarital sex*? (You can add to the list.) Do they have neutral, positive, or negative connotations? How can these labels affect how the act (or the person committing the act) is perceived?

8. Use an ethnomethodological approach to discuss norms of monogamy/fidelity in marriage based on the stories. Ethnomethodology is the study of how norms of the social world are created and understood (Garfinkel, 1984). Ethnomethodologists deliberately breach social norms to underline the rigidity of those norms. How can we see norms about monogamy/fidelity at play in marriages when those norms are questioned or violated?

9. Berger and Luckmann (1966) highlighted that reality was both objectively socially constructed through the processes of institutionalization and legitimation, and subjectively socially constructed through the internalization of reality by socialization. Legitimation indicates justifying something by religious, moral, or other kinds of arguments. Institutionalization means that a belief or practice is supported/legally sanctioned by an institution, such as marriage, for instance, and is seen as if existing as an inherent truth, entirely outside of human/social influence. Through socialization (by our families, education, religion, etc.) we learn to accept things as absolute truths. Explain how definitions of faithfulness and adultery might be viewed as socially constructed. What kind of legitimation processes are taking place? What is the role of institutionalization and socialization? How can approaches to adultery as socially constructed explain differences in views on adultery across the globe and over time?

10. What is your definition of cheating? Is it any different depending on whether it is in a romantic relationship or marriage? How could circumstances impact what you consider cheating? How do you think your environment (family, education, media, church, etc.) has influenced your definitions of cheating?

Find the Answers

Go to https://ifstudies.org/blog/americas-generation-gap-in-extramarital-sex to find answers to the following questions.

1. What is the difference in the numbers of Americans believing that extramarital sex is always wrong versus those who reportedly have cheated?

2. Who seems to engage more in extramarital sex, younger or older Americans? Report the actual numbers, too.

3. What might cause the generation gap in extramarital sex?

4. How have polyamory rates changed over time?

Mini Research Assignments

1. Survey at least seven individuals, asking them to rate their agreement with the following statements on a scale of 1–10 (1 meaning complete disagreement and 10 indicating full agreement): 1. "Cheating in a marriage is always wrong." 2. "Cheating in a marriage is worse than in an unmarried romantic relationship." 3. "Emotional infidelity is just as bad as physical, sexual infidelity." 4. "It's less acceptable for a woman than for a man to cheat." Summarize the results, discussing the potential impact of gender, age, education, and other similar factors in the answers. Draw parallels with the stories as well.

2. Watch a documentary on adultery or honor killings outside of the United States. How is it depicted? What are the circumstances? Who commits the adultery or honor killing? Discuss the role of gender, culture, tradition, religion, social class, and other similar factors. Explain the role of norms, prejudice, and stigma. Draw parallels with the stories as well.

3. Do some research on statistics and geographic location for adultery or honor killings across the globe. Summarize your findings. Discuss the role of gender, culture, tradition, religion, social class, and other similar factors. Explain the role of norms, prejudice, and stigma. Draw parallels with the stories as well.

References

Berger, P. L., & Luckmann, T. (1966). *The social construction of reality: A treatise in the sociology of knowledge*. Garden City, NY: Doubleday.

Blumer, H. (1969). *Symbolic interactionism: Perspective and method*. Englewood Cliffs, NJ: Prentice-Hall.

Garfinkel, H. (1984). *Studies in ethnomethodology*. Malden, MA: Polity.

Goffman, E. (1986). *Stigma: Notes on the management of spoiled identity*. New York, NY: Touchstone. (Originally published 1963)

Wolfinger, N. (2017). America's generation gap in extramarital sex. Charlottesville, VA: Institute for Family Studies. Retrieved from https://ifstudies.org/blog/americas-generation-gap-in-extramarital-sex

Zerubavel, E. (1991). *The fine line: Making distinctions in everyday life*. New York, NY: Free Press.

CHAPTER 16

"I love her. And her. And her."
POLYAMORY AND POLYGAMY

Kashvi wiped her hands after peeling some vegetables to put in to-day's dinner. She had a relatively large family, so she was used to preparing large portions for each meal. She didn't mind cooking; in fact, she truly enjoyed it, and it relaxed her most of the time. While she always had a lot to do around the house, she never felt overwhelmed, espe-cially because she had help. Being the only grown woman in the household didn't mean that she had to handle everything on her own.

Kashvi's immediate family consisted of her three husbands and three children. She lived in a part of Nepal where polyandry, the practice of hav-ing multiple husbands, was not unusual. In fact, in her community most marriages were polyandrous. She had grown up in such a household and was raised to most likely enter a polyandrous marriage herself.

When the time had come, Kashvi's family and her future husbands' fami-ly agreed on the marriage, and soon after, Kashvi married Ayush, Arpan, and Ankur. The three men were brothers. This was a common form of polyandry. When the husbands were all brothers, it was called fraternal polyandry.

Kashvi had known the brothers and their family for virtually all her life, and she was aware of how hardworking and honest they were, and that's what mattered the most. She also trusted her parents' decision. She considered herself lucky that her fate was taking such a good turn and that she had the fortune to marry into this family.

A few select regions in Nepal weren't the only place where polyandry existed; it could be found in other parts of the Himalayas, too, such as some pockets in Tibet and India, as Kashvi had heard. Historically it was apparent in some other cultures as well. At the same time, Kashvi was also cognizant that the practice had declined some. It didn't flourish as much as it used to.

Polyandry was predominantly practiced for pragmatic reasons. In Kashvi's community and at other similar places, the harsh, mountainous terrain didn't leave much room to cultivate crops. Land was scarce, and farming required an incredible amount of work. Once a family obtained a piece of land, it wouldn't have made economic sense to divide it between their children once they were grown. For example, if three brothers inherited a third of their family's land and got married, they probably wouldn't have been able to support their families. It was much more logical to keep the land in one piece. Also, if three brothers married three different women, they would end up with much more children to feed. However, by marrying only one, they could keep the population down because one woman can't get pregnant so often and bear as many children as three women.

The prevalent causes for polyandry applied to Kashvi's case as well. Her husbands' family owned a relatively good-sized piece of land. While it took back-breaking work to cultivate it, the land supported their family handsomely. They weren't affluent, but they always had something to eat and didn't know scarcity. In addition, they only had three children so far, which could have been three times as many in a different marital arrangement, involving three women. If polygyny—that is, having multiple wives—were

Anton Jankovoy/Shutterstock.com

widespread in this area, instead of polyandry, that could be a disaster, leading to a population increase that their community couldn't tolerate.

Ayush was the oldest of the brothers, who took a slightly dominant role in the family. He functioned as the head of the household, and his brothers accepted it. This used to be different in Kashvi's family of origin. Her mother had married two brothers, and as far as Kashvi could discern, they performed very equal roles; neither of them was more dominant than the other. Ayush's dominance was barely noticeable, and it worked very well in their family. It seemed that it made his brothers work more efficiently and the household run more smoothly.

Ayush differed from his two brothers in another way as well. He didn't resemble them at all. He was taller and heavier than them, and his facial features were more pronounced than theirs. He had bigger hands, feet, nose, and lips than them, too. Arpan and Ankur looked very much alike, almost like twins. In the beginning, Kashvi nearly mixed them up a few times, especially in the dark. She chuckled a bit when that happened, but it didn't matter too much anyway, and the two brothers didn't even recognize her momentary confusion.

The three brothers all worked on the land, but Ayush seemed to work even harder than the other two, and usually he was the one to divide tasks between the three of them. As there was only one of Kashvi and three of them, and also because it was customary, all three of them did some chores around the house as well and participated in childcare.

Kashvi had grown to love each of her husbands and appreciated different things about them. In a way, she didn't separate them in her mind. They were all her husbands just the same, and the four of them functioned as a marital unit. Their family was complete just the way it was, with their three children.

While her husbands might have had their unique ways of showing their appreciation and respect for her, she didn't feel that one of them would love her any more or any less than the others. She never experienced jealousy from any of them, but it would have been unusual and senseless anyway. Jealousy was generally not a part of polyandrous marriages. At least Kashvi had never heard of any families where that would have been the case.

Sex tended to be regulated by an unspoken schedule. At least the schedule remained unspoken to Kashvi; she didn't know if the brothers had discussed it among themselves. She did notice, however, a certain regularity in the brothers' conjugal visits: Ayush tended to come to her bedroom on particular days, and a similar pattern seemed to be apparent with Arpan and Ankur as well. There were some exceptions here and there, but the broth-

ers appeared to follow the schedule for most of the time. As it was customary for a husband to leave his shoes by the bedroom door when he visited his wife, there could be no confusion as to whether the conjugal bed was occupied or not, and two, or all three, brothers couldn't have attempted to approach Kashvi at the same time.

Kashvi had never wondered which brother biologically fathered each of her children because it didn't matter anyway. They were all relatives, and all of her husbands were considered to be fathers to the children. The children called all of them "father" just the same. Kashvi did notice fleetingly that her two sons bore a great resemblance to Ayush, whereas her daughter seemed to be a mix of all of them. However, she didn't dwell on such observations and didn't attribute any significance to them.

Kashvi considered herself lucky to live where she did and be part of the family she belonged to. She felt cherished and respected by her husbands and children, and their family functioned very well. She couldn't imagine it any other way. Sometimes she heard whispers about the world outside of their village, and she was shocked to learn that in many parts of the world people had only one spouse, or none, they usually tied the knot to pursue romantic love and passion, and they often divorced. Kashvi could hardly believe that such things existed, and she felt deep compassion for those poor individuals who experienced those issues. She was happy that she wasn't one of them and never would be.

*

Wolther sighed contentedly. Relationship-wise he was finally at a place in life where he had always dreamed of being. He had grown up in a traditional family in the Netherlands. His parents had been married and raised him and his brother together. His mother stayed at home after she had had her children. She went back to work part time when the boys were both in school.

While his upbringing was peaceful and stable, even as a child, and especially as a teenager, Wolther sometimes wondered if this kind of family arrangement was the only way to live. He saw a documentary on polygamous families in his midteens and was fascinated. When he remarked to

Gender, Marriage, and Families: From the Individual to the Social

his parents that he didn't understand why such a family form wasn't legal, or at least an option, in the Netherlands his parents looked at him, stunned. He quickly changed the subject and didn't mention polygamous families at home again, at least not for the next few decades.

When he started dating in his late teens, he began to experience struggles with monogamy. His relationships tended to end because he cheated. He didn't necessarily consider it cheating, though, because he usually told his girlfriends upfront that he didn't like to limit himself to one woman. He was a true extrovert, and he had many friends. He couldn't understand why he was allowed to have multiple friends, but not multiple romantic partners. He was always honest, but the girls generally thought he was kidding, too young, immature, and hoped that he would change for them and become willing to commit and be exclusive. They were sorely disappointed when they learned that he did mean what he had communicated and did end up dating someone else at the same time.

By his late twenties Wolther was getting tired of being labeled a cheater and a jerk, and his heart had been broken several times by then because multiple women that he had truly loved, but couldn't stay faithful to, had left him. He was becoming almost hesitant to date and get involved in serious relationships because he didn't want to disappoint anyone or risk his own feelings either.

After a 1-year relationship hiatus he had met Betje. He fell head over heels in love with her. She was the most attractive, smart, funny, confident, and independent woman he had ever met. He couldn't resist her, and their

CHAPTER 16: "I love her. And her. And her." Polyamory and Polygamy

351

relationship was progressing at light-speed. They moved in together after 3 months of dating. During 3 years of living together Wolther felt incredibly fulfilled and never thought of other women. He began to hope that he had become mature enough and found the right woman to be able to practice monogamy. This hope gave him the boost to propose to Betje, but he did mention to her that he had had some difficulties with fidelity in the past. She laughed it off; she was too confident to worry about him cheating on *her*.

They were very happy for nearly 3 years after their wedding. Then, after a promotion, Betje started to work more and more, and their intimate moments had begun to dwindle. Also, they were having some debates about having children; Wolther wanted a baby, whereas Betje preferred to wait and focus on her career. Wolther caught himself missing emotional and sexual closeness and dreaming about other women. He still loved Betje and intended to stay with her, but he had some needs that weren't being fulfilled in his marriage.

As he had pledged loyalty to Betje, he swore not to go out and simply cheat on her. He loved and respected her too much for that. He hesitantly brought up the subject with her and suggested a temporary open relationship. Betje rejected his suggestion, but, to his surprise, she came up with the idea of visiting a swingers' club. They went a couple of times, but Wolther noticed that Betje wasn't really into it, and he still didn't feel completely fulfilled either because while he got some sexual release, there were some emotional needs still unmet. He didn't just want sex; he wanted another relationship, just not instead of Betje, but in addition to her. When he told her this much, she was very upset and eventually suggested a divorce. He tried to fight for their relationship a while longer and was almost ready to give up his desires for other women at this point, but, for Betje, there was no going back. She was irreversibly disappointed in him.

After the divorce Wolther fell into a depression, which was difficult to overcome. He went to a therapist, and as they analyzed his past relationships, the therapist pointed out that it sounded like Wolther might be happier in a polyamorous relationship, where he had the opportunity to be romantically, emotionally, and sexually involved with more than one person. The therapist stressed that some people just worked that way, and it was a legitimate choice for them. Wolther felt relieved and began to explore polyamory. He read a lot about it online, and he realized that it indeed might be the best suit for him. It was all about honesty and openness, so he wouldn't have to feel like and be labeled a cheater.

When he met Anneke a few months later, he told her upfront that in the long-run he was looking for a polyamorous relationship, and if they got involved, sooner or later most likely it wouldn't just be the two of them. Anneke smiled and agreed that it would be fine, as long as they always kept open communication. She hadn't been in a polyamorous relationship in the past, but was open to the idea.

After about 4 months of dating, when their relationship was turning more serious, Anneke revealed that she couldn't bear any children. She had tried with her ex-husband, with no success, and she was diagnosed with a condition that made it almost impossible. Wolther was a bit shaken, as he really wanted children and was hoping to have them with Anneke, but he loved her dearly, and her admission didn't change anything about his plans with her. He thought in passing that if and when another person entered the picture; if this relationship turned into polyamory, it could be someone to have children with.

Approximately 9 months later Wolther met Liese. He fell in love with her instantly, but it didn't affect his feelings toward Anneke one bit. He told her right away. She seemed truly happy for him and wished to meet Liese as soon as possible. Wolther introduced her after 3 weeks of dating. Anneke really liked her, and they quickly developed a friendship. As neither woman was bisexual, it was never a question whether they would get involved sexually, but their emotional connection was very strong from the very beginning.

After Wolther had been seeing Liese for 5 months, he discussed with Anneke whether he could ask her to move in. Anneke didn't object and

Liese accepted the proposal, so she moved in. There was some strain and a few debates in the beginning while everyone got used to the new arrangement, but in about 2 months the tensions subsided, and their polyamorous relationship flourished. They all truly loved each other, just in different ways.

When Liese got pregnant a year later, Anneke struggled with jealousy. She wasn't jealous of Wolther's relationship with her, but she did envy Liese's ability to bear a child, which she couldn't do. She had several discussions with Wolther and Liese alone, and the three of them did as well. Anneke even considered moving out, but she couldn't bear to lose Wolther, or even Liese, who she had begun to view not only as a close friend, but as a family member by then. She visited a therapist a few times, too, to sort out her feelings.

Something changed by the beginning of the third trimester. Anneke got over her jealousy and became almost as excited about the baby as Liese. She realized that this was the next best thing. She couldn't have a biological child of her own, but she could become a second mother to the child of the two people that were the closest to her in the whole world. She could participate in raising this child because the four of them would be a family, just as the three of them had been functioning as a family for a while.

When Anneliese was born, Anneke was bursting with exhilaration. She was extremely proud and moved that Anneliese was named by combining Anneke's name and Liese's, indicating that the little girl had two mothers. Anneke could even joke by then that she was lucky that she could become a mother without the excess weight, morning sickness, and a painful childbirth.

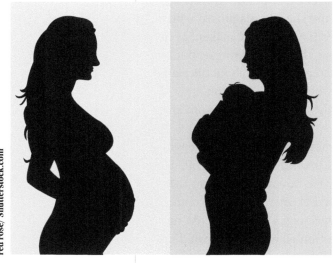

Their life was like a fairytale from then on. Anneliese had completed their family, and they were happier than ever. The only thing was that their fairytale didn't involve one prince and one princess. This fact didn't bother them one bit; in fact, they preferred it this way. However, there were some people who judged them, especially their decision to raise a child in a polyamorous family. They couldn't get legally married, but it would have been possible for the three of them to enter into a civil union. They considered it, but they didn't think it could make them more of a family, so they decided against it. They agreed that if Anneliese or any future children wanted it later on, they could still do it. And who knows, by that time polygamous *marriages* might become legal in the Netherlands as well.

When the three of them were invited in their hometown to an open forum on polyamory, they gladly agreed to participate in hopes of educating people and potentially debunking some myths or misconceptions about polyamorists. They were slightly nervous because they didn't know what to expect, but they were prepared for everything and vowed not to react negatively no matter what anyone posed. The forum started with a brief introduction of their family, then a Q&A session followed.

The first question came from a tall man in the audience, "Is this about sex?"

Wolther gave a nervous laugh, then responded, "Great first question. You know, I'm actually glad you asked that question because usually that's what many people think, so I'm happy to address sex. The short answer is no, it's not about sex. It's not primarily about sex. Sex is only part of the picture as much as it is in any other romantic relationship. If I were looking for as much sex as possible with as much variety as possible, there would be other, even easier ways for that. To give you an example, and this is very personal, but it looks like we're getting personal, my ex-wife suggested a swinger club to satisfy my unfulfilled desires. At least she thought that would satisfy me. It didn't. If it were only about sex, it would have. I wasn't looking for meaningless sex; I was seeking meaningful, intimate relationships, and somehow I could never quite get that, at least not enough of that, from one woman."

"And if it was only about sex, what would be in it for me?" Liese interjected. "Or for Anneke? We are both involved with just one man, and before you ask, no, we don't have sex with each other."

"What is it about then?" asked another man in the audience.

"Just as the term, polyamory, would suggest, it's about love. Lots of love," Anneke replied quietly.

"Yes. Why do you have to be restricted to loving only one person?" Liese added. "If you have several siblings or children, you love all of them, not just one. You may have a great number of friends and love all of them. In a monogamous romantic relationship you can only love one. Why wouldn't you share your love if you have a lot of it?"

"Yes. I love her. And her. And her," Wolther said pointing to Anneke, Liese, and Anneliese's photo that they had brought. "I'm a loving person, and I can show even more of that in a family like ours."

"So, what would you say to people who wonder if this is euphemized cheating?" a plump woman asked.

"This is not cheating," Wolther stressed. "We all know about each other, and we have given consent. There's open and honest communication. So, it's not cheating."

"Was there ever any jealousy?" the woman inquired.

The three of them glanced at each other and laughed.

"There was maybe a little in the beginning," Wolther admitted. "Just because we're poly, and we're mature, we're not immune to jealousy. We're only human. I believe it was the hardest for Anneke. Liese had known from the get-go that Anneke was in the picture, but for Anneke, Liese was a new addition, and our relationship dynamics changed somewhat when she became our third member."

"We call it new relationship energy," Anneke added. "It can be a difficult transition in the beginning, but it's only for a short while. Things are shaken up with a third person, and they have to settle. But they eventually do. And it helped that I genuinely liked Liese. And soon Wolther wasn't the only thing that connected us; we had emotional bonds of our own. And, you know, if you really love someone, you are delighted to see their happiness. It warms my heart to witness what Wolther and Liese share."

"What about your child?" the same woman asked.

"Anneliese is such a happy and confident child," Liese emphasized. "She has the benefit of having three people who love her, not just one or two. And she has two mothers, double the nurturing."

"And we've never had to hire a babysitter," Wolther smiled. "Never. There are enough of us to watch her."

"And children who grow up in polyamorous households are usually more flexible and open-minded than other children. Anneliese is too young to demonstrate that, but I've read that it's true," Anneke elucidated.

"Are there any challenges in your everyday life?" another woman wondered.

"Of course," the three of them said in unison, laughing.

"We have all the challenges that any family has," Liese explained. "Plus, in spite of all the benefits, there are some difficulties sometimes, such as scheduling."

"Yes, my schedule is extremely full," Wolther grinned. "We have family time scheduled for the four of us, then there's time for the three of us adults, then private time with Anneke, private time with Liese, and alone play time with Anneliese. I'm a busy man."

Stokkete/Shutterstock.com

"But what about the women here?" a young woman asked. "Are you open to potentially adding another man? If you are both poly, are you fully satisfied with the way things are now?"

Anneke and Liese looked at each other, then Anneke replied slowly, "We never say never. It's not impossible that someone else might join one day. But for them to become a live-in partner, a part of our family, they would have to meet a lot of criteria. A lot."

"Yes, definitely," Liese echoed. "We don't discount the idea, but, for the sake of simplicity, and for him to really work for our family, he would have to be someone that both Anneke and I are very attracted to and could fall in love with. And how likely is that? Although maybe pretty likely if we consider that we're both in love with the same guy now. If only I or Anneke were involved with him, it might not work very well for our family dynamics."

"Also, I'd have to like him at least," Wolther interjected. "It'd be pretty difficult if I hated him."

"So you wouldn't object to the idea?"

"No, why would I?" Wolther wondered. "I'm poly, and it doesn't just work one way. I would be fine with an addition, but I'd hope to find someone that I can develop such a close emotional bond with that Anneke has with Liese. And that's a tall order. Possibly harder for guys as well."

"And, of course, Anneliese would have to like the man," Anneke added.

"Of course," Wolther and Liese echoed.

As they left the forum and returned to the home that they shared, they hoped that they could bring some enlightenment to people and eradicate a few stereotypes. Either way, they were happy to live in harmony, which was unfortunately not true for many other families. They knew how lucky they were and looked forward to many more years together.

Discussion Questions

1. How do you envision the families in the two stories in 5 years? How about 20 years?

2. Discuss the role of gender in the stories. Would the stories or any important aspects of the stories change if the sexes of the protagonists were switched? For instance, what if the first story described one man with multiple wives and the second one woman with two partners?

3. West and Zimmerman (1987) explained that gender was a routine, everyday accomplishment, something that we performed in interaction with others. Discuss a few examples of how characters in the stories do gender, and how society/culture impacts their gendered behaviors.

4. Do you find polygamous marriages and/or polyamory deviant in any way (different from social norms in a given society at a particular time)? Why/why not? Do they seem to be deviant in the countries featured in the stories? Why/why not? Does it depend on whether they are lawful or not? That is, if something is against the law, is it automatically deviant, and if it is not, it is not deviant? Why/why not?

5. Do you think that there is any stigma regarding polygamy and/or polyamory? Remember, stigma is a strong, stubborn, negative label that is used to describe individuals who break social norms (Goffman, 1986). If yes, does the stigma vary by different factors and circumstances? Why do you think the stigma is stronger at some places than others? Does one seem to involve more stigma than the other? Why/why not?

6. Use an ethnomethodological approach to explore norms of monogamy/fidelity in marriage and romantic relationships based on the stories. Ethnomethodology is the study of how norms of the social world are created and understood (Garfinkel, 1984). Ethnomethodologists intentionally breach social norms to shed light on the inflexibility of those norms. How can we see norms about monogamy/fidelity at play in marriages and relationships when those norms are questioned or violated?

7. Multiphrenia is defined as splitting into multiple self-investments (Gergen, 2000). Discuss examples of multiphrenia from the stories.

8. Emotion work (or emotional labor) is what we do to suppress or evoke emotions we are "supposed to" or not supposed to feel in certain situations (Hochschild, 2012). Discuss examples of emotion work from the two stories and how emotion work might relate to polygamy and polyamory in general.

9. How do you envision the future of polygamy and polyamory? Do you expect them to be more widespread or less widespread? Why? Do you see polygamous marriages legalized everywhere? Why/why not? Do you think monogamy might fade or even die out in the future? Why/why not?

Find the Answers

Go to http://www.livescience.com/27128-polyamory-myths-debunked.html to find answers to the following questions. You'll need to click on the numbers to read each page in the article.

1. About what percentage of Americans currently practices consensual nonmonogamy? What are some of the different types of it?

2. List at least three myths about polyamory.

3. What is the relationship between jealousy, commitment, and polyamory?

4. What does research show about the impacts of polyamory on children?

Mini Research Assignments

1. Watch at least one documentary and/or TV show on polygamy or polyamory. How are the featured relationships depicted? Discuss the role of gender, culture, tradition, age, religion, social class, and other similar factors, too. Explain the role of norms, prejudice, and stigma. Draw parallels with the stories as well.

2. Search the web for polyamory dating sites and/or support groups, blogs, etc. Select at least three, and compare and contrast them. What kind of messages do they send about polyamory? What kinds of issues do they emphasize? Discuss the role of gender, culture, tradition, age, religion, social class, and other similar factors, too. Explain the role of norms, prejudice, and stigma. Draw parallels with the stories as well.

3. Survey at least seven individuals, asking them to rate their agreement with the following statements on a scale of 1–10 (1 meaning complete disagreement and 10 indicating full agreement): 1. "Marrying more than one person is wrong, even if it's not against the law in a country." 2. "Being in a relationship with more than one person is cheating even if they all know about each other and consent." 3. "It's less acceptable for a woman than for a man to have multiple committed relationships or be married to multiple people at the same time." 4. "Raising children in one household with multiple committed romantic partners or spouses could have negative impacts on children." Summarize the results, discussing the potential impact of gender, age, education, religion, and other similar factors in the answers. Draw parallels with the stories as well.

References

Garfinkel, H. (1984). *Studies in ethnomethodology.* Malden, MA: Polity.

Gergen, K. J. (2000). *The saturated self: Dilemmas of identity in contemporary life* (reprint ed.). New York, NY: Basic Books.

Goffman, E. (1986). *Stigma: Notes on the management of spoiled identity.* New York, NY: Touchstone. (Originally published 1963)

Hochschild, A. (2012). *The managed heart: Commercialization of human feeling.* Berkeley, CA: University of California Press.

Pappas, S. (2013). 5 myths about polyamory debunked. New York, NY: Live Science. Retrieved from http://www.livescience.com/27128-polyamory-myths-debunked.html

West, C., & Zimmerman, D. H. (1987). Doing gender. *Gender & Society, 1,* 125–151.